The Role of Brain Hemispheres in Architectural Design

Ali Khiabanian

Ali Khiabanian © 2015

All Rights Reserved

All rights reserved. No part of this book may be reproduced or transmitted in any form or by any means, electronic or mechanical, including photocopying and recording, or by any information storage and retrieval system, without permission in writing from the author.

Title: The Role of Brain Hemispheres in Architectural Design

Author & Designer: Ali Khiabanian,

Translator (from Persian): Chadorkafouri, R.

ISBN: 9781939123053

LCCN: 2015906541

Publisher: Supreme Century, Los Angeles, CA

Prepare for Publishing: Asan Nashr

www.ASANASHR.com

Dedicated to Professor Cyrus R. Sabri & Mr. Mehdi Zahed with a heart full of color & beauty.

Email: Ali_khiabanian@yahoo.com
Website: www.iduarchitects.com
Pages in Facebook:
- Interdiscipline Design Universe
- Parametric Architecture +
- Conceptual sketches in Architectural Design

Instagram: IDUarchitects

Table of Contents

A Review of Creativity Definition	10
Brain Right and Left Hemispheres	12
How to Strengthen Left Hemisphere:	15
How to Strengthen Right Hemisphere:	15
Creative Thinkers' Particulars	16
Stages of Creative Thinking	17
Creativity Role in Architecture Designing	18
Fundamental Principles in Creative Instruction in art & architecture	21
Critical thinking in design process	26
Critical thinking and judgment	43
Architectural judgments	44
Decision making strategy in architectural design process	45
Architectural Designing Process	48
Designing process	51
Thinking about Architecture Designing through Diagrams	54
Architectural Diagrams	55
Diagrams in Architecture Designing Process	57
Creative Process Diagram in Architecture Designing	59
Project Recognition	62
Purification	66
Analysis	66
Synthesis	66
Idea	67
Four Stages of Idea Production	72
Role of Creativity in Producing of New Ideas	74
Idea Changing to Form	75
Concept	85
Features of Concepts	91
Spatial Structure	95
Architecture Creation Cycle	99
Creative Process in Architecture Designing	104
Trade center of Iran national industries	106
Sustainable house in Iran's desert	125
Sketch	145
What sketches can be effective	147
Conceptual Sketches or Mental	152

Drawings
Fundamental Principles in Sketching	166
Conceptual Sketches of Neda Mansouri	171
Exercises for Better Understanding of Space	176
Examples of student projects	187
From Sketch to Architecture	226
Art Center Design Process	253
References	265

To me architectural endeavors have always been a symphony of brick and mortar but not without tipping function over form and rightly so. As part of my teaching assignment one day, there I was trying to know a book that was as pedagogically authentic on form as it is reliable on the functionality of design for my students' reference. One of my colleagues, upon knowing, mentioned The Role of Creativity in Architecture Designing Process written by Ali Khiabanian and Leila Manzouri. In the beginning I was as deeply reluctant as my experience navigating through this book was owing only to the non-English language it was available at the time. I am over joyed to see this work is lately available in English and is therefore out to invite more readership.

It has been for so long time that waves of books asserting the importance of safeguarding architectural design have bombarded us from all directions. Without dismissing the importance of those beautifully written books, this single volume has been holistic enough to induce my student's likings and is set to make its convincing mark. The Role of Creativity in Architecture Designing Process is very captivating and holds the promise of strengthening the knowledge base of architectural design. Slowly but steadily, I evolved myself into knowing that this books was not simply an accumulation of facts, it actually enables change in the way we think about and practice architectural design; not change for the change sake but intelligent innovations that respond to the needs of the future and unmask a new layer of quality to building design. Let's commit to a quick glance but not too fleeting to decipher the latent value of the message therein.

This book initiates journey by riveting readers to a solid framework on the importance of creativity in Design. An elaborative multi-pronged easy to grasp agenda on how to bolster conceptualization process while at work is rich in its essence. All the more important dimension of this book was to underpin everything around the basic building blocks of hand-eye coordination to left and right brain personalities and their comparative analysis. In the following chapter, we find a treasury of ideas and practices that enables designers to respond to a diverse range of socio environmental concerns. Indeed, today architectural practice is heavily surrounded by the on-going discussion on how to get high performance buildings which are a step forward to a less resource intensive urban life style. The primacy of second chapter on Architecture Design process is demonstrated by what can be achieved when basics are well taken care of. Consider the new chapter on sustainability. This section provides perspective on the informed application of climatic characteristics as well as designing approaches necessary to achieve desirable human thermal comfort level though architectural design. Incoming solar radiation and its impact on buildings is descriptively discussed and subsequent to that a section about strategically located shading devices and design interventions aimed at mitigating the radiating hard impermeable surfaces' effect on design have been very well explained.

This book supplements argument and graphic representations with embracing case studies showcasing work from the library of well-respected design professionals from across the breadth of architectural field. This book has all the ingredients to becoming a well-used resource. There may have been sections in this book hinting to advocate a simplification in totality but this work is relieved of all the accessories of hortatory works and is not so technical to make it too tedious to go through it.

Naveed Mazhar- MRAIC
B.Arch, M.L.Arch

Instructor, Project Lead – Proposed BTech Landscape Architecture
School of Sustainable Building and Environmental Management
Department of Landscape Architecture Technology

During recent decades, creativity as one of the most important educational factors has attracted more attentions. Psychologists and instructional thinkers try to define and set methods and systems to strengthen individuals' creativeness. This was discussed and analyzed in art and architecture areas for a long time so that different solutions on training creative artists and architectures have been offered in several books and articles by now. The first and most important question we face at the beginning of discussion in classes and specialized arguments relates to methods of strengthening creativeness and whether creativity can be trained and learned.

Recent findings of psychology make it clear that unlike the ancients' ideas, creativity process is not inherent; rather it can be educated.

Psychologists and experts of educational sciences believe that:

Through education, we can teach children to think about unusual ways, think about problems and find solutions through taking benefit of brain right hemisphere and divergent thinking. Creativity process is not a premade one; rather it is a generative and changeable process.

In subsequent arguments, the posed questions will be answered. The first section of the book will consider creativity role in training, specially art and architecture, through obtaining a brief knowledge about creativity and creative thinking. We will try to reach a correct and comprehensive knowledge and analyses about function of brain hemispheres in architecture designing process by resorting to our experiences and learning.

A Review of Creativity Definition

It is necessary to know aspects and features of everything even a concept if it leads to a better application and conclusion. For this reason, we cannot ignore a category like creativity. Considering that performing every creativity-based task will have a valuable result, so acquiring knowledge on creativity, defining features and analyzing its characteristics is an appropriate prelude for every measure. Availability of several definitions and interpretations on creativity is a main problem. Of course, none of them are comprehensive and clear by themselves. Some points or descriptions should be added to each of these definitions so that they can be regarded as a comprehensive one which includes all aspects of creativity.

For instance, E. Paul Torrance- researcher and author of books on creativity- uses elegant interpretations in defining this concept in his book under title of "creativity skills and talents and how to test and nurture it" as deeper digging, watching again and crossing out the mistakes, entering deeper waters, coming out of closed doors and shaking hand with future. These nice interpretations, in fact, are efforts to describe a newly-appeared action which has never been conducted and met all needs toward aesthetic through its appearance.

Torrance also offers more applied definitions about creativity leading to perceptions on processes available in creativity. Torrance suggests that: "creativity is an action occurs after a mental image. When there is a problem and it is clearly explained, creativity will also exist. Creativity takes place while trying to solve an explained problem and then it realizes through continuing. Creativity cannot be called so until the activity required for its identicalness has been completed. It will be called creativity when the problem is identically solved, its solution accepted and also its uniqueness discovered. It means that every action could be regarded as a creative one and even particularly, every action is a creative one. The problem is only that no one has discovered its creativity".

As it has been mentioned, authorities and psychologists have offered several definitions in this regard. Michele Shea states that creativity means seeing what does not exist in advance. You should find out how to call it back to existence and therefore turn to be partner of the existence. Michael Wertheimer defines creativity as capability of having a new and different view on a subject and, in other words, breaking up and rebuilding process of one's knowledge about a subject and obtaining a new insight toward its nature. In Dan Gilliam's view, creativity is discovery process of what has not yet considered and establishing novel relationships. Joy Paul Guilford- American contemporary psychologist- introduces creativity as a divergent thinking (against convergent thinking). De Bono Edward, a Maltese psychologist, physician and author, defines creativity as a lateral or horizontal thinking against vertical one.

Finally, experts' comments on creativity can be divided into two sections:
1- Creativity is synonym with problem solving or creation,
2- Creativity is means for problem solving or creation. Some definitions consider creativity regarding product and its result while others describe it considering process aspect and its quality.

In past, psychologists' arguments about creativity focused on "creative person or process". At present, although most of scholars consider creativity as a process, their definition about creativity is based on "generative" feature. However, all psychologists are not unanimous in creativity definition and consider it from different aspects. Some believe that creativity means emancipation from presumptions, frames and necessities. Others state that creativity is the product of the supreme level of human knowledge.

Some believe that creativity is not talent. They think that talent is limit and guide person just in specified channel of capabilities, mental and intellectual facilities while creativity is wide and forces the creative individual to think about different arguments and disciplines.

Creativity means dynamism and extent like water and river. Creativity is similar to extent, flexibility, activity and uproar of water in the river. It widely and unstably moves toward discovering unknowns. It does not know the destination but is very bold and brave.

Some psychologists state that creativity is the soar of human thinking capability which can promote him toward progress and develop and help him in solving all problems of life. Samples of creativity could be observed in wall paintings of cavemen, creating of an art work, industrial machineries, cooking and dressmaking ...

With these descriptions, psychological framework let us believe that creativity process is not an inherent one; rather, it can be trained. In William James' idea, we all have creative capabilities and talent but unfortunately we learn to be uncreative during life and training course. In other words, learning environment including home, school and society generally inure us to convergent thinking.

Brain Right and Left Hemispheres (Divergent and Convergent Thinking)

Creativity and learning does not merely result from knowledge, experience and practice; rather, other factors such as genetic, brain function and the same are also effective in this regard. We can direct their effective on creativity and learning through recognizing these factors. Human brain is a complex system which its function details have not been known yet. This system has composed of two right and left hemispheres.

Left hemisphere deals with discipline, logic, planning and consciousness, and right hemisphere manages affairs related to art, imagination, creativity and unconsciousness.

These hemispheres are like cycles of a bicycle in which both of them should work in order to move. But, it is possible one of them precede the other for a short time in different persons and situations.

Convergent thinking is duty of brain left hemisphere. This hemisphere focuses on words, symbols and figures. It is analyzer and follows logic, takes benefit from words to remind, remembers names instead of faces, processes thoughts subsequently and orderly, logically deducts the information step by step. Initially, it verifies details and then considers generalities. It is interested in preparing inventory and planning, blindly follows regulations, is efficient in following up and maintaining time and always has preplanning. Data collecting and classifying, reasoning, concluding and issuing of command are the most important tasks of this hemisphere.

Therefore, all functions of the left hemisphere are a completely defined process occurring according to documentations. As a result, novel thoughts are less emerged in convergent thinking. People see and accept phenomena as they are.

Brain left hemisphere does not demonstrate an appropriate function in spatial understanding, exact observation and recognizing of patterns, developing and combining of figures and pictures and establishing relationship,… In particular, in responding to the subject of designing it uses common and repetitive volumes and figures rather than creative forms and combinations.

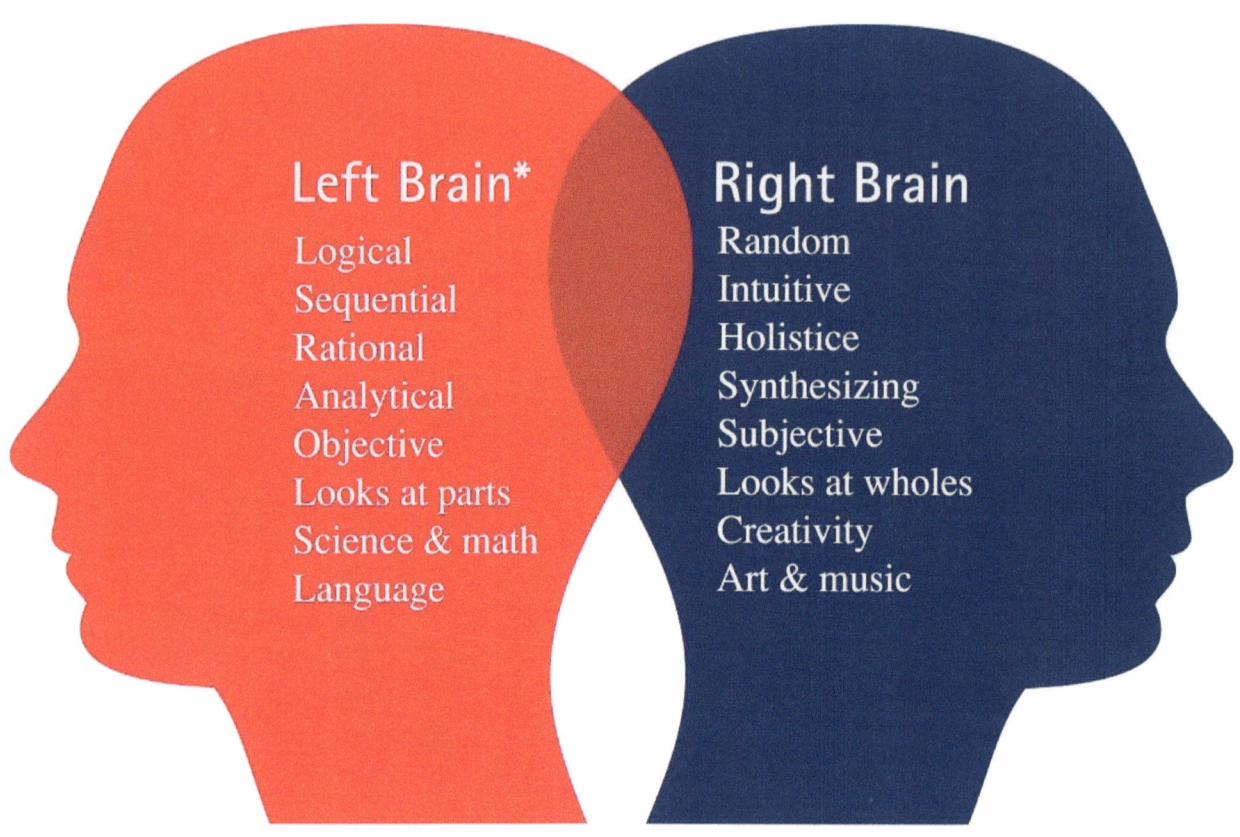

*Source: Funderstanding.com, Inc., New Jersey

How to Strengthen Left Hemisphere:

1- Solve crossword puzzles.
2- Write down daily routines in detail and follow a plan.
3- Prepare a summary while reading and studying.
4- Try to memorize what you hear.
5- Strengthen logical thoughts.
6- Divide the tasks into smaller parts and perform them step by step.
7- Plan to study mathematics and philosophy as part of your programs.
8- Practice chess and puzzle.
9- Learn management skills.
10- Use your sense of hearing in nature for more enjoy.
11- Practice speaking and lecturing. (Psychological Society of Isfahan)

Divergent thinking is duty of the brain right hemisphere. This hemisphere focuses on pictures and patterns. It reaches intuitive perception through following emotions. Concurrently processes different subjects and connects the information. Initially, it deals with generalities and then considers details. It takes benefit from free association and looks for reasons of laws instead of following them. Function of this hemisphere is such that it can produce a big cocoon just equipping with a clue and it uses all related and unrelated things to do so. Creative thinking, in fact, is in a direct relationship with divergent thinking. Individuals with divergent thinking do not accept phenomena, affairs and thoughts as they are. They try to exactly analyze the subject with a different view and even add their own comments to it. Interestingly, most great elites such as Van Gogh, Einstein and Emilia Dickinson (American famous poet) mostly benefitted from their brain right hemisphere.

How to Strengthen Right Hemisphere:

1- Consider problems generally rather than in detail.

2- Ask "if" or "then" questions and find different answers.
3- Provide the opportunity of imagination and fancy for yourself.
4- Enjoy from being in nature and pay attention to sounds and smells.
5- Use mental games.
6- Learn always by drawing and designing.
7- Learn painting and sketching.
8- Read novels and review stories in your mind in images. (creative imagination)
9- Look and observe more rather than just listening.
10- Imagine your dreams and wishes in future.
11- Look for relations between individuals, objects and subjects. (Psychological Society of Isfahan)

Creative-based instruction requires working on divergent thinking features. In fact, training creative individuals in all aspects will be realized when strengthening divergent thinking will be considered from initial stages of instruction and experience, discovery, analysis, evaluation and combining of concepts and subjects be regarded more important than grade, memorizing lessons and acquired materials which their correctness or incorrectness has previously been known.

Creative Thinkers' Particulars

Creative thinking is seeker and adventurous. Emancipated from regulations and arbitraries, it is attracted by unknowns and passives. And it is incited by risk taking and doubt. Creative individuals embrace risks in their endeavors and efforts, frequently reject clear conditions and try to clarify ambiguities because they want to exceed their knowledge and talent bounds.

Motivation to progress at higher levels, abundant curiosity, enthusiasm, discipline, capability for self-expression and self-dependence, informal and uncommon character, stamina and discipline in affairs, autonomy, critical thinking, brimful emotion, aesthetic and intuitive thinking are attributes found in all creative individuals. It is possible to find four specific features through classifying these attributes:

"Flexible thinking" is one of these features and means that creative thinkers, in spite of difficulty of creativity, have learned to take it easy because they know that fun- spiritual flexibility and imagination- makes creativity easier. Also, creative individuals are internally motivated. **They usually enjoy creation and grade, money and even satisfying others are not important to them. What is valuable for them is the creation per se**. For this reason, most of their motivations are internal.

"Risk taking" is another feature of creative individuals. Knowing that risk taking is different from carelessness and impudence, they accept some amount of risk and dangers. Of course, they may mistake. These mistakes indicate their more ideas: successful ideas and failed ones. Pablo Picasso, Spanish painter of 20th century, had more than twenty thousand paintings; but all of them were not masterpieces. Creative thinkers accept their failures and learn a lesson thereof.

Finally, creative individuals try to identically evaluate their works unlike this dominant imagination which state that they are self-based and follow minds. They appreciate judgments of respectful and reliable individuals and find out whether they are in appropriate course leads to success.

Stages of Creative Thinking

Authorities often consider creativity as a five-step process:

1- **Preparedness:** This stage includes data collection, problem definition, offering alternative solutions and consciously studying of all available data. How to deal with the first stage makes the main difference between skillfully and creatively solving the problem and its rationally solving. Creatively solvers of the problem act more flexible in data collection, problem definition, offering alternatives and studying of options. It is in this stage that, in fact, instruction on creatively solving the problem can be significantly effective.

2- **Training:** It often includes unconscious mental activity in which the mind combines unrelated thoughts following a solution and there is no conscious effort. Some ideas occur to your mind and in this stage, sometimes, you find an unusual relationship between affairs.

3- **Insight:** This is the same "Aha" stage; a moment in which a person finds relation between stages and the problem is solved; i.e. all parts of the puzzle are set together.

4- **Evaluation:** Now, you have to decide which one of your ideas is valuable and should be continued.

5- **Development:** This is the last but the most difficult and long stage in creativity, meaning that it should be generalized, embodied and correctly offered under a structure or concept. Typically, curious and creative artists repeat the mentioned stages several times and try to find better ideas. (Firouzbakht, 2004)

Creativity Role in Architecture Designing

Being highly creativity and having active mind has a special place in the process of art works creation. Therefore, each artist gives importance to its stimulation and productivity consistent with his/her artistic characteristics. On the other hand, recent studies demonstrate that creativity can also be trained. It is possible to strengthen creativity through use of ways consistent with individuals' characteristic and mental features. This has resulted in a new approach in instruction aims at training a creative and dynamic mind in different aspects of life unlike ordinary methods of education.

Great architects such as Frank Lloyd Wright, Le Corbusier, Mies van der Rohe and others have been praised for their creative works. Their works have been considered as samples of individual genius, and role of schools including instruction of their works general principles and cultivating genius seeds found in every student.(Soltanzadeh, 2000)

Creativity and creation in art and architecture is kind of directed activity i.e. artist or architect works to create a design in an organized and aimed way. Clearly, this activity, considering its organized form, will not solely be regarded as a design or idea unless the architect or artist pay attention to innovation as a strong means and design by its help because designing is impossible without innovation. Considering these descriptions along with other factors which are effective in architecture formation, role of creativity and innovation in forming all kinds of art works and specially architecture ones cannot be ignored since artful power of human mind is a generative one. This is genesis and creativity of artist being which has formed and is forming art history.

Le Corbusier has granted special position to creativity in his definition of architecture:"… it is an undeniable fact that architecture is created in a moment of creativity. When mind is busy about how to guarantee stability of a building and also provide comfort and convenience requirements, it is stimulated to reach a goal which is superior than supplying merely functional needs and prepared to exhibit poetic capabilities which stimulates and pleasures us.(Ghazi, 1990)

In creating an art work, thinking and imaging capability is regarded as a potential power performed by aid of efforts, practices and aimed activity. And, it changes from a mental concept to an evaluable identity. All artistic creations result from realizing artist's thoughts and perceptions. More exactly, this is architect that demonstrates reflex and effect of different factors in architecture. An architect, as an artist coordinates his/her knowledge and perceptions with available facilities and directs them by help of brain hemispheres in the process of architecture creation. He/she takes benefit from all his/her posses such that they change to an integrated and new phenomenon after passing through filter of architect's creativity and personal viewpoints. Finally, this novel phenomenon is creativity in architecture designing which can be built from elements and details similar to thousands of other designs, but creativity has been enlivened like a soul to these elements and details and has made it a creative generality. (Khiabanian, 2010)

Fundamental Principles in Creative Instruction in Art

(Creativity is the most important feature of art and architecture students)

Providing conditions resulting in strengthening of creative thinking in educational spaces has a wide domain which ranges from attitude changes to teaching methods and self-assurance. Some of these cases will be discussed later.

1- Creating interest in students: Art instruction experts introduce two elements of excitement and interest as the main motivation in education. This is the same of famous philosophers statement that indicate a person cannot know a thing if he/she is not in its love. Nowadays, imitation, obedience and unquestionable following have no place in creative instruction principles unlike traditional educating system which was based on tedious and boring repeat and imitate. Therefore, creating interest and excitement for learning is one the most important duties and obligations of educational instructors. (Khiabanian, 2005)

2- Only creative teachers can train creative students. "Being creative is an important condition in architecture teaching. An instructor who steadily repeats a designing process to the students without considering time, space, mental and social conditions cannot be successful. If we expect our student to be creative, we, ourselves, should be creative and always try to create an ever-increasing process by understanding student's environmental and spiritual conditions. (Hojjat, 2004)

3- Confronting prejudgments and practicing critical thinking

4- Comparing with aesthetician philosopher, creative designing teacher should have more comprehensive understanding. He/she should advocate independently-thinking aesthetician because it is just "liberalism" that fertilizes imagination faculty and art.

5- Creating a free space for discussion, negotiation, independent thinking and freely expressing emotions

6- Creativity blossoms with liberty.

7- Creativity is strengthened with capability for establishing relationship among different things: completing and developing architectural sketches or three-dimensional incomplete structures can be referred as useful practices in strengthening creativeness. In this method, we can use two-dimensional or voluminal, simple or complex compositions considering capability of individuals. An incomplete combination of volumes and figures is provided for the student and he/she is asked to complete it; of course as he/she recognizes. In similar exercises, relation between volumes or horizontal and vertical extension of the suggested structure can be asked from the students. (Khiabanian, 2010)

8- Believe innovation and imagination so that conditions required for appearing creative activities in society are provided.

9- Pay attention to metaphors and figures. Everything is capable to demonstrate a concept which exceeds what appears. Look for concepts.(Mohammad Panah, 2007)

10- Creating self-confidence and self-assurance.

11- Thorough focus to realize your aims and dreams increases your excitement and self-confidence.

12- Classrooms can be managed as learning-based rather than teacher-based.

13- Sympathy of teacher and student (guiding student to recognize capabilities and develop ideas)

14- Mind dynamism (mind dynamism drives the student toward unknowns, finding answers and recognizing talents)

15- Recognizing valuable traditions

16- A peaceful, far from anxiety and stressful environment is suggested as the educational environment. It is advised to set instructional conditions such that students can express their ideas with liberty, interestingly listen to others, think about different issues and organize their mental concepts so that their thinking faculty is strengthen. Providing enough facilities for students and asking questions by the teacher for challenging students to find their answers through use of the facilities and acquire the required skills is recommended.

17- There is a sensational pleasure in teaching and learning, try it. Make every moment of classroom unrepeatable and sweet in your and students' mind. Enter the class with plenty of energy, greet joyfully with students, teach excitedly, and enthusiastically provide answer to the questions. Let your students touch completely your eager in teaching. Remember that even time stops when you enter the class reluctantly.(Pur Ali, 2007)

18- Tenderizing and strengthening teacher-student relationship: increase students' trust toward yourself so that they can believe your statements carefully. "Initially, I thought how I can teach my students better, now I think how I can establish a good relationship with them so that they can believe their capabilities and internal growth through this relation and act accordingly".

19- Put aside good and bad. Think well and design more as possible. Class discussions help students to learn how to listen, read and comprehend better, ask their questions, offer their comments, criticize their friends arguments, bear their critiques, argument, take care of fallacious reasoning, ...

20- Set the chairs in circle rather than in parallel and rows

21- More emphasize on positive points of students' work

22- Respecting students' thoughts and leaving the result to them

23- Creating a sense of being socially worthiness: unlike children, teenagers are worry about their social position. They want to have a specified position among their peers and feel worthy. For this reason, their emotional conditions will be better if they feel that they can be paid attention and be confirmed in the school. This results in easiness of social consistency and lessening life disciplinary problems. They try to make maximum use of available facilities in school to strengthen and stabilize this social position and fulfilling this main need.

24- Practicing patience in carefully listening to students and their problems enhances their self-respect; makes them happy and fresh; make them to feel worthiness, comfort and convenience; and certainly they will not face any mental critical condition in strengthening their weak points.

25- **Your character follows your thoughts**. Always remember that your character follows your thoughts and attitudes about yourself. Your works are directed by your thoughts. You are the same person you imagine, and others think about you in the same way you think about yourself. Always try to remind your norms and values and accept that you are excellent, you can do everything at its best, and you can be better than now.

26- **Emphasizing the importance of thinking process and architecture during the semester not its end. Route is more important than the**

result. When the results guide the route, we will reach a place where we are. But if the route determines the result, it is possible that we do not know where we are going but we know that we want to be there.

27- Typically, focusing on destination deviate the individual's attention from the environment.

28- Instruction means fair judgment about what you and others do.

29- Evaluating of students at the end of semester should be based on their progress during the semester and just a little percent of grade is dedicated to their final presentation. Generally, university is a place for learning and experiencing and is responsible to help students as a mother helps her child in walking. Finally this child will be successful in establishing his/her balance resorting to the acquired experiences and efforts. At subsequent stages of the child's growth, he/she begins other physical activities based on primary principles (experience, courage and effort) who remember from walking training. Overemphasize of some teachers in architecture instruction on complete learning of students may have negative effects such as reluctance and unwillingness. In creative instruction, avoid comparing students with each other and evaluate them considering their progress during semester. (Khiabanian, 2005)

30- More weakening of grades importance for making personal capabilities valuable

31- Drawing conceptual sketches to strengthen brain right hemisphere

32- Always learn through drawing and sketching.

33- Free writing which helps students in their mental solidarity

34- Determining class procedure and curriculum regarding students' capabilities and through consulting them

35- Preventing from repeating their own works or imitating their classmates or teacher works. Imitating does not lead to creativity. Rudolf Arnheim (German-born author, art and film theorist and perceptual) is severely against copying and finds no value- even in realistic reflex- therein. In his idea "there is no faithful imitation of physical reality". Thoughtful effort to understand realities and obtain inherent nature of objects cannot be replaced by copying. Architecture student should be encouraged to act independently considering imitative, adapted and eclectic experiences and prevented from bounding and dogmatism about subjects- whether logical or illogical. (AI, 2010)

36- In some stages of designing, typically, the designer suffers from mental vacancy and cannot continue. In such a situation, showing a rigor behavior to the students and threaten them to drop the course at the end of the semester is unhelpful. The teacher should be exactly consider the students' mentalities and solve the mental problems; otherwise, they will still continue repeating of previous designs or imitating their classmates.

37- Do not afraid of fail and failure of design. Use all your ideas boldly.

38- If you want actually understand a thing, try to change it.

39- Use simulation to connect the phenomena in your mind.

40- Enjoy from being in nature and pay attention to sounds and smells.

41- Be enthusiastic and believe in God's support. When a friend comes to help you, do not reject it. Considering that most of us carry this terrible idea that our creativity is worthless from God's viewpoint, do not underestimate creature's help to its peer.(Cameron, 2010)

42- Create conditions required for thinking in classroom. In theoretical or practical courses, for example, the instructor can discuss about an architect's designing method, his/her ways in dealing with a site, project function and ask the students to introduce a better alternative to decisions of that architect. (Khiabanian, 2005)

43- Provide the opportunity of imagination and fancy for yourself. Imagination is defined as human capability in creating forms, images and ideas. It is a wide concept and is responsible for breaking current frames. However, quitting habit is one of the imagination techniques.

44- A person who completely accepts new experiences and does not take defensive position can always be full of novelty.

45- Always be curious and look for new solutions.

46- Be positivism and full of energy.

47- Students should be advised to try to have a positive and kind view toward their environment and those who surround them, treat compassionately and love them because our creation is nice. In this case, they will be success in their personal life, works and social affairs.

48- A good instructor is who does not think and decide instead of students.

49- Do not think about just one answer in replying the questions.

50- Take serious students' strange and extraordinary questions.

51- Ask questions from students which have several answers and let them discuss in this regard.

52- Carefully look at your students' faces to understand their expectations and find out their problems. Create a capability in yourself so that you can be in their shoes.

53- Do not have inappropriate expectations from yourself and do not introduce yourself as jack-of-all-trades. In other words, avoid absolute perfectionism which results in anxiety, feeling disability and weak.

54- Move from yourself to yourself. Avoid every mental frames and designing special patterns. Look for reality inside yours.

55- Understanding theoretical materials and concepts and their practical experience on architectural designs instead of their mere memorizing (coordination of theoretical and practical courses)

56- Teachers should restrain themselves from showing partial views about students works specially in designing courses

57- Students should not confine themselves to their teacher's comments and also ideas stated in architecture books. In most architecture designing classes, there is a challenge between imaginary works and state economical and constructional facilities. Some teachers have a professional and practical view on the subject and force students to follow their thoughts and demands, while others believe in more liberty to students through having inclination toward western common movements and styles. Both of these methods influence students' recognition of their capabilities and delay or destroy formation of their architectural character. As it can be observed, an architect with independent ideas and thoughts is rarely found among high level architects of the country.

58- Mental tempest: it is defined as mental attack to a subject. Select a subject, ask students to draw or write what comes to their mind regarding the subject in a limited time. Ask them to rely just on their right hemisphere. Then, discuss about drawn works and materials with students. Prepare the conditions so that students can consider the subject from different aspects and offer new ideas and analyses. Time control and creative viewpoint is very important in this method. A student's ability in drawing more sketches- with acceptable quality- in a determined time interval indicates his/her creativity and this student can enhance apprentices capability and creativity in space understanding and organization.

59- Visual thinking: diagrams are kind of visual thinking. Following picture demonstrates the author's mental process in drawing diagram of designing process. Use of figures and lines with different thicknesses increases information stability and more proficiency on understudy subject.

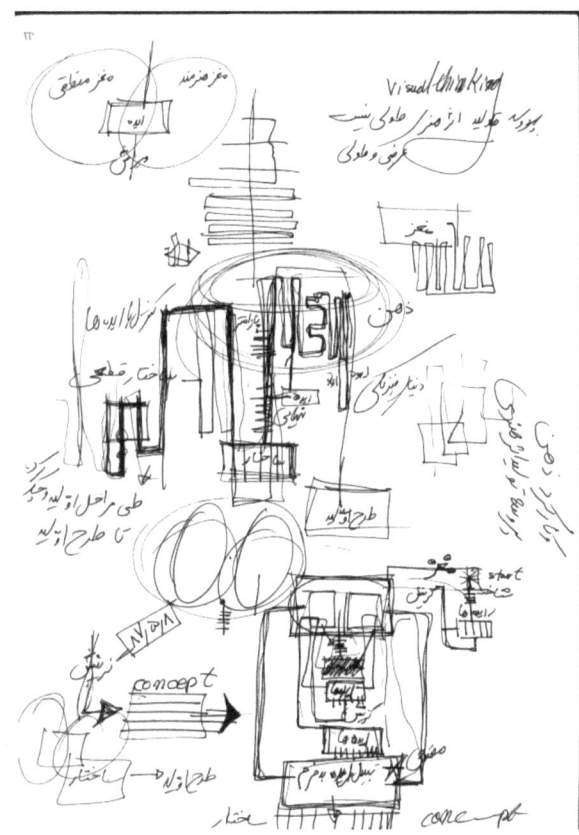

60- Creative embodiment or active imagination

(Embodiment of a space, being there and moving)

Embodiment is a daily activity in our life. We design and direct our life based on imaginations found in our minds. All efforts, desires, wishes and demands are mostly based on our mental imaginations. We frequently imagine- consciously or unconsciously. This activity has a special place in everyone's life. Your imagination is regarded as a function whenever you think and decide about what you can wear in a party or at work. When you decide to go to a known place such as your office, store, shopping centers or your friends' house, your mind unconsciously observes that place and guides you there. Before going a place where you have not previously been, you usually preplan for this event. How do you do it? You use your imagination, take benefit from your ability for imagination, and imagine rods and streets you are going to pass and even traffic lights. You plan your route by help of maps and imagination capability.

Imagine a person asks about a known address. You show the route while imagine the way in your mind. When you decide to bake a cake, buy a new pants, change decoration of your home, select a car to buy, plan about your holiday, relate a story or summary a movie, you do all of these by your imagination.

Fancy; how is it?

We imagine events and scenes of a movie in our minds. When we imagine, it is possible that these imaginations appears real to us. If we repeat the same fancy in a period of time, we will fall into the habit of it, we will believe it and we will accept it as a fact; in particular, if this fancy associates with strong emotions. When positive fancies realize, they will have good and positive results. Fancies can also be about problems and unfavorable events. In this case, they will be called worry. If these kinds of fancies are repeated, it is possible to realize and lead to unhappiness and dissatisfaction.

What we imagine affects our viewpoint, mentality and mind state. It means that we should be very sensitive to what comes into our minds. Thoughts are regarded as visitors of minds. When the same thoughts are repeatedly created in the mind, they became to its permanent residents. Do you let a person come to your house and stay there? If not, why do you allow the thoughts to do so?

Scientifically, creative embodiment means imagination process of a figure in mind which manifests it on the related plate through use of mental and natural regulations. In other words, creative embodiment means process of images and thoughts creation - consciously or unconsciously- in mind, and then sending them to body as orders or signals. (Khoshdel, 2008)

Deciding about what we actually want to occur and its imagination with focus, believe and interest will be very effective in practice. Creative imagination is a strong instrument and we should know how appropriately and positively apply it. This is a natural process used unconsciously by us. Thoughts create our life. It is possible to learn, accept, think about and embody just positive thoughts through teaching and practicing. In this way, we can fill our life with happiness, success, health and love. In order to effectively use mental faculties, called as mind magic, there is no need to charm or formalities. Thinking faculty, imagination, emotions and intentions are the most important elements in this regard. Whenever we focus our mind on special thoughts and add special emotions and senses, we use mind magic. Our strong thoughts have a definite effect on environment and those who surround us. It can be stated that all of us are magician somehow. However, few people understand this and consciously use it. Also, creative imagination can be effectively used in art and architecture instruction. For example, a summary of an architectural space description is offered to the students in some exercises and they are asked to imagine themselves there, move and complete or change there as they desire and state their findings in words or sketches. Students' mind is usually full of different ideas and spaces but they cannot express them correctly. This results from lack of exact imagination and mental focus on the subject. Imaging an uncreated space in mind with more details and correct scale will be very effective in more quick and exact imagination and designing. Enhance imagination power of your mind by practice and repeat. (This is not limited to imaginary courses; rather, it can be useful in most of life affairs and increase stability of information in long-term memory).

61- Dreaming (it is civilizing).

Dreaming provides opportunity for appearing of excessive passion of moral senses and sometimes even metaphysical ones, supports them, grants them liberty and manifests them. The most elegant sensation of human relations, refined differences, learning the best culture and finally, a conscious logic which have very nicely been explained and it can be obtained just with a vigilant movement. Dream is an uncivilized story takes its rise from very civilized emotions. (Roland Barthes, The pleasure of the text)

62- How to watch better (strengthening visual capabilities): in everyday life, we see what we like to see. It results somehow from our brain function. We delete some part of information because of need to stability, ignore other ways, interpret all things based on our current viewpoint from existence, and classify the received data according to our traditional methods. **This is while a creative mind should learn to exactly watch the environment and understand details of nature. A creative person accepts nature as it is and looks carefully and enthusiastically for discovering of unknowns. This process is highly affected by our methods of seeing, and amount of our care and understanding.**

63- Take photos from different subjects and perspectives. Try to create different spaces and figures by use of collage technique. This will be useful in strengthening brain right hemisphere and your visual sense.

64- Before presenting a subject and through exercises posed in the class, the teacher should try to force students to indirectly prepare some of the required concepts in their minds and even analyze them.

65- Old methods of training prevent creativity: A person who looks for creativity and innovation in good or bad, initially should start with destroying values.(Friedrich Nietzsche)

66- Write down and draw all architectural thought and ideas coming to our minds without any judgment. It is necessary to write its date.

67- Always keep the class lively through playing music, reciting poems in chorus, use of emphasizing words,… Such activities can be done in theoretical and practical classes with some changes. This is regarded as one of the instructional necessities which result in enhancing coordination and cooperation between students. On the other hand, performing such exercises will result in refreshing of students who were busy for drawing and designing for hours.

68- Promoting state of cooperation: manifestation of new and novel thoughts and ideas cannot be expected until students do not feel security and belonging among their friends and also the classroom. This will grant more courage to students to state their thoughts and ideas.

69- Enter yourself more than one route.

Do not think about just one answer in architecture designing. Try different ideas, even when you think this cannot be an appropriate idea in this regard. Remember that a logical brain initially tries to classify ideas and data of the project resorting to its reasons and analyses and then offer some of them as desired options of the project. In contrast, an artist's brain considers the apparently inappropriate ideas and tries to adjust them with demands of the project. In addition to strengthening creativity and enhancing self-assurance, designer faces many ideas and results through passing this way.

70- Encounter realities and problems of project and do not change the question.

71- Do not work on what your friends have focused on.

72- Work on different projects in a period of time.

73- Always look for new ways in designing.

74- Be excited and look enthusiastically at events in your surroundings. Learn to be excited with a fragment of music, color of a leaf, an incomplete sketch and smile of a child.

75- Create a weblog for yourself and let others observe and criticize your works and thoughts.

Critical thinking in design process

As stated, creative thinking is responsible to create new ideas and solutions as well as better ideas. In addition to empower the creative imagination, another kind of thinking is required to help us in selecting, evaluating, and assessing the findings. Critical thinking is a divergent thinking providing logical reasoning, differentiating facts, determining ambiguities of problem, and recognizing contradictions. In fact, creative and critical thinking are wings of an architect to found his/her creative works on mental, logical, and applicable bases.

Critical thinking does not mean negativism and criticize; rather, it is a thinking dealing with evaluating reasons and causes. Critical thinking emphasizes ideals of a reasonable person, i.e. a person who can think independently and without others control (Fischer, 2007).

In his book (How we think), John Dewey defines suspend judgment or healthy skepticism (constructive criticism) and avoiding from hasty judgment as nature of critical thinking. In other words, he defines critical thinking as exact, sustainable and active evaluation of all ideas and knowledge (Dewey,1982). Chet Meyers, in his book known as "teaching students to think critically", defines it as identification of incorrect reasoning, avoiding from stated and non-stated contradictions and assumptions in others discussions, lack of emotional excitement when encountering the problem and believes that asking questions about problem and criticizing and evaluating solutions without referring to alternations are the main factor in critical thinking (Meyers, 1995).

Robert Ennis, author of "critical thinking", defines critical thinking as rational and logical thinking focusing on deciding about ideas and actions. He believes that thinking becomes critical when the thinker analyzes subjects exactly, looks for valuable evidences, and reaches healthy judgment and results. He suggests that teaching to think critically aims at educating persons who are far from personal biases and are precise in their work (Ennis, 1985).

Critical thinking necessarily includes analysis and evaluation. To find evidences and criteria in critical thinking, data is initially searched, collected, and analyzed and then validity and conformity of what has been found are judged based on the selected criterion (Bear, 1987)

What has been stated by Barry Bear (author of several books about thinking) about function of critical thinking corresponds well with what occurs in design process. If creating of idea, form and novel structures, or finding ways to realize ideas are known as results of creative and divergent thinking, thus, critical thinking will be responsible to analyze findings and select the most accurate of them. Critical thinking is an activity mostly done in the left hemisphere and progresses logically.

Ten skills of critical thinking stated by Barry Bear are considered to make clear what should be dealt with in analyzing and evaluating of data in design process (the descriptions come after every skill are written by the author):

1. Differentiating confirmed facts and value claims
   - Considering real needs of society against ambitions and value desires
   - In evaluating implemented samples, works of some famous architects are usually referred to and the efficiency of projects, especially foreign ones, is not studied considering society
2. Differentiating related and unrelated information, claims or reasons
   - Especially in renovation and urban development projects where it is very important to evaluate historical information and their verity and untruth.

3. Determining real accuracy of statements
   - Recognition stage of design process usually deals with data collection and classification rather than discussing about reality of findings. Unfortunately, there is not any course or curriculum focusing on the mentioned points and skills.
4. Determining validity of references
   - In recognition stage, there are some oral references (or other forms of references) with no required validity and they may not be used as a basis for scientific study
   - In climatology, for example, it should not suffice to some books written during recent decades and possible changes should be traced from meteorological organization.
5. Determining ambiguities of claims or arguments
   - It is better to provide in written the discussions, meetings, and arguments about great projects of the country
6. Determining the specified assumptions
7. Discovering of inclinations and biases
   - Style, custom, and desire of special groups without any scientific and logical roots should not be accepted and designs should not be based on them. A problem faced by Iranian architecture where employers of private or public sector guide Iran architecture and architects execute employers 'requirements rather a creative work
8. Determining logical sophistries
9. Recognizing contradictions in reasoning
10. Determining power of a discussion or claim

Uniformity of critical thinking skills with that of design thinking during recognition stage of architectural design process

Describing and analyzing thinking, Jennifer Needler refers to following skills and believes that they are necessary to empower critical thinking. She divides skills into three main parts and describes them completely. These descriptions specify train of thought and titles which should be considered by designers in recognizing the problem:

a. **Defining the problem and clarifying it**

1. Recognizing main viewpoints: capability to recognize main idea of articles, discussions, or political movies, capability to recognize reasons and results of discussions
- Drawing diagrams, compiling accurate physical program, analyzing of site, and evaluating the region climatically
2. Comparing differences and similarities: capability to compare similarities and differences of several thoughts, objects, persons, or occasions in a special time or during different times (Shabani, 2010, p.83)
- Evaluating different viewpoints and ideas about design (e.g. residential complexes)
- In design courses, one kind of thinking and attitude toward design (usually dominant attitude of the instructor or society) governs the design studio and different thoughts and ideas are not discussed about. Additionally, there are few books about design of museum, hospital and etc. which discusses the case theoretically
3. Recognizing information related to the problem: capability to recognize related and unrelated or

reviewable and non-reviewable information about the problem

4. Posing appropriate questions: capability to design questions resulting in better and deeper understanding of the viewpoint or occasion (Shabani, 2010, p.83)

- Questions asked by architects during project design process especially at recognition and idea production stage may be really helpful in stimulating creative mind and securitizing the students
- In drawing up of questionnaires used to collect data from a specific region, whether generalities are collected or this is done in several stages and new questions are asked and evaluated in line with the project progress

b. Judging about information related to the problem

5. Differentiating between facts, beliefs, and documented judgment: capability to use scientific criterion in order to determine quality of observation, deduction, and judgment

- Unfortunately, most assessments including that of university corrections and higher decision making levels in governmental organizations and departments do not significantly consider it and projects are commonly dealt with based on personal values and ideas

6. Evaluating conformity of concepts: capability to recognize conformity of concepts and context of information, for example, whether points mentioned in a political discussion have logical conformity with each other and with the main viewpoint (Shabani, 2010, p.83)

- For example, do architectural ideas confirm with culture and climate of the region

- Does the presented plan confirm with logical requirements of employer and project
- Conformity and interaction of building with the site should be considered from initial stages of design to prevent from future problems
- Corresponding of site plans provided by organizations or consulting engineers companies with each other and governing conditions

7. Recognizing of unstated assumptions
8. Recognizing of fixed stereotype beliefs about persons, groups or ideas
9. Recognizing of emotional and advertising factors as well as biased materials (Shabani, 2010, p.84)

- The West advertisements are not limited to selling of goods and showing of movies. Scientific societies of the West advertise their dominant thoughts and beliefs through holding of seminars and workshops and, unfortunately, the East deals with this emotionally and thinks that being inattentive to them directs them toward retardation
- There are different ideas opposing with some aspects of sustainability in architecture in the West. However, they are not evaluated by scientific society of Iranian architecture and they blindly, repeatedly and superficially (as the author thinks so) use ideas of western thinkers and rely on their ideas (Refer to "determining accuracy of statements", the skills stated by Barry Bear).
- An obvious example is application of a special approach related to West architecture in executive or

university projects without any sufficient research about it during second half of 1990s such as deconstruction and folding architecture in architecture faculties of Islamic Azad universities, or recent focus on green architecture and sustainability in spite of gaps found in this regard (especially in quantity and efficiency of executive plans, their cost-effectiveness and generalizability to other societies). Most instructors ask their students to design sustainably in their designs and thesis.

10. Recognizing value systems and different worldviews
- Paying no attention to the above-mentioned subject considering how to think about architecture and urban development results in irretrievable shocks to development plan of most Iranian cities conducted with a modern attitude and ignoring organic structure of cities.
- Influence of modernity and human-based beliefs in Iran changed design methods and architectural education system as well as architects orientation toward West such that most look at past architecture of Iran reluctantly, unwillingly, and even inefficiently. As stated in previous pages about worldview, lack of thinking and generation of though in society opens the way for influence of lifestyles and thoughts. While, being equipped to such skills promotes recognition and decision making capacity of the society and leads to its progress.

c. **Problem solving or extracting results**
11. Deciding about sufficiency of the collected data
12. Predicting possible results
- Predicting future development of the project
- Predicting needs and requirements which will be brought up in future (for example, adding a new ward to a hospital or developing of one of the current wards such as laboratory).

Critical thinking and judgment

Judgment is of important factors in design process and is capable to change direction of design or subject of project. As stated, critical thinking is divergent and operates based on reason and logic. The role arises from cerebral activity of the left hemisphere of brain. Considering activities of the left (logical brain) hemisphere and its strengthening ways, information about critical thinking skills especially judgment, logic and decision-making, which will be observed in coming pages, may empower us in using logical brain capabilities and reach better and more accurate results.

Judgment, known as discovering of contradictions, is a kind of differentiating between reviewable and non-reviewable information. Quoting from Mac Quinn (1985), Barry Bear defines it as interpreting of information and detecting biased statements (Bear, 1985).

In other words, judgment may be distinguished from differentiating, discovering, interpreting, recognizing, and identifying and essentially used for all skills of critical thinking.

Architectural judgments are introduced as follows:

It should be noted that architects are familiar with following cases. However, their accurate evaluation with a judgment and critical viewpoint is of high importance especially at academic level. They should be discussed in design studios and judged and selected logically. Relying on these trainings, creative and critical thinking may be converted to an inevitable tradition in academic and mental system of architecture society and change its value, personalized, and one-dimensional format.

1. Judging about nature and quiddity of project
2. Judging about assumptions of project
3. Judging about needs and requirements of society and employer
4. Judging about physical plan and construction function
5. Judging about project site in city and location of building inside the site
6. Judging about validity of observations (Shabani, 2007, p.85)
7. Judging about explicitness of statements
8. Judging about refinement, analysis, and options
9. Judging about results of every stage of design process
10. Judging about presented alternatives
11. Judging about quality of plans and ideas
12. Judging about consistency between architectural plans and climate and culture of the society
13. Judging about economic justification of project
14. Judging about construction principles of the country.

Decision making strategy in architectural design process

Decision making is of the most important strategies in design process. According to thinkers working on thinking training, the strategy is often discussed and evaluated in line with problem solving. All solutions carry kind of decision making and no results will be concluded without decision making and final selection. Judgment and decision making are along each other and are merged in a way since accurate judgment contains what which should be selected or used for decision making.

In every design studio, there are usually some persons who have problems in selecting of their designs and even change their design within the last weeks of the semester. It indicates to weakness of logical thinking, accurate judgment, and decision making. Similar cases may be seen in the society varying from buying clothes to deciding about the spouse (it is one of the reasons for slow progress in our society). In addition to studying of thinking topics and practicing the mentioned skills, the readers should use other sources of thinking and the related courses. Thinking will not be achieved through studying of one or more books or practicing for some weeks, rather, it is a process which should be dealt with during life.

Designers always emphasize on multi-dimensional thinking and offering several solutions, pre-design, and idea to lessen the mistakes through increasing options. It will serve as a clue for more activity of the artists mind. In this regard, selecting of appropriate cases requires critical thinking operating through relying on some skills including judgment and decision making. Characteristics of decision making strategy are as follows:

1. Selecting some accepted alternatives when there is not any special or accurate alternative
2. Concurrent evaluation of the selected alternatives instead of continues assessment of potential solutions

3. Using qualitative and quantitative criteria in analyzing of different alternatives
4. Repeating sources to test criteria application

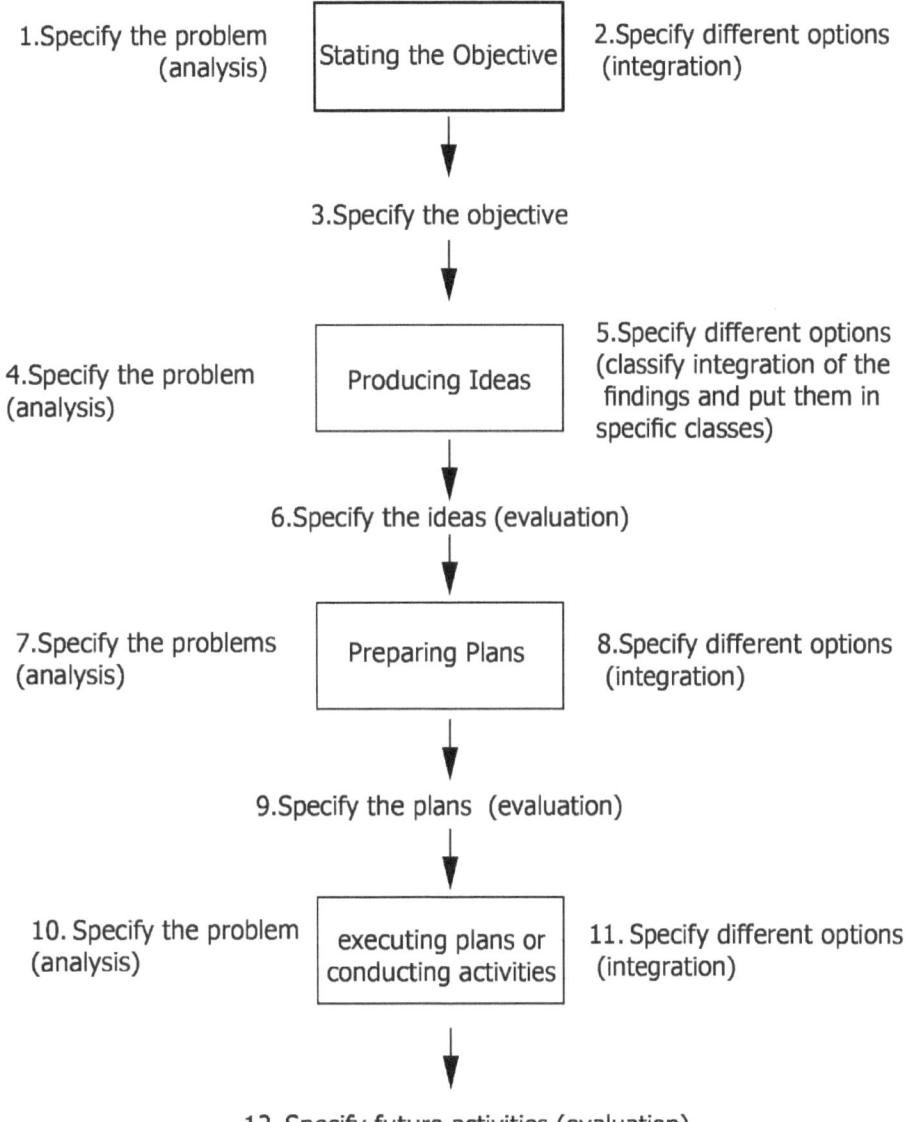

The waltz, Nardi, and Stager pattern (1986) for decision making

Architectural Designing Process

It is for a long time that this question has been posed in minds of architecture theoreticians whether architecture designing or process for reaching architecture body is merely a kind of innovative mental practice and it is not possible to clearly describe its structure generality or it is possible to explain a fixed and specified process in architecture designing through thinking on architects' ideas and functions considering designing?

An architecture's act as a creative character is passing through a continuous process of artistic creation which start from a main motivation derived from a set of other motivations and lead to creation of a final design. Designer does not create something from another thing; rather, he/she creates a new entity and takes benefit from his/her "imagination" potency in this process. Therefore, it is not possible to know a design beforehand or set a complete regulation or specified course for how to design. This is one of the most important points observed in sketches without a special theme (conceptual sketches) performed based on some kind of inner excitation.

Contemporarily, most of those dealing with descriptions on designing process have specified stages thereon. Different individuals pass these stages through a variety of ways. Most of them introduce designing process as a completely intuitional and indescribable one. Others describe designing as a rational process, while another group think about it as a controversial one. Each of these ideas requires separate discussions. Almost all designers, however, agree with the importance of intuition in designing process. This is exactly the common point between architectures and their works. Communication with existence and emancipation in nature result in creating ideas and thoughts in artist's mind in a special moment and he/she starts to create while inebriated with energy. This is a condition observed in most successful architects.

At the first step, the architect uses instruments like pen and computer to incarnate what is in mind. Designing is the first tool provides the architect to combine his/her ideas and thoughts with requirements and needs of the project and to portray the result. Architect is, in fact, a designer designs his/her ideas in order to make and respond to users' requirements. An architect should know designing for architecture and know how to present it exactly because of this feature that his/her design will be used in a construction. In other words, definition of designing has a unique concept to an architect considering necessity of its applicability, so it is inevitable to determine a specific process and course during designing.

The architect does the same with designing that an author or poet does with words, a painter with paints and a composer with notes with a difference that his/her work is not to be part of life. Rather, results of an architect's designing will be container for life occurrence if it yields and is performed. Designing is as a bed for architect in which he/she demonstrates his/her knowledge along with his/her creativity with the hope of making and offering facilities and enhancing life quality of part of population of a society, though this bed is not last stage of an architect's work.

What's designing?

Designing as the first and most important approach of an architect to transfer his/her mind has been studied and evaluated from different aspects for several times and there are many definitions thereon whose expressing will be useful.

Designing is expressing thoughts and emotions through use of points, lines, contrast and relationships governing them which are conducted for creating space, introducing and communicating with the partner.

Designing has been defined in Oxford English Dictionary as follow: architecture designing separately refers to a sequence of distinct able moments in the process until the idea is formed in the mind, until elementary sketches are prepared and presented as instructions for making something which leaves the details to be worked on later and preparing required plans and drawings for constructing a building etc., workers should work in its accordance.(Madani Pur, 2000)

Queen Lynch (1918), a contemporary American urban-planner defines designing as:" designing is creation along with powerful imagination of a possible form aims at realizing serving to human in some social, economical, aesthetical or technical ways". At another place, he explains this definition as:" artistic creation and evaluation of possible forms for something including how they should be made".

Designing process

When an architect decides to design a work until the final result is present to be executed as a sketch, it is not just designing which has been occurred rather there are many events inside it referred to as designing process. Designing process is a set of stages and activities performed consciously or unconsciously by the architect to present his/her mental findings in the frame of a specified body.

Wonderful feature of architecture designing has always been emphasized as a process. As it has been mentioned, designing process is a step by step or even parallel occurrence of events each of them helps the other in completing the idea. These events may sometimes be along and even they can disregard each other and lead to decorating the final result in a similar function. (Khiabanian, 2005)

Designing process, in fact, consists from several stages exactly woven in each other. Although each step is self-dependent, they act in coordination and unity and are under control of the designer's creative mind. All designing stages have the same values and there is no preference. Accordingly, it is possible to refer to several stages in explaining designing process but it does not mean considering order or preference to these stages. Also, existence and nonexistence of each stage in designing process of each architect directly depends on his/her procedure and customs. In real, preferences and order of events in designing process bear less importance. What is more important is existence of this process which is an inevitable necessity. Unfortunately, little attention has been paid to this necessity or in most cases has been ignored in architecture faculties.

Necessity of process for designing stems from inability of the architect in imaging details for a design which does not exist. Details are in service of generalities. At the first stages of designing process, generalities of the work should be formed and then the details should attach it after complete coordination. Therefore, designing is similar to see a person who approaches us from far away. At first, we observe a general and vague figure, as we approach it and with any step toward it, the vague will disappear and more details appear step by step. Sometimes, architecture designing is similar to bringing up a sapling. Your idea sapling should pass its special stages so that change to a fructiferous tree. Recognition of these stages can create a more appropriate and direct process in designing. The first stage is watering the sapling which is regarded as primary idea. In turn, the course should be prepared to approach more exact thoughts and ideas. At the next stage, the architect should wait for occurring what which should occur. Hurry is useless since the ideas will let the architect know when they become powerful. More creative architect's mind, greater, quicker and deeper artistic productions will be observed because the architect or designer connects to endless treasury of knowledge for his/her artful mind.

It should be remembered that designing is the same as unveiling a fact and should be conducted exactly, finely and step by step.

Architecture designing is a multi-structure and complex process requiring both knowledge and creativity. It is difficult and somehow impossible to determine a comprehensive and specified method for architecture designing because of extensive and various areas and concepts in its common space the architecture and designing has been placed.

As it has been mentioned, it is not possible to consider an exact and detailed designing process for architecture designing. It is also cannot expected from architects to operate on the basis of a specified process. The presented diagram which will be completed and scrutinized at next pages is a general statement of stages passed by the designer to reach the specified goals. Performing all stages is not necessary. It is likely that some architects combine the stages or perform them concurrently owing to their powerful mind and hands.

Meanwhile, the mentioned phasing can be changed: for instance, designer repeats stages of idea and structure production several times or adds parameters such as others' experiences and directions to the designing process to reach an appropriate concept. **What is especially important in designing is how to control the mind, have a specific process in designing at the initial stages, having accurate information from designing process and their correct performance at the next stages.** The drawn diagrams, in fact, are excuses for analyzing mind function and what occurs during designing process. Designers can evaluate and draw a specific process of designing via exactly recognizing function of brains hemispheres and time and place of their correct performance.

Thinking about Architecture Designing through Diagrams

An architect thinks by means of sketches and drawings. Relation of pictures with brain right hemisphere (artist mind) makes creation of ideas and new solutions possible for him/her. Meanwhile, indelibility of information and their recalling is done easily in this method (this will be discussed in detail in arguments on creativity and visual thinking).

Traditionally, an architect is responsible for offering executive plans including profiles, executive details and so; but images offered by designer while drawing in order to verify and evaluate the alternatives are often abstract and are less important in constructing a building comparing with executive plans.

At initial stages of designing, the designer draws diagrams to register ideas, develop and connect them, analyze functions and prioritize in accessing to spaces, understand available plans and drawings, find new forms and correspond them with the main design, analyze the site, ecology and other cases. In this regard, paper and pencil play an important role in embodying architect's mind findings.

Betty Edwards- designing instructor- states that: plans and designs not only are regarded as a means for communicating with others but also sketches and drawings help designers to observe, understand and evaluate forms which are thought about.

At this stage of designing process, the designer draws diagrams about different subjects. Diagrams are a series of images for thinking, data analysis, problem solving and establishing communication in designing courses; they form primary grounds of designing; and are a simple and quick way for expressing structure or hidden relationships in a physical set. Diagrams are almost similarly used in different majors such as mechanical engineering, graphics, urban planning and others.

Architectural Diagrams

Architectural diagrams are drawings in which geometrical elements are used for absolute presenting of artificial phenomena such as noise, light, wind, rain; construction elements (walls, windows, doors, ..); furniture; human behaviors like population, range of vision, independent understanding, internal limits of a room or functions.

A diagram may represent a visual phenomenon such as wind, rain, specific landscape; or human perception from environmental phenomena like noise, heat, ventilation; and also functional aspects of the environment. Such diagrams present physical elements and their relations and demonstrate forces and potentialities such as direction and angle of sun light radiation or accumulation and scattering of population in architectural space which should be considered by designer. Therefore, we face with lines, vectors and other representative images of forces and potentialities in most diagrams which exhibit spatial features of the project in form of size and direction. These are useful in more complete understanding of the project. (Khiabanian, 2010)

A diagram is absolutely presented without offering detailed descriptions about scale or realistic images of project volume and form. Working with diagrams, we face indefinite figures approximately demonstrating some relationships of architectural spaces. In contrast, a sketch often discusses about appearance of an architectural space; offers information about three-dimensional features of the internal and external parts of a building; and considers details of the building plan and profile, its fitness, materials and its elements.

An architect considers figure, form and dimensions of spaces in sketching a plan and refers to diagrams of spaces relations for decoration of spaces and their function. It should be mentioned that drawing and analyzing of diagrams is a background for more exact sketching. Establishing communication and interaction between diagrams and sketches take place easier because they are of image type. It is possible that designer obtain newer ideas in space definition through these analyses and drawings.

It should be remembered that appearing of new ideas is possible in every stages of designing process and an exemplary designer should always be ready to accept and receive new thoughts and events.

Designing theoreticians' comments on role and importance of diagrams:

- Kirby Lockard in his book "*Design Drawing Experience*"(W. W. Norton & Company, 2001) states that: capability in drawing diagram of the project site features depends on designer's knowledge in related areas such a sun, wind, plant coverage, traffic and perimeter. He says that diagram drawing can be used to study differences of designing problems. This empowers the mind to visually observe, understand and response more than what can be remembered from verbal signs. Diagrams are, in fact, embodiment of verbal signs in graphic images.

- In "graphic thinking for architects and designers" (Wiley publications, 2000), Paul Laseau- architecture instructor- introduces use of diagrams as a method for solving designing problems, establishing and developing of communication with others. He states that like a verbal language, a diagram as a graphic language has also words and grammar which should be considered in drawing diagrams. He expresses that **"verbal language"** is sequential while elements of **"graphic language"** operate concurrently, i.e. all their symbols and relations should be considered at the same time.

- Lain Fraset and Rod Henmi in "*Envisioning Architecture* introduce"(Wiley publications, 1993), through analyzing of techniques and drawings affect architect's works, diagrams as drawings which offer a specific interpretation by summarizing and deleting unrelated information from the author's viewpoint. Architects put abstract cases like motion, access, noise, view, function and time in a diagram form as symbols through drawing diagram and, therefore; offer a perfect and comprehensive summary of information related to the project and use them to analyze and synthesize their ideas.

- Daniel Herbert- a university instructor and theoretician in architecture designing- define diagrams in the frame of analytical images including synthesis of graphical signs and written notes. A diagram translates verbal meanings to a graphical text and tries to offer approaches for solving architectural problems. "Diagrams are more than an appropriate strategy for solving architectural problems and used as a designer's main instrument in thinking".

Diagrams in Architecture Designing Process

Architectural diagrams are drawn during a designing process, before production and verification of the idea, and along with analysis and recognition of an architect's mind from a project. In fact, diagram is the first embodiment of the architect from analyses and problems which challenge the mind about desired problem and is an excuse for developing and scrutinizing performed activities.

Most architects start their designing process by drawing general diagrams from their architectural program; this process continues through studying project details and changes to a series of more complex graphic image. In such a method, designing is defined as a process of transformation and joining diagrams and the designer's effort in drawing, completing and synthesizing structural, functional and motional diagrams. Bryan Lawson- a deigning theoretician- has interviewed ten famous architects in "*Design in Mind*" (Architectural Press, 1994) book and studied their designing methods. He concludes that drawing plays an important role in designing process. **Designers state that thinking is difficult for them without having a pencil in their hand. Drawn images enhance mind solidarity and increase their control on different aspects of project,** a method which has faded among architects and students and replaced by verbal games and computer drawings.

Each diagram consisted of just some lines or symbols, while most of these diagrams, together, indicate variety in meaning and can express or at least demonstrate application of a series of models or spatial relations. Sketches and diagrams are methods for visual thinking and imaging a perceptive frame for analyzing, changing and replacing of designs. Number and variety of drawings and attention of designer to their quality provides more space to evaluate, select, interchange and develop of images in other parts of designing.

Architectural diagrams result in focusing of designers on knowledge and subjects related to designing, they clearly show designing route as a guide and offer results and regulations which help designers to prepare themselves for future analyses and designing. It can be stated that diagrams are always accompany designer during designing and are not limited just to the mentioned operational stage. Artist's mind is always engaged in analyzing and producing new thoughts which should not be neglected. We should not confine ourselves to fixed findings.

Creative Process Diagram in Architecture Designing

In the diagram which will be presented, it has been tried to offer a relatively specified and flexible structure of mind activity, idea production process and architecture design. Comparing with other designing process, specific features of this diagram can be found as follow.

- Creative process is not a linear one. Returning to previous stages or their combining with regard to mental capabilities and designing experience is possible at every moment. The most important is that the result of all stages including idea, concept or structure before confirmation should be compared with information and analyses of recognition stage by the brain left hemisphere and finalized in case of consistency.
- In creative process, it has been tried to offer details which are effective and important in designing process in addition to general discussions and put them in their appropriate places (idea production stage is an example).
- Creative process is a flexible one and designers can use it considering their brain hemispheres and designing methods. It is possible to combine designing stages or repeat the previous stages during the process considering mind function. Both hemispheres of brain attend in designing stage. Space required for function and selection of findings without any priority should be done exactly.
- In most designing processes, starting point of designing and how we can have a strong start is forgotten. Use of conceptual sketches during designing and recognizing function of brain hemispheres provides specific conditions for starting and continuing designing.
- Circular motion can be observed during all stages of the process.

- Circular and supplementary motion during designing process. For example, designer can return to ideation stage and repeat the stages, if not satisfied with the resulted structure.
- Research, possibility and tree-shaped attitude in idea and information analysis, structure stage, concept and… are also reminded like architecture creation circle in every stage.
- **Synthesis** and **experimentation** are points added to creative process after analyzing at the end of each stage.
- Creative mind is always ready to produce new ideas. The resulted concept and structure can be used as a new idea for other projects. Production of more than one concept or structure should always be expected.

Specific Stages in Designing Process

- Recognition: Drawing of diagrams, analyzing and processing of information
- Purification
- Information analysis
- Ideation
- Concept
- Spatial Structure
- Layout
- Architecture final design

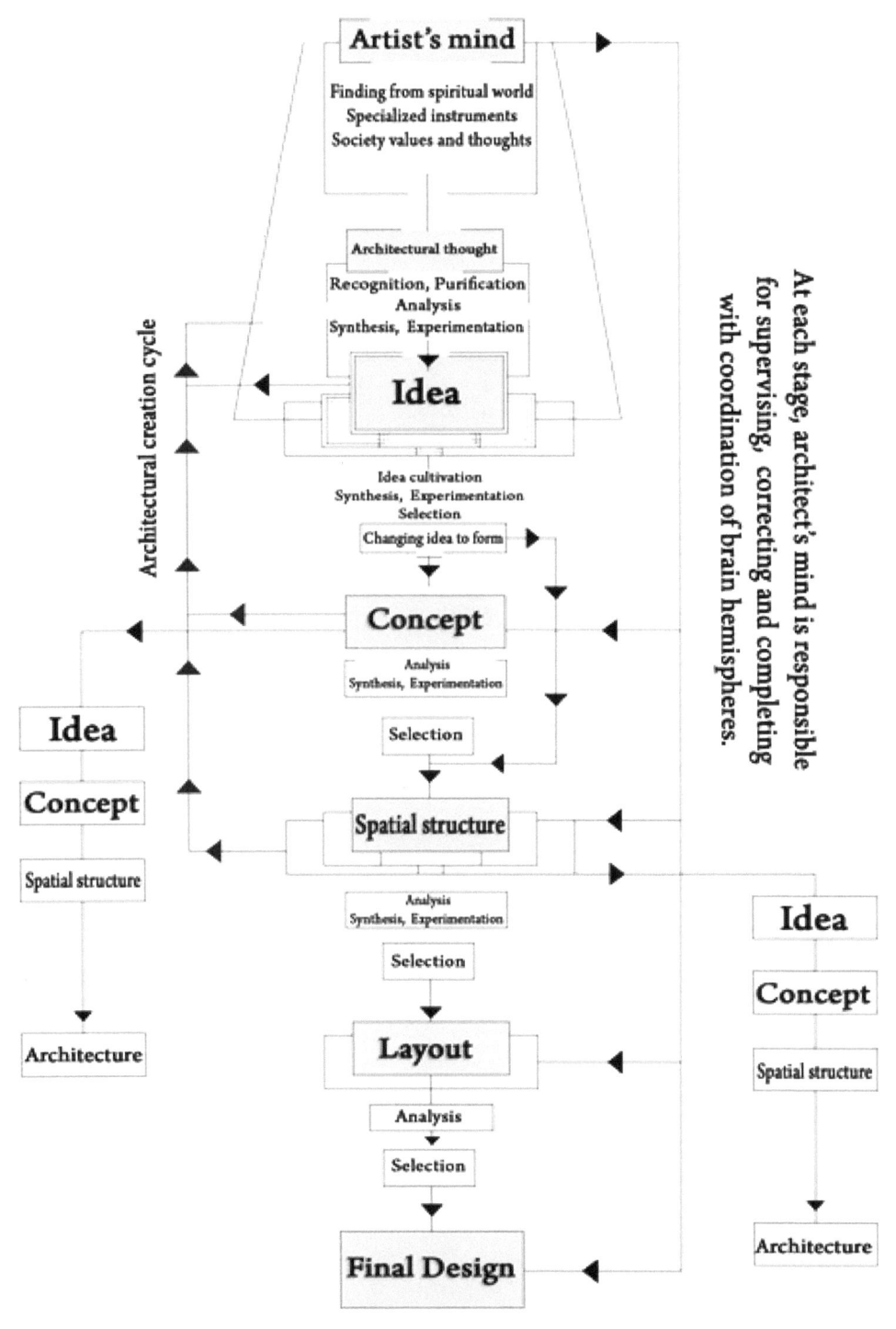

Project Recognition

Project "recognition" and analysis is the first stage in designing process. Every architect and designer initially looks for recognizing and studying different aspects of the project. The more knowledge and proficiency of designer in this regard, the more accurate and nice works. Creative embodiment and drawing of diagrams are considered as the most important and efficient instruments in recognition stage specially quality analysis of functions, realm, site position and project spatial divisions.

Following cases should be correctly analyzed in full recognition of an architectural project:

- Realm (recognition of process and natural circumstances of region)
- Project site: history of site and region inside it, land topography, buildings and natural complications such as trees and rivers found there, view from outside into the site and vice versa (landscape), surrounding streets and alleys and how to access the site
- Studying of adjacent points, geometrical pattern of the region and current applications
- Evaluating the site considering building localization, relation of site with the building and vice versa
- Accurate analysis of accumulation or scattering of buildings in the site
- Features of buildings found in the region considering oldness, structure, designing and construction style and method, confronting with ecological and material problems, culture and viewpoint of the residents toward architecture
- Urban-planning standards: comprehensive and detailed plan, region develop and change in past, present and future (correct localization control of project by the employer)

- Architectural standards of organizations and municipalities such as density and occupation
- Cultural and social conditions of the environment, paying attention to mentalities, physical and mental needs of residents Psychological analysis (relationship of human with space, human with human in a designed space, and space with space)
- Project and employer demands
- Physical program of the project, diagram of spatial relationships, circulation, spatial hierarchies, analysis of priorities, infrastructure of the project
- Financial and economical problems of project: corresponding of architecture design with the budget considered for construction, economical justification of the project and capital return
- **Formal analyze**
  Studying similar patterns and finally studying type of architecture which can respond to the environment. (next page images)
- And ….

Formal analyses of landscape design Designed by Farzaneh Rahmat Dust

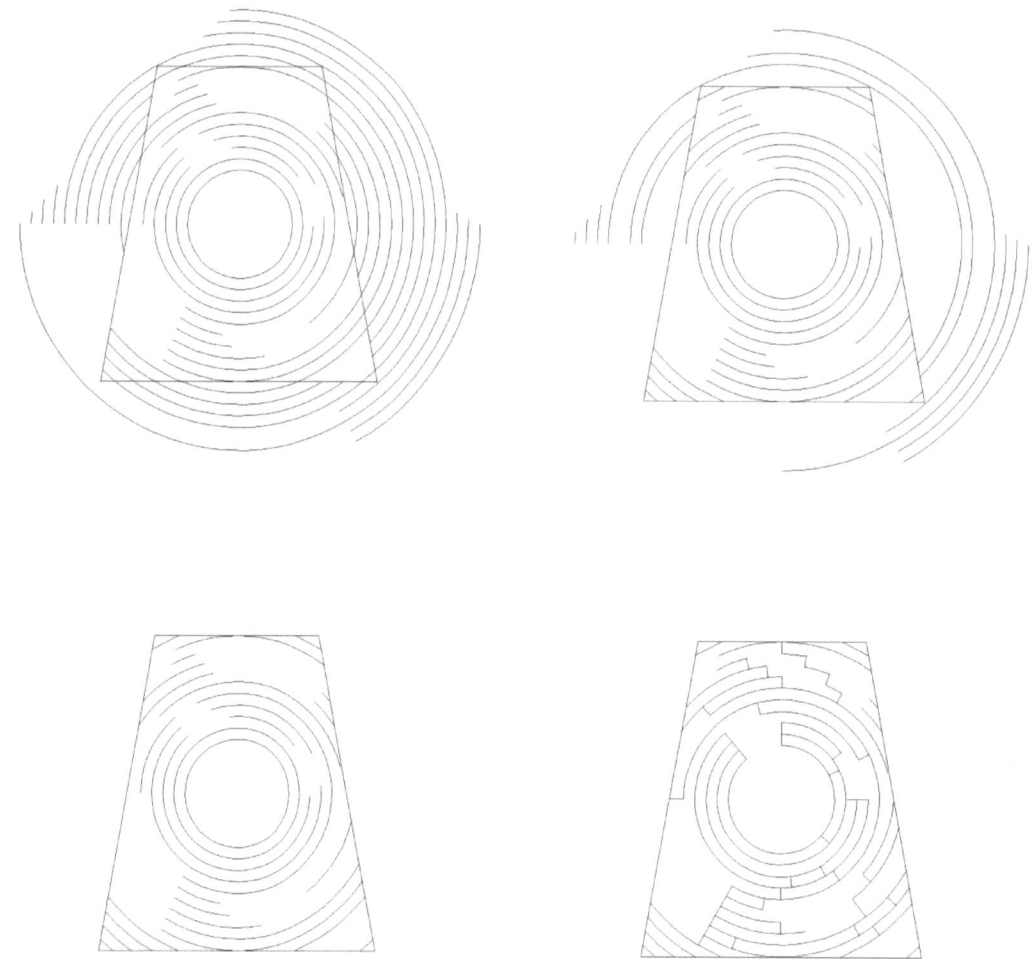

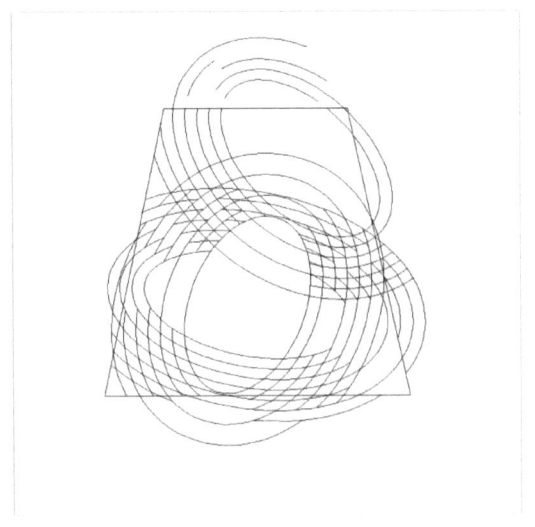
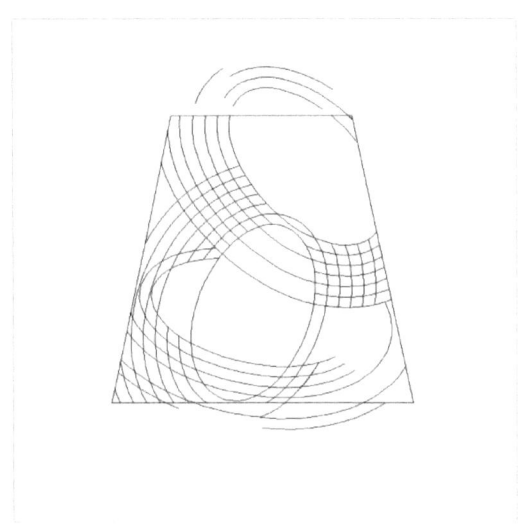

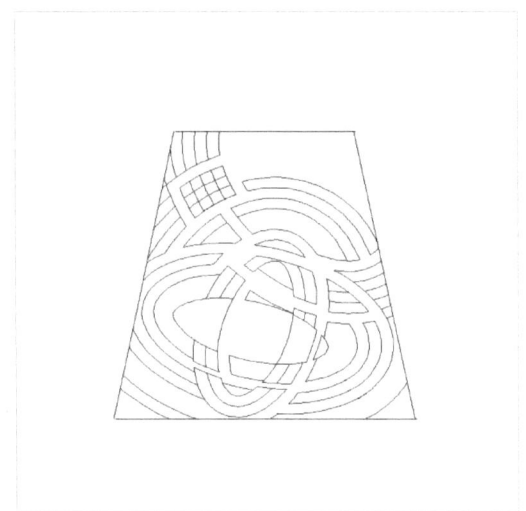

Purification

At this stage, the collected data should be purified and classified. Pure and impure information are separated. Use of visual thinking can be helpful in this stage. Initially, all information is displayed on a big blackboard or computer screen at once and their priority reasons are clearly specified.

Next, the person tries to classify the desired materials in common groups considering their features and importance. Incorrect information is omitted from designer's mind cycle.

Analysis

Informational groups are being discussed and studied. Their efficiency in idea production is verified. Brain left hemisphere (logical mind) has the most duty and should determine time and location of information use for designer; which discussions will be needed where or how they can be effective in designing. Of course, some part of this effort done unconsciously, artist's mind unconsciously analyzes the posed subjects and subsequently introduces ideas.

Synthesis

At synthesis stage of this process, necessary cares should be taken to synthesize, insert, integrate or coordinate available information considering ratios obtained from analysis of the previous stage.

Experimentation

This stage considers more details of designing process and deals with cases such as experimentation, testing besides information analysis and project constraints. Typically, several ideas can be produced during designing; but, analysis and experimentation of the findings practically can reduce possible errors in designing, and increase project quality.

Idea

As it has been mentioned, phasing designing process and considering it as a terminated one after passing through the stages is not possible. Recognition phase is one of the most important stages in production of new ideas and thoughts in architecture. The offered diagrams and analyses present new methods for problem solving. Drawing diagrams, in fact, provides designers' mind to deal more clearly and carefully with their findings and knowledge of the project. This time interval which often neglected by architects and consultants is an opportunity for activity of the brain right hemisphere and production of creative ideas.

It should be remembered that logical mind, considering its specific structure, quickly uses architect's mind archive and presents previous studies and experiences for problem solving or deals with the project when faces with municipality standards or ecological problems. Within this time, little activity is observed from the brain right hemisphere due to continuous and hard activity of the left hemisphere. Considering imagism function of artist's mind and time passing, drawing of diagrams reduces function of logical mind and creates a balanced condition for function of both hemispheres. It is at this moment that appearance of new ideas in dealing with ecological problems, municipality standards and so can be expected.

Idea is the result of knowledge, thinking, awareness and information found in designer's mind and is in direct relation with the world and perimeter surrounding him/her. Information acquired by senses from outside and come to the mind will be organized in thinking process and led to appearing of idea in case of presence of creativity. All phenomena such as buildings, a natural form, even a story or poem found in the world can operate as catalysts for cultivating idea in mind.

For an architect or designer, idea production process and concept formation are as the most important and effective stages in designing process. Searching and discovering new ideas and their embodiment in a graphic language which determines constancy and developing route of the project is more sensitive than other stages. It is exactly regarded as the most important stage in forming an artist's mind, creatively retelling processed information of the logical mind, and offering new solutions for some problems and questions.

Ideas are definite or imaginary thoughts originates from observations, perceptions and thoughts such as methods of buildings directing, positioning of a kitchen in a residential unit, use of air natural flow, value of energy and its saving, methods of dealing with the site, considering potentials and restrictions of project, locating project volumes in interchange, and coordination of site and architecture. Architect can use everything and everywhere, life daily objects, nature, different sciences, historical buildings and especially all that are present in program and site to create ideas.

There is always appropriate opportunity for imaging ideas at initial stages of the project, especially if the mind is capable to accept unusual and imaginary creative thoughts which can solve most problems. At the next steps, when architects obtain more acquaintance with the project and get information about its problems, recognize that some imaginations and ideas are more important and appropriate and change them to architecture during designing process or involve them in their architecture. Stability, constancy and dynamism of ideas, and depth and content of the architect's thought are a guarantee for proper and appropriate presence of an architect.

Existence and control of a stable thought which is capable of offering new ideas in a determined frame of time and location and even can prove its being against immenseness of existence exceeding every presence is the most important need of human being specially in continuing the selected route. Study of deigning process and methods of mind control can provide answer to most of architects' questions regarding architecture designing.

Synthesizing ideas and information to make something is really gratifying. Much energy is spent for moving and developing thoughts and more and more ideas are produced. Therefore, changing methods of thinking, extending choosing ability, leaving judgment aside to add more information and ideas to ours can have desired results. In progressing from ideation to putting them in practice, we should be steady and try hard so that we can observe their realization.

Ideas as human directors can be influent just when be essentially dynamic and can bear and face with other ideas. Logic, correspondence with realities, rational evaluation, understanding capability and testing based on nature and realities can specify value of an idea.

To exactly study idea, we will have a glance on ideation and architecture of Zaha Hadid:

Working with land is one of the main characters of Zaha Hadid. The idea of land leveling of design (in philharmonic Hall of Luxembourg, for example) form main ideas of her designs. It is a method for accessing a new geometrical organization that makes creating of new and unknown spaces possible while the site and environment are coordinated; a method for developing of architecture in all directions rather than being confined in a bottleneck.

For example, Zaha Hadid has used field and force idea (land remoulding idea) in designing of Qatar Museum of Islamic Arts and Modern I.I.T Academic Center. In design of Rome Museum of Contemporary Arts, delta-shaped force fields operate like boundaries and take place in horizontal routes. This is while in Rainasofia Museum development, force fields are interwoven and rigidly rest on each other. Therefore, a treasury of figures is available to designer that result in coordination of designer's works due to general solidarity of their language and their generating from a single bed in spite of many differences in concepts or figurative sets.

Leveling, site slope, topography lines (depth, width, synthesis and even material) are concepts operating as ideas in spatial organization of the project through different analyses in architect's creative mind.

Dubai opera house
Zaha Hadid

Architecture method and the route passed by each architect in architectural production is often different with other architects' especially in "idea" production in which personal experiences and viewpoints are more involved rather than a specified and documented method. Neither it is possible to consider a specified time and location for production of artistic works nor recognition of sources of inspiration and communication of the artist with spiritual world. It is evident that successful architects have always widely worked in different artistic and theoretical aspects and created architecture in multi-dimensional spaces which is in coordination with other fields. Painting, sculpture, literature, philosophy, psychology, music and … have always been regarded as forces to stimulate and scrutinize architect's mind and as tools to express his/her findings.

From Michel Angelo to Le Corbusier, Friedrich Hundertwasser, Marcel Breuer, Peter Eisenman, Zaha Hadid, Santiago Calatrava, Hushang Seihoun, Kamran Diba, Bruce Mao, Hani Rashid and most other successful architects of the world have repeatedly used other arts as important instruments in creation of ideas and concepts such that Le Corbusier introduces painting as principle basis of his practices and architectural thoughts.

Four Stages of Idea Production

At this stage, mind starts producing of creative ideas through referring to its resources (recognition, purification and information analysis) collected during a specific process at the previous stages. Four stages can be considered for idea production:
- Idea finding or creating
- Idea cultivating
- Idea selecting
- Concluding or returning to the first step

Idea Finding or Creating

Inspiration resources in idea production:
- Paying attention to concretes: Architectural works, natural figures and forms, arrangement of topography lines, project landscape, ecological problems (offering appropriate solutions), artists' works and comments (painters and sculptors)
- Conceptual dealing: Psychologically analyzing space, considering philosophical arguments and their structural function
- Use of artists' mind: In this case which can be at the same direction or accompany the mentioned discussions, the architect uses mental-conceptual sketches for finding new ideas. Designer sketches considering ideas (from previous stages) and spatial requirements of the project without activating of logical mind for thinking. Experiments demonstrate that continuing of these sketches gives full appearance to new ideas originating from the architect's unconscious mind or prepares structures with capability of ideas embodiment for the architect.

Example: At the stage of site analysis and volume locating and after studying technical and ecological aspects, the students are asked to sketch with an aesthetical view and purpose of deeply understand lines and structural capabilities of the site. As it can be observed, it is possible to access different structures in the third dimension in a trapezoid with developing and completing capability.

It should be remembered that principle foundations of project designing are based on analyzing and sketching of the project site. It is gradually completed with designing of the plan and project volume. Building designing has direct relationship with site and surrounding environment. Plan site designing should not be postponed to final stages of the project.

Most of us are sensitive to role of synthesizing in reaching unity and integrity in designing buildings and drawings. Unity is obtained in perimeter through aesthetic regulations, figures, patterns or specific details divided by elements which forms this environment. Knowledge of aesthetic system found in our drawings is developed through sketching and a similar sense of disciplinary is added to it.

Idea Cultivation

This stage takes place through selecting the resulted ideas, their adding, changing and synthesizing which lead to creating more complete and new ideas.

Designing process is not a definite linear one which a start and terminate point can be defined for it. At every stage, whether structure or concept, a creative mind can have innovative ways and methods. The produced ideas do not act abstractly and without changing; rather they are active part of an architect's mental process. Considering specified time and frame is not possible for idea production. New ideas may appear until final moments of project completion.

Idea Selection

Ideas selection and their correspondence with the collected information done mostly by the brain left hemisphere. It should be remembered that "writing" and "drawing" of ideas and the resulted outcomes is very important at every stage of designing process, and offering mental diagrams as words, sentences or sketches are appearance of idea evolution process and make changes, synthesis of concepts and conclusion easier for the architects and their addressees.

Conclusion or Return to the First Stage

It is possible to repeat 4 stages of idea production. At each restart, we can reach novel thoughts in addition to idea completion and acquiring more skills. This is the same for whole of designing process diagram. Apparently complete ideas and thoughts should not prevent us from repeating. (Khiabanian, 2010)

Role of Creativity in Producing of New Ideas

Generally, new ideas are created through thinking in which the mind deeply involves in a problem, embodies it and helps in illuminating a new idea through emitting or synthesizing of available facts. The resulted insight will nourish imaginary faculty in finding new thoughts. The new thoughts originate from imaginary faculty rather than human logical power. The obtained clues are evaluated and related to obtain the best thought.(Bidokhti, 2005)

Definition offered for creativity and idea formation process will pose the question about reasons of scarcity of new ideas at present and their foundation on western patterns, if any. Directing of us toward repetitions and sometimes surface copying of ancient architecture or western samples by today architecture is related to lack of appropriate grounds for thinking and passing through complete process of creativity in offering new ideas.

Architecture students observe less creative samples from their instructors, and for them the resulted outcome in any order is usually more important than designing process. Assuming that architecture instructors are creative, what they teach their students is not related to how to use imaginary faculty to change information to new ideas. A few students learn during their education how to process information required for creating architecture based on new ideas. Therefore, most of those graduated in architecture have problems in changing their perceptions from the environment to architectural ideas. Architecture students and architects are aware of most news, information and new phenomena in architecture area due to living in communication era, but they are not fully capable to reach correct thoughts and opinions through this information and create novel ideas. In fact, what happens to these architects is access to great information in a short time and disability in extracting thoughts and opinions from this information and their processing. These architects face problems in updating or localizing thoughts and opinions because they do not know procedure of information processing and passing them through imagination and embodiment filter, or the opportunity required for reaching new clues from what they have is not provided for them for several reasons.

Idea Changing to Form

Importance of passing through idea stage to form is similar to having good ideas for an architect. Initially, the idea may be available as a pure thought and is imagined with known non-architectural elements, and then changes to an architectural and finally to a normal idea. (Conceptual sketches or architectural concepts are of this category).

In order to change idea to form, it is necessary to pass through required routes. Therefore, having information about how to extract ideas from known categories and environmental phenomena and change them to architectural form is very important. Directly changing of what attracts our attention to architecture is sometimes impossible and also a superficial one. The most important point in designing process relates to identification of main characters of phenomena that considered as resources for creating architectural ideas by the architect. Ideas can be appeared in different forms. This appearance is determined with designing strategy rather than with form. Therefore, it is possible that the same idea lead to two different designs through taking different designing strategies.

Capability of formation initial ideas and designer's knowledge and skill in changing idea to form can be referred to as two essential conditions for changing idea to form. The first point in changing idea to form is related to formation capability of idea. This capability is in relation with idea resource and designer's mind. The second step in changing idea to form requires designer's knowledge and skill. Knowledge refers to designer's information of creativity and synthesis techniques and so can be learned by everyone through study. The issue of skill is more complex and related to talent and taste cultivation and gradual acquiring of capability in applying forms.

For example, Alvar Aalto is one of the architects that introduced nature as a great resource of different figures, volumes and ideas, dealt with drawing and scrutiny during his architectural life, and changed his viewpoints and understandings to structures in form of lines so that they can be changed to architecture. Creativity created as a result of considering hills, clouds or natural phenomena and sets of figures and concepts help the architect regarding architectural meaning, embodiment and imagination.

Alvar Aalto used different interpretations including integration with land complications through coordination, integration through applying appropriate materials, efficiently and thoughtfully combining of materials to enrich and coordinate internal/external spaces and even nature enhancing strategy while working with nature. He believed that building, sometimes, should change to its landscape such as ceiling of Lapila's house in Rovaniemi and pyramidal ceiling of auditorium and engineering building of Rovaniemi Technical University (Aalto's successful idea in coordination of architecture with environment). Aalto was always busy for sketching and drawing the nature and made love to his homeland, by fishing and hunting around there from childhood. (Ay, 2010)

Considering effects of visual arts specially painting on architecture, it should be mentioned that Mondrian's style, syntheses and paintings opened a wide window for architects and designers in a new expression and novel tradition at the beginning of the 20th century. Efforts of the Dutch artist and architect, Gerrit Rietveld (1888-1964) in three-dimensional imagination of these syntheses in the form of furniture specially chairs directed mental and creative process of architects from considering spaces and identical and historical findings to inside of their mind such that Mondrian's works are not regarded as mere artistic writings of a lonely and hard-working pious; rather these are reflective mental practices and exudations in universe system which present reports about coordination in existence with a knowledgeable insight and tries to exhibit some concepts of majestic world as form and color.

His works has been considered as an important resource in selection and production of concepts even for contemporary architects due to their deep meanings and accurate structures. Mondrian's violation to the available structures is regarded as an important event in architecture (a new approach in production and embodiment of ideas, selection and creation of correct and appropriate concepts). A rectangular canvas can be compared with architectural site. Each site is a ground and each ground includes horizontal sight (plan and site plan) and vertical sight (landscape and profile). Coordination of ground and figure such as locating volumes and their relation, placing windows on landscape, division of plan such as subset of other figures, colors and figures contrast, accumulation and ambiguity, and positive and negative space of painting, all include different degrees of painting approach toward architecture. Mondrian's works are regarded as powerful and appropriate imagination of basic and fundamental concepts. Some of them are referred as follow;

- Stable balance with straight and perpendicular lines
- Methods of dividing canvas
- Locating painted surfaces
- Rhythm, repeat and synthesis
- Valuation on surface
- Reality, definiteness, clearness
- Simplifying the figures as possible, a subject which can be observed in modern architecture and previously in the works of architects and artists of minimalism movement

In fact, painting, sculpture and conceptual sketches/ mental drawings act as a bed in production and a means in registration of ideas passing from mental to identical in helping the architects. Le Corbusier believed that: main principles of researches, my intellectual production, and secrets hidden in them can just be found in continuous painting practices. His paintings include architectural ideas and thoughts.

Such a method is not the only way for designing, and the mentioned architects have used other methods during their architectural life. Analysis of such discussions will bring us nearer to their designing process and architectural thinking and help us in finding a complete and appropriate procedure of architectural process. In pictures of the next pages, it is possible to observe a specified process of effectiveness of thoughts of Mondrian, Victor Vasarely and other modern artists up to the contemporary era in architecture.

Piet Mondrian 1921

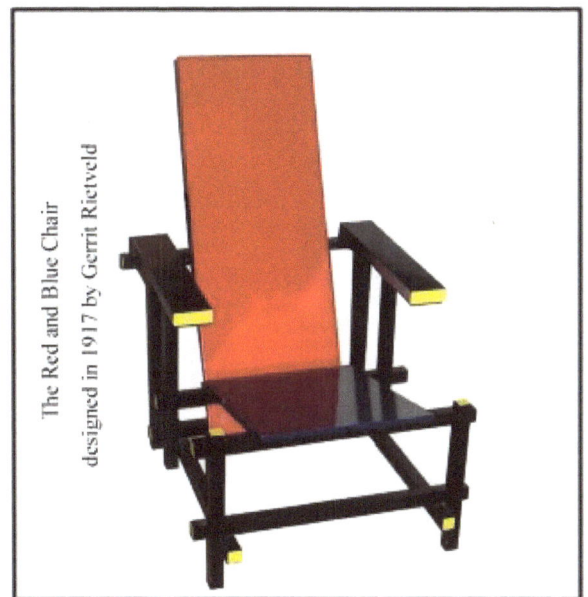
The Red and Blue Chair designed in 1917 by Gerrit Rietveld

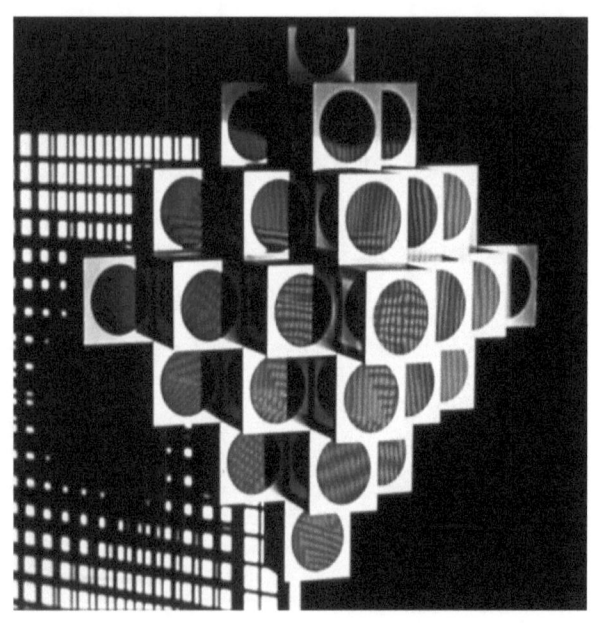

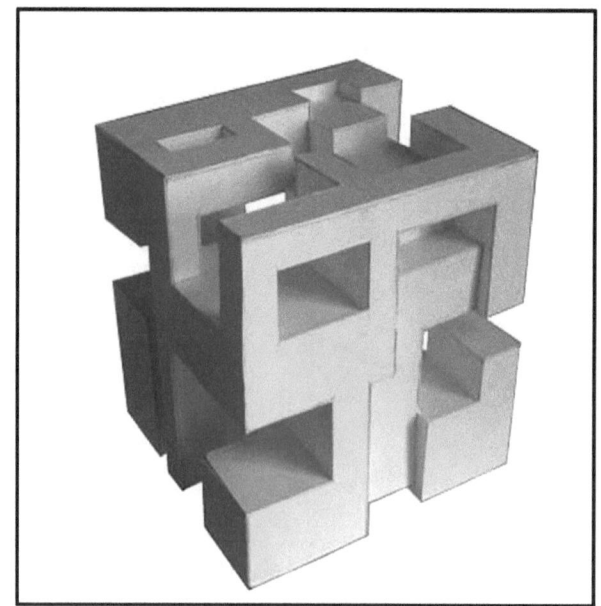

An example of a design process based on the above topics

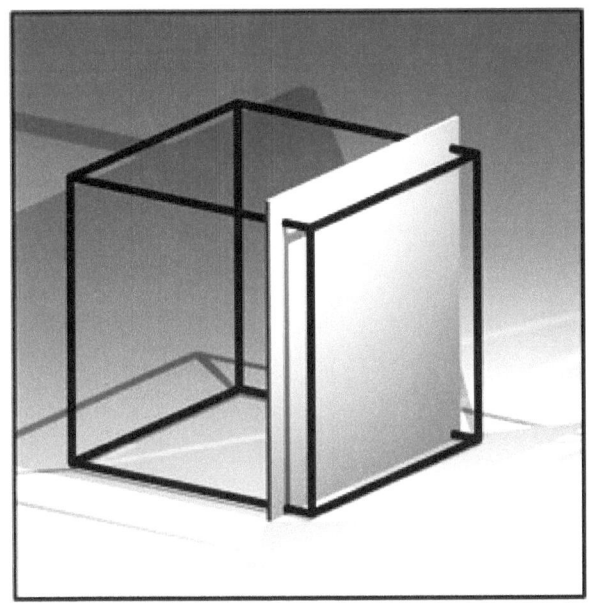
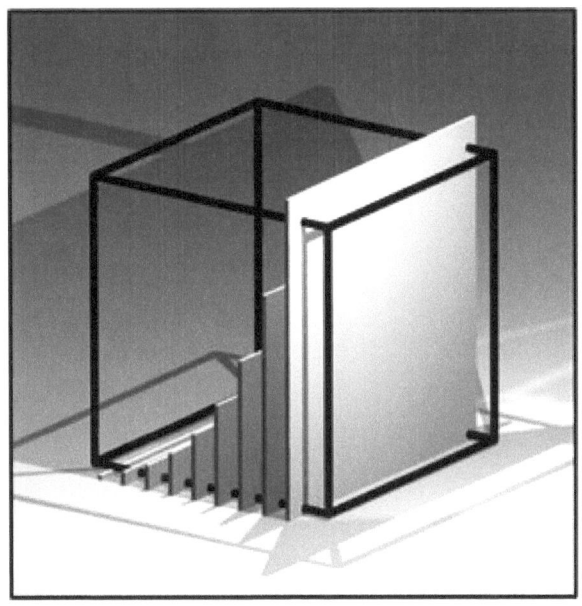

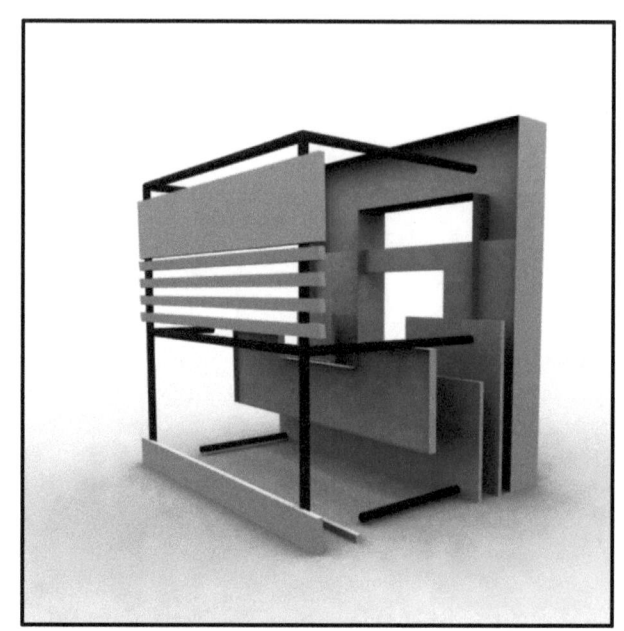
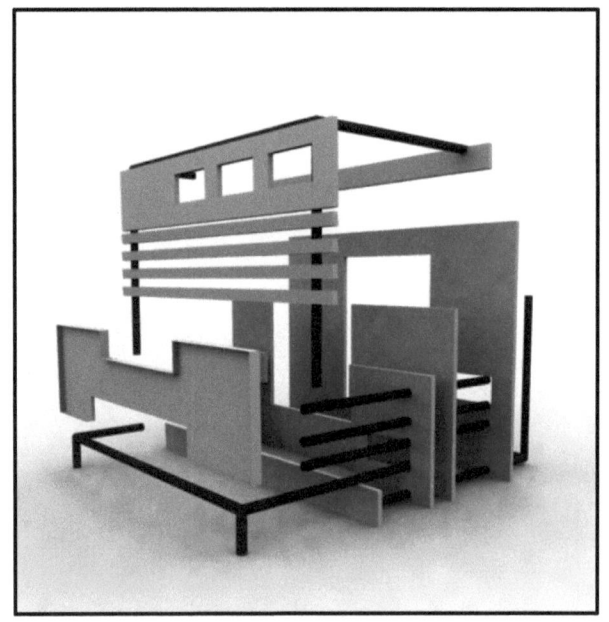
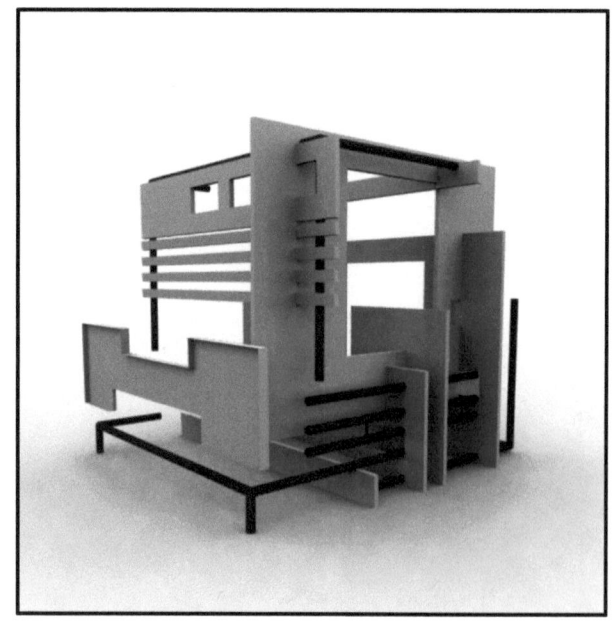

Concept

(Mind & Body Meeting)

"Concept is an extract of the architect's mind and embodiment of ideas in the real world with the capability required for producing, developing and completing spatial structure of a project"

Architecture take benefit from two types of expression: "mind" and "body" or in other words "word" and "image". Each of these expressions with their features and instruments travel a specified route in developing and elevating of architectural scope whether as characteristic of an architect or mental infrastructures of the society, undergo changes and evolution, precede each other and finally embody in architectural framework. Coordination and interaction between an architect's mind and hand is an important and determinant category in architecture quality. An architect is a thoughtful person trying to exhibit his/her mental findings in outside world considering predetermined goals. Architecture is not merely a theoretical or practical course and it cannot be make any difference between these two. Unfortunately, as it can be observed in today society of our country, theoretical concepts are limited to academic issues and doctorate theses and just body and architecture construction are considered in professional world.

What makes an accurate architecture possible should pass through interaction of these twos. Ignoring or preferring one on another resulted in forming of an incomplete and problematic phenomenon in architecture and urban planning of the society within recent years. How often negligence committed in accompanying and coordination of these two subjects during the last two decades and led to form and spatial disturbance and failure of indoor and outdoor of buildings of our today cities resulted in undesirable mental and social outcomes considering behavior and relationship of citizens and staining history of architecture in Iran.

Identifying and expressing "mind" and "body" meeting is one the most important stages of designing process which includes a sense of meaning. Concept is a stage of designing originating from figurative backgrounds and human inner challenges and accompanying ideas embodiment through passing through limitations- demands of real world.

In other words, concept refers to embodiment of thoughts resulted from perceptions and findings of architect's creative mind which tries to express different elements and features of needs and potentialities of project in a determined whole. Passing through an abstract and mental category to a tangible one is a magic moment determines destiny of project in different stages of designing and construction.

Architects differently consider concept and its role and position in designing process. Their viewpoints have changed at different eras.

Concept is a turning point in architecture designing process accompanying architecture all over its history, gathers different elements of designing in a solidified whole, and makes the architects capable of apply it in designing important aspects of a project through direction of resources and their own potentialities.

Of course, severalty of different ideas and possibility of expressing a fixed idea in different forms and figures resulting in availability of several supplementary or independent concepts for designer should also be considered. For instance, how an architect deals with nature and ideas formed in his/her mind from water flow to patterns of birds flying differ from each other and have an independent expression.

Artists' inspiration resources, quality of idea and concept production and cultivation are sometimes a personal characteristic and compiling a specified process for it is not possible. But it is evident that every artist requires excuse, position and instruments for embodying the mentalities such as natural and artificial volumes and forms which can reflect their ideas and thoughts in the physical world. From Mondrian's colorful compounds to birds flying- considering project conditions and demands- can operate as a mediator between mind and body.

Generally, concept can be divided into two general types:
- Concepts resulted from curiosity and thinking of architect in the real world (including natural and artificial)
- Concepts originate from architects' creative mind and their restless spirit in spiritual world. Conceptual sketches are of this type. It should be mentioned that artists' mind plays a significant role in both cases and considers second type as more conceptual and intact (not in all cases, of course)

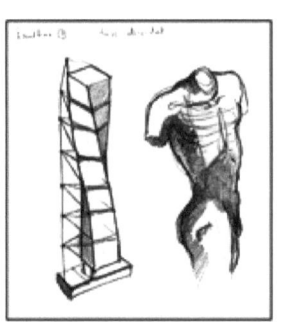

Santiago Calatrava
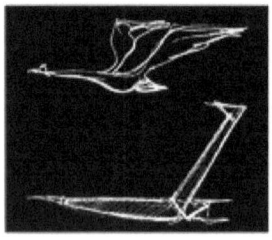

Abstract sketches and paintings of Zaha Hadid, paintings of Le Corbusier and Friedrich Hundertwasser and selections of Santiago Calatrava from natural forms and creatures are actually regarded as mind and body meeting. Most of these roles can be changed to an architectural structure, and it is possible to extract a comprehensive generality of the architectural space.

Next, we will consider structural experiences in Santiago Calatrava's architecture:

Santiago Calatrava, a person who has been known for his architectural activities, considers art as a motivation and stimulant for his works creation; his infatuation and interest in art can be observed in surprising number of his designs and statutes by now. Within the last 20 years, he has collected over than 65000 sketches and designs in his archive. Calatrava states that diversity in his designs reflects that how important is every detail for him such that size and quality of paper creates a dialogue between architect and designing. Initial sketches of Calatrava cannot be considered so much as architecture, and it is just in main stages of designing that realism of these sketches are manifested. It should be mentioned that from very initial he was looking for artistic expression, he did not put the realistic thoughts away and tried to establish an interchange between artistic and technical aspects of architecture. Calatrava has thousands of designing from human body; most of them reflect architect's imagination from human body without using a specific model in their designing. His strong interest in this regard has been reflected in portraits, individual and group bodies, evolved and involved in an architecture designing process. Some other designing of him include colloquy of cubes and human body in different positions. The most outstanding of these works is a dynamic tension created by approaching a runner's body and number of cubes. (Khiabanian, 2010)

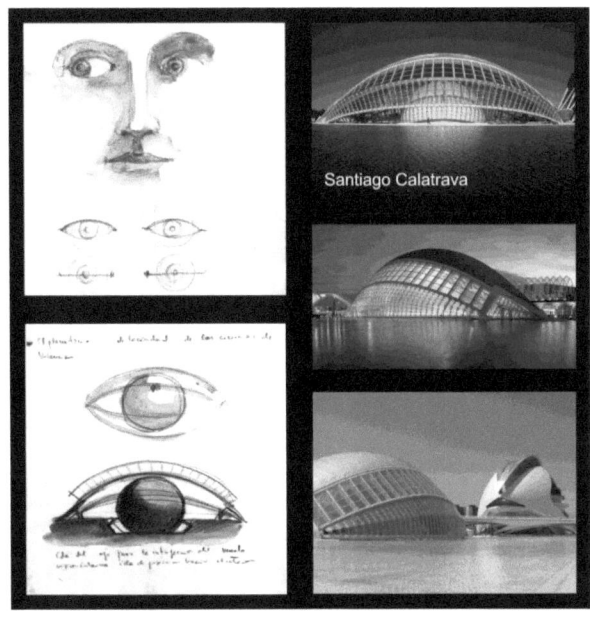

Santiago Calatrava does not introduce himself as a designer; designing has been mingled with his work and considers it another way to obtain potential of ideas attracting him. For instance, his tables are among the most dynamic designs of furniture. Significant number of his sketches and tables built by him are based on human body which its knees, arms or head tolerate a glass on their upper part. These drawings are, in fact, statutes that functionally changed through putting a plane on them such that turned to a main part of whole. His designs and statutes should be considered from artifacts viewpoints. Meanwhile, the mentioned cases operate as a laboratory or space for developing and directing of concepts at the initial steps of creativity and designing process so that they can play a mediator role in animating of thoughts and analyzing of forms.

Features of Concepts

Identity or expression can be transferred when whole of building is comprehensively interpreted. Like other artifacts, a complete and strong concept should dominate whole of an architectural work and all elements should be actively part of this whole (creating an appropriate structure derived from the concept or the concept, itself, should have complete structural features).

This is true for the most substantial and initial elements such as plan or structure system to the final ones like color of indoor walls or door handles.

Cases should be considered in selecting or creating of a concept:

- Considering issues posed at cognition stage
- Defining and determining designer's ideas
- Generating novel ideas
- Capability of producing or extracting spatial structure thereof
- Flexibility, develop and change on account of the project demands
- Synthesizing elements and coordinating different features of a design in a whole unit
- Coordination with society culture
- Considering content rather than just form. (Khiabanian, 2010)

An example of the architectural design process

Concept: Snail

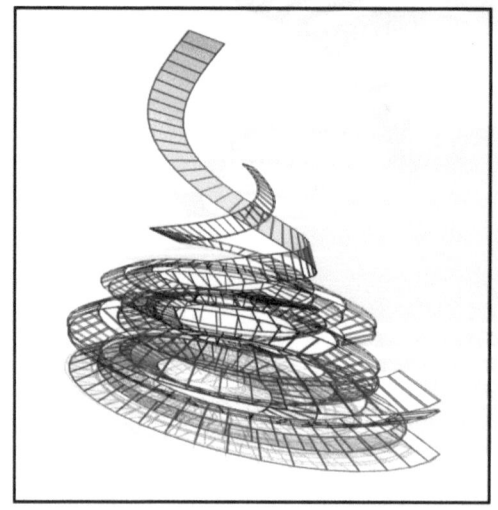

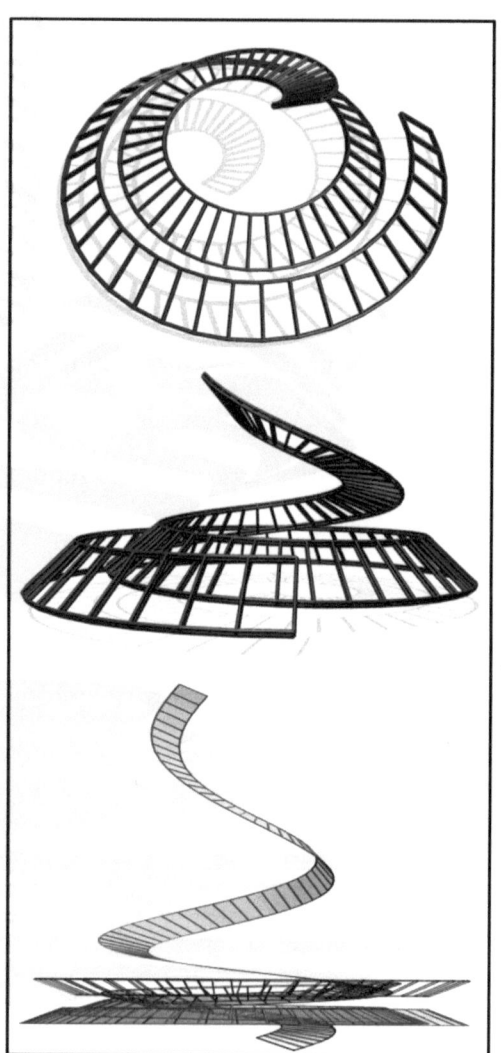

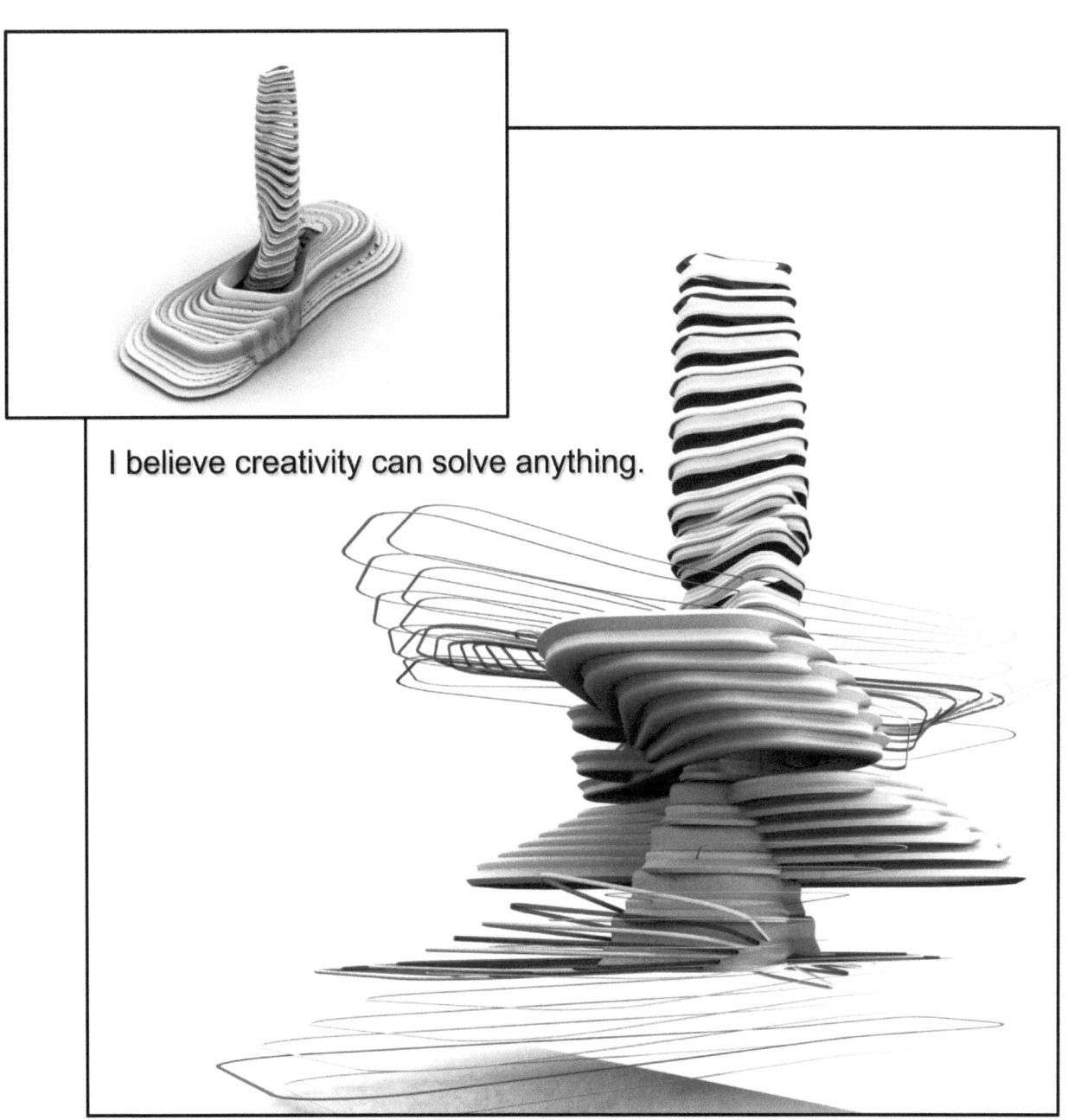

I believe creativity can solve anything.

I believe creativity is the highest form of intelligence

Spatial Structure

A concept created for an architectural project provides a general structure for designing of the desired subject. A structure direct us toward reaching lines and surfaces which is a scheme of project form and spatial generality and quality through its development and evolution; **structure is a mediator between abstract language of concept with real body of architecture.**

If mind scope can be divided into sections, it can be concluded that some layers of mind enter operation at initial stages of a work creation which are more figurative. Thought and logic take more room while it gradually approaches to identity of an artifact. Contrary to the initial stages of architecture which are figurative and abstract, secondary layers affecting a project are more experimental and mental. Concept tries to embody architect's mind and mentality; but, the resulted structure is looking for to create physical patterns and frameworks rather a mere mental one to the designer.

It should be mentioned that some architects have especial potentialities in changing ideas to dynamic and perfect architectural structures and do not feel any need to having a specific concept from nature or their environment. This is while other groups commence their conceptual sketches from very beginning of ideas embodiment and select desired concept or structure through their sketches.

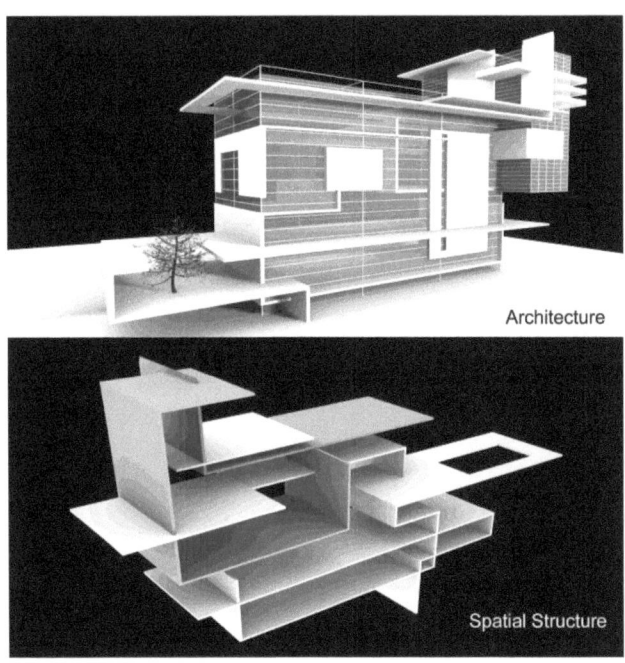

Examples of Spatial structure

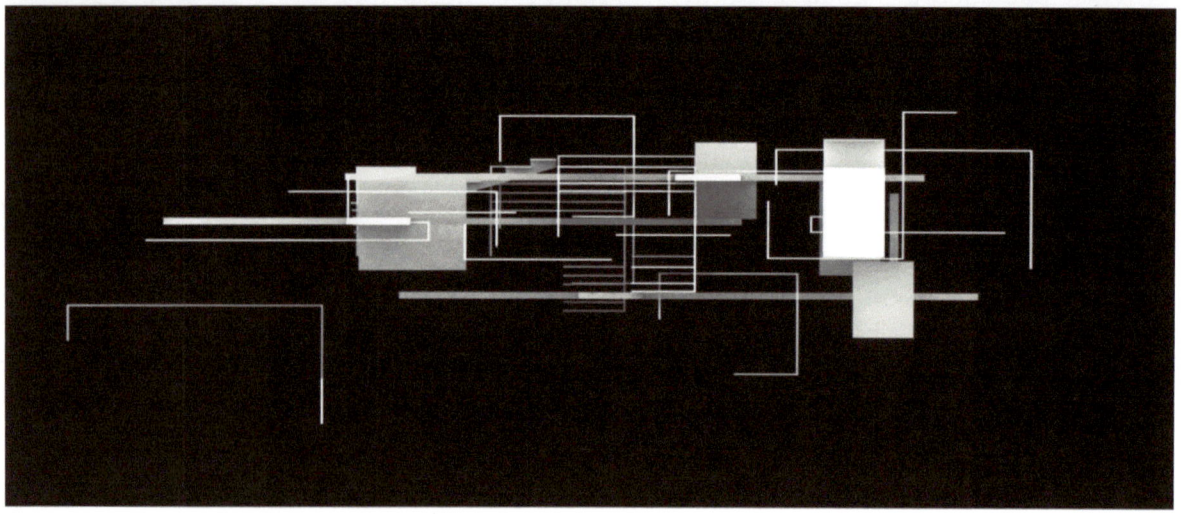

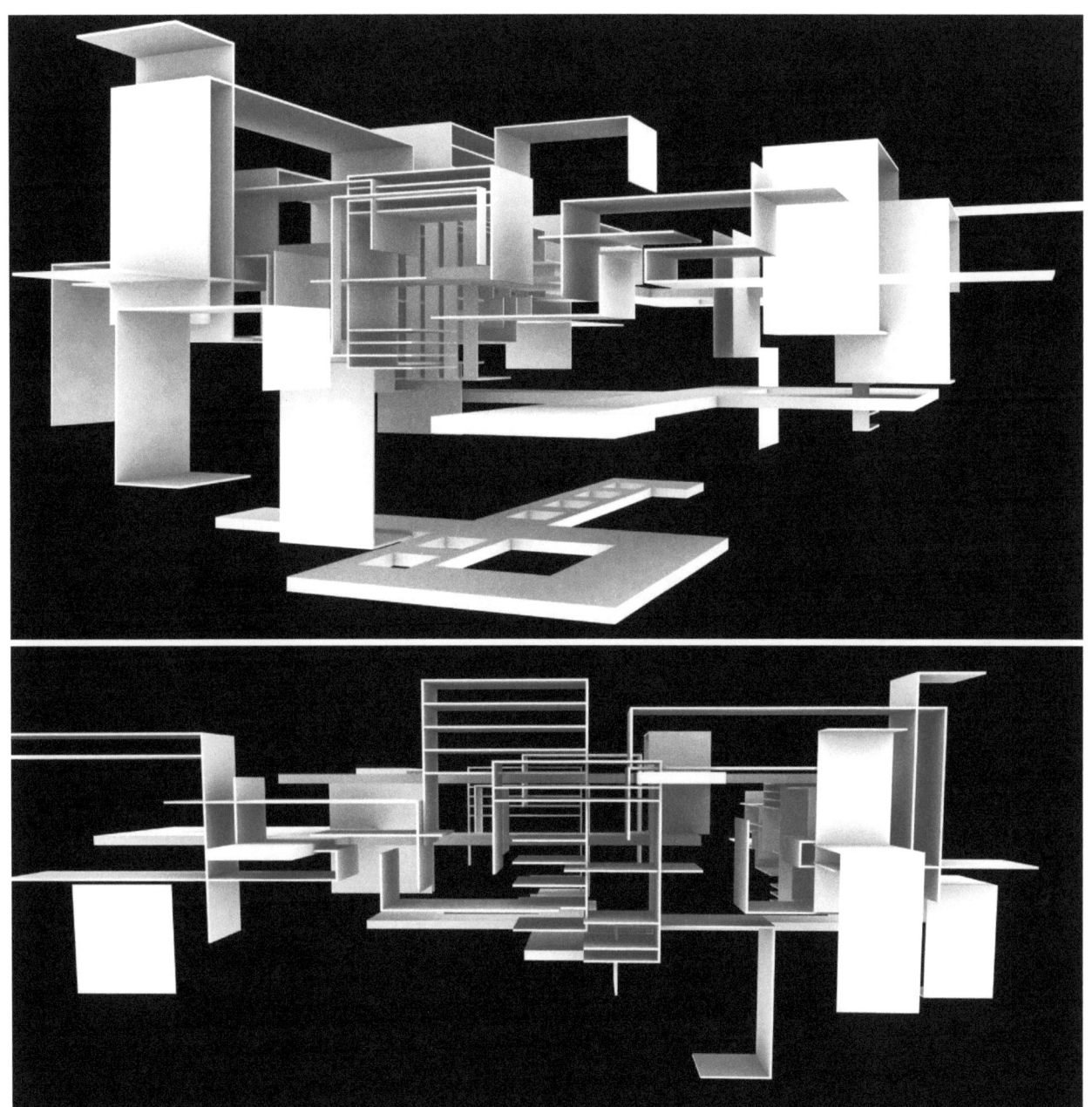

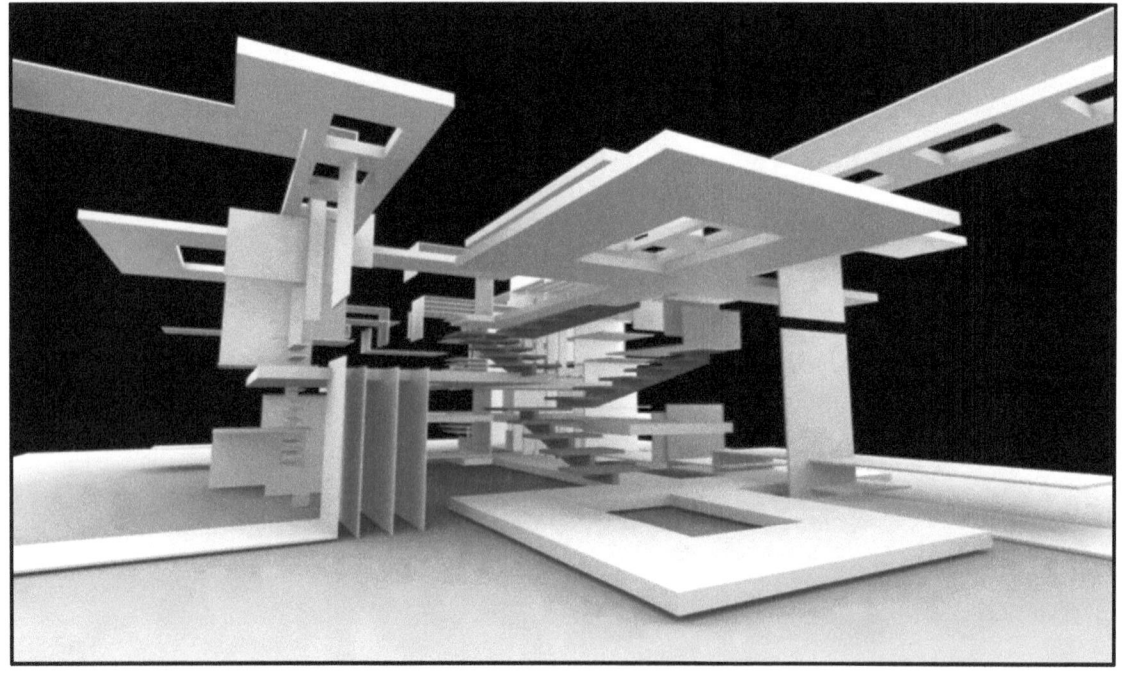

Architecture Creation Cycle

(Repetition and restarting from initial stages of designing process)

It is possible that designer swiftly passes through all designing stages and reaches several suggested designs which are effective in solidifying of information, responding to employer's demands and requirements and dealing with project limitations and can be helpful in developing, completing and selecting of the final design. But, there is another process indicating repetition and review of previous stages of designing process.

A designer moves several times in designing cycle in order to reach a prefect and ideal design. Each time, discussions and analyses seem more logical, advanced and well. More satisfactory solutions are provided at next reviews.

It should be remembered that this process is not confined in a limited time interval and specific project which result in termination of designing process with its ending; rather as it has been mentioned, new ideas and approaches are produced in every project which should complete their evolutionary process as mental activities and conceptual sketches besides main idea so that can gain the capabilities required for performing other projects in addition to strengthening designer's mind. Therefore, similar to other artists, architects spend most of their time for sketching and studying, experience different ideas, do not wait for offering a specific and acceptable project and begin planning, studying and designing. Considering rotational nature of the mentioned designing process, artist or architect's thoughts and character require reactivation and review so that be sufficiently prepared to deal with new issues and questions regarding professional capability and offering novel thoughts. (Khiabanian, 2010)

It should be noted that desired diagram just indicates a general scheme of a process passed by an artist as a creator, and it is possible that it lacks sufficient capability or can not be responsive in special conditions. So, in completing the offered discussion and filling available vacuums, it is necessary to state that all mentioned stages are rigidly united and merged such that in some cases it is not possible to separate and study them in details. There are some cases of architects' works that we face with synthesizing or omitting of some stages of designing process.

Presence or nonuse of concept is not regarded as inevitable conditions of architecture. In evaluating of a work or verifying verity and untruth of its formation, presence of concept neither is a reason for design superiority nor indicator of incapability of the architect or architectural work. Availability of a specific process in perfect designing and embodiment of ideas is the only most important and effective problem which provides approximately fair judgment for the architect and others.

Layout

Layout is drawn differently from diagrams and sketches with more exact dimensions and scales, includes information found in diagrams and sketches, and makes observing of generalities of design and architectural details possible. Possibility of availability of more than one design should be taken seriously in this stage.

Designs selection is often done by logical mind rather than artist's mind. However, if two hemispheres operate through full coordination during designing process, no significant difference will be observed in results and offered designs.

Final Design

...

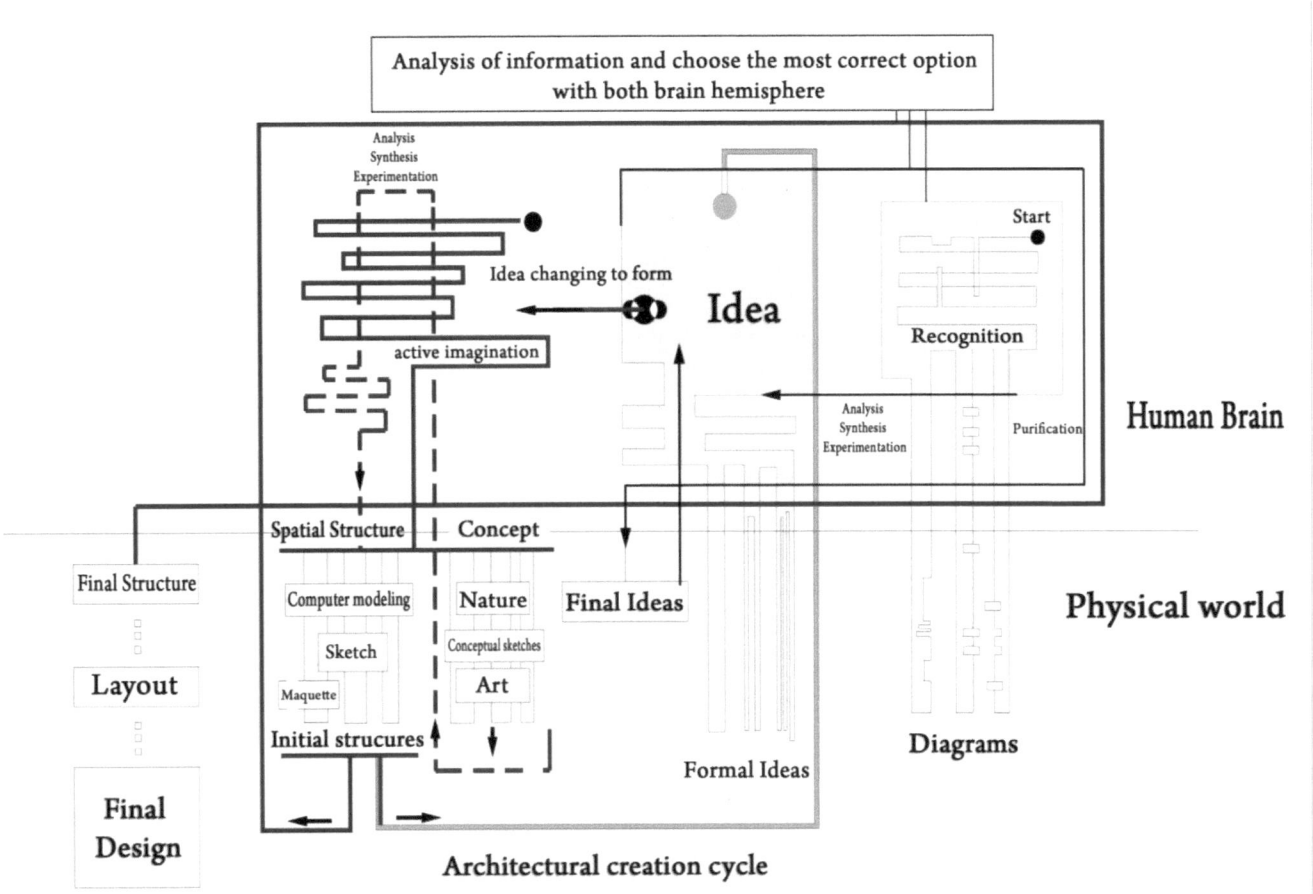

Enlarge idea production phases

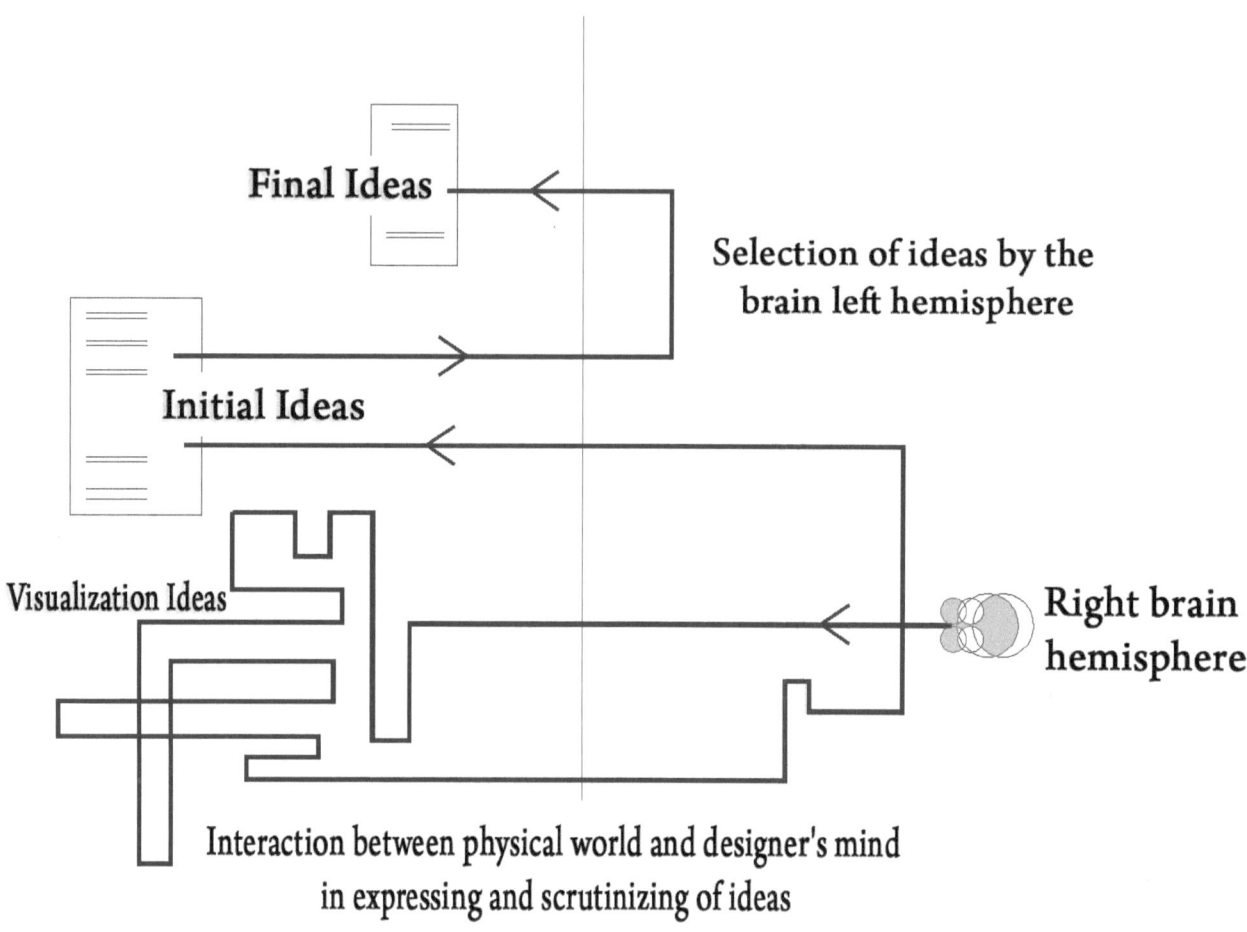

Ideas embodied in the concept

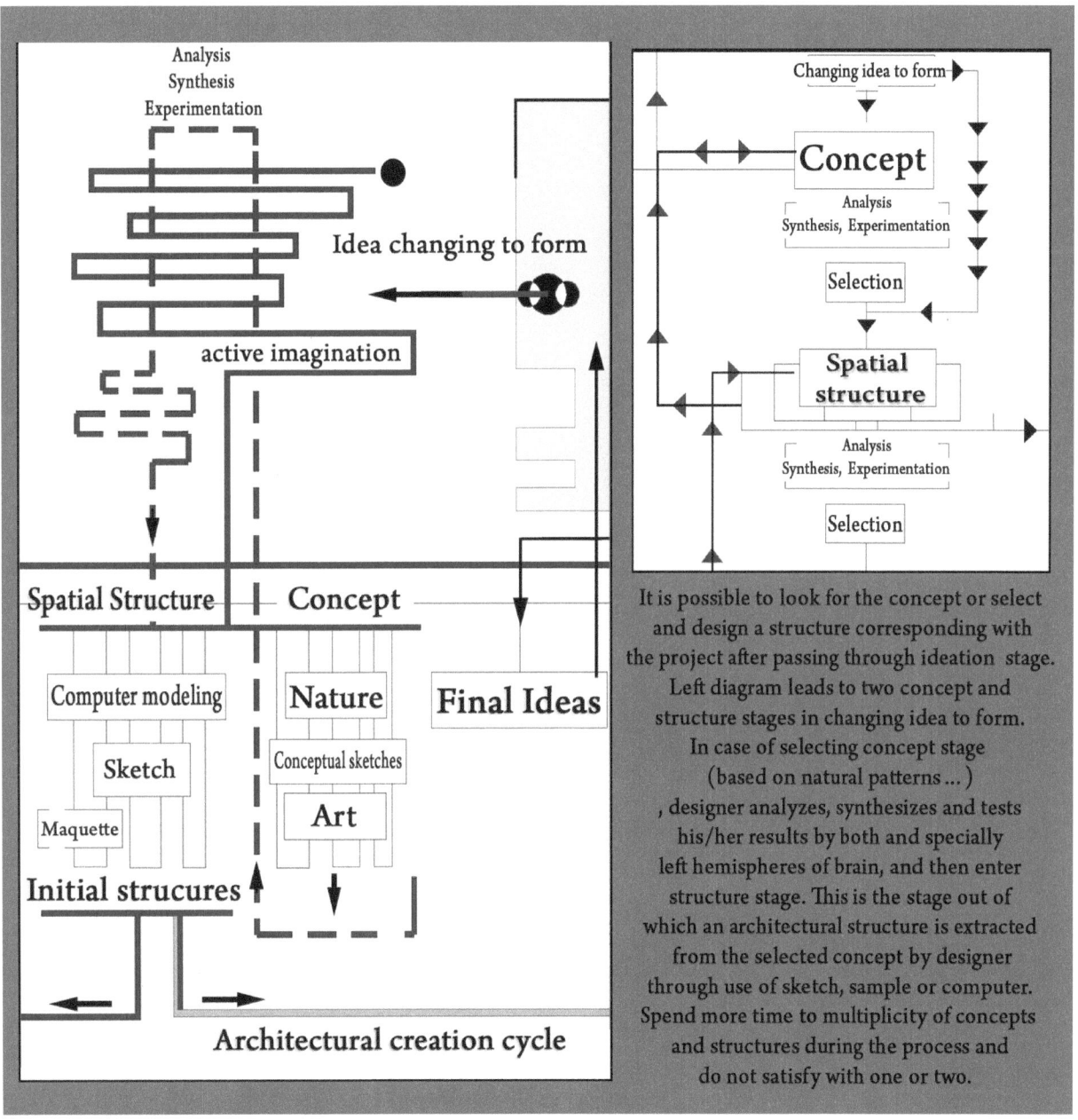

It is possible to look for the concept or select and design a structure corresponding with the project after passing through ideation stage. Left diagram leads to two concept and structure stages in changing idea to form. In case of selecting concept stage (based on natural patterns ...), designer analyzes, synthesizes and tests his/her results by both and specially left hemispheres of brain, and then enter structure stage. This is the stage out of which an architectural structure is extracted from the selected concept by designer through use of sketch, sample or computer. Spend more time to multiplicity of concepts and structures during the process and do not satisfy with one or two.

Creative Process in Architecture Designing

Creative process in designing starts from project identification in human mind and are expressed as diagrams and sketches in the physical world. There is a dynamic interaction between architect's mental space and real world to reach a perfect recognition of the subject. The outcomes resulted after analyses, required and effective cases are selected.

Information obtained from recognition stage is regarded as an important factor in idea producing. Again, brain hemispheres start their activity at other aspects of the process and offer ideas to the designer considering more perfect recognition of the project, efficiency and experiences of the right hemisphere. The ideas may be mental or formal, and some of them will be selected as final idea after passing through stages such as analysis, synthesis and testing. Effects of brain hemispheres in idea production process has been specified in diagram

The mentioned process in stages of changing idea to form, concept, selecting of the final structure and layout operates as above. Considering evolution of the process and amount of use of brain hemispheres in an appropriate time of designing is very important. Coordinative function of hemispheres is the best activity of the brain. Separating or omitting of activity of one of the hemispheres (e.g. mere attention to right hemisphere and creativity issues) in putting the ideas in practice and producing an appropriate spatial structure creates some problems to the process.

Conceptual sketches are emphasized in the first book because of their significant role in starting architectural task and idea embodiment on one hand and developing and strengthening of creative mind in confronting with different subjects and barriers of designing on the other hand. Therefore, relying on artist's mind and extracting design ideas, concepts and structures from designer's mind along with concepts from the physical world will be very effective in creating of a good, efficient and novel architecture. In selecting of concepts, do not satisfy yourself with just one; rather try the similar cases, too. Synthesizing of concepts and, more important, doing conceptual sketches in interaction with selected cases will create combinations belonging to designer's creative mind.

Trade center of Iran national industries
Design Process

Because of special importance at national and international aspects, the collection being designed while being mass index, should designed in sight of futuristic concepts and universal patters and especially for the sake. Factor, should have special face power. (Middle consoled mass at commercial sit)

Ecological parts and light absorption of space:

- Light radiation direction was effective on direction of residential blocks.

- Rising and coming down at commercial bulks is a factor on good light absorption spaces and it makes a good situation on the landscape.

- Locating the green septum at western side of the collection is the suitable covering against unfavorable winds.

- Considering the green house and usage of the yard at commercial and residential stories (refer to related sections), increase the finesse and space variety at the inside and faces while considering ecological issues.

Commercial and office spaces of collection:

- The spaces didn't have separated from each other and at any bulks of low stories, shops and at 3terminal stories have located offices.

- Conformity of dividing planes with spatial structure of masses is important case which increases the out and inner versatility of building and cause its architectural identity.

- Considering the moving line, inner circulation and good sight into collection site and having good sight and high spaces profit from designing commercial planes.

Taking into account the installation cases and ensuring the numbers of desired units of the project, the height of commercial stories has been considered 4 meters, and only at the north bulk of the collection, the highest height at tip of arch reaches to 27.5 m because of sinking bulks into the ground in height 1.5 m (because of ecological matters) and at rest cases it was 25m or lower. The numbers of shops and offices are mentioned beside planes of stories

Ideas:

- First of all at designing commercial area, the case of exteriority and at residential complex, the aspect of its exteriority has been considered green space around commercial collection and inner area at residential site, which has surrounded by apartment blocks, indicate for the case.

- At other stage, because of total lines of extensions site at highway edge and the way of occupying and good dividing of site after doing multi sketches, the result is a liner organizing which necessary spaces are defined at one spatial balance; so this way of function is considered at residential collection and 42 degree rotation has done in order to maximum use of south light.

- Adjacent of site with FATH highway which is symbol of fast move and speed, has effective on extension of north edge bulk and frame lines of fraction face, into the bulk, make possible the perception and looking into the complex.

Locating the complex near the airport, have been an important factor at shaping bulks

- First there was possibility of bird sight into collection, because of collection importance, index bulks with perspective to future has been considered.

- The way of rising and coming down of airplanes at adjacent to the site, while conforming around activities .

Of course, it's to be noted that parallelism of mentioned spaces at this structure have been considered. **(Khiabanian, 2011)**

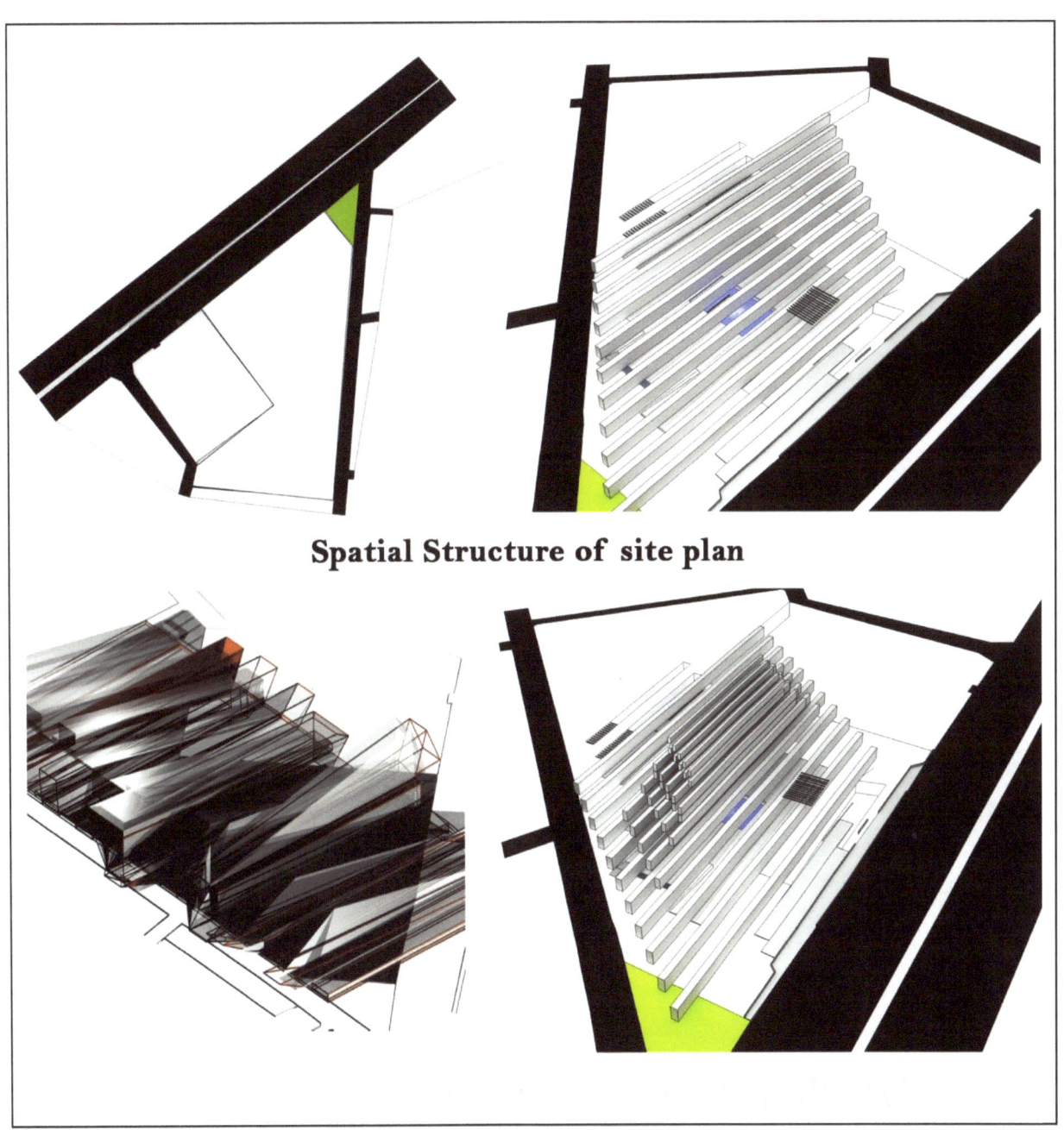

Spatial Structure of site plan

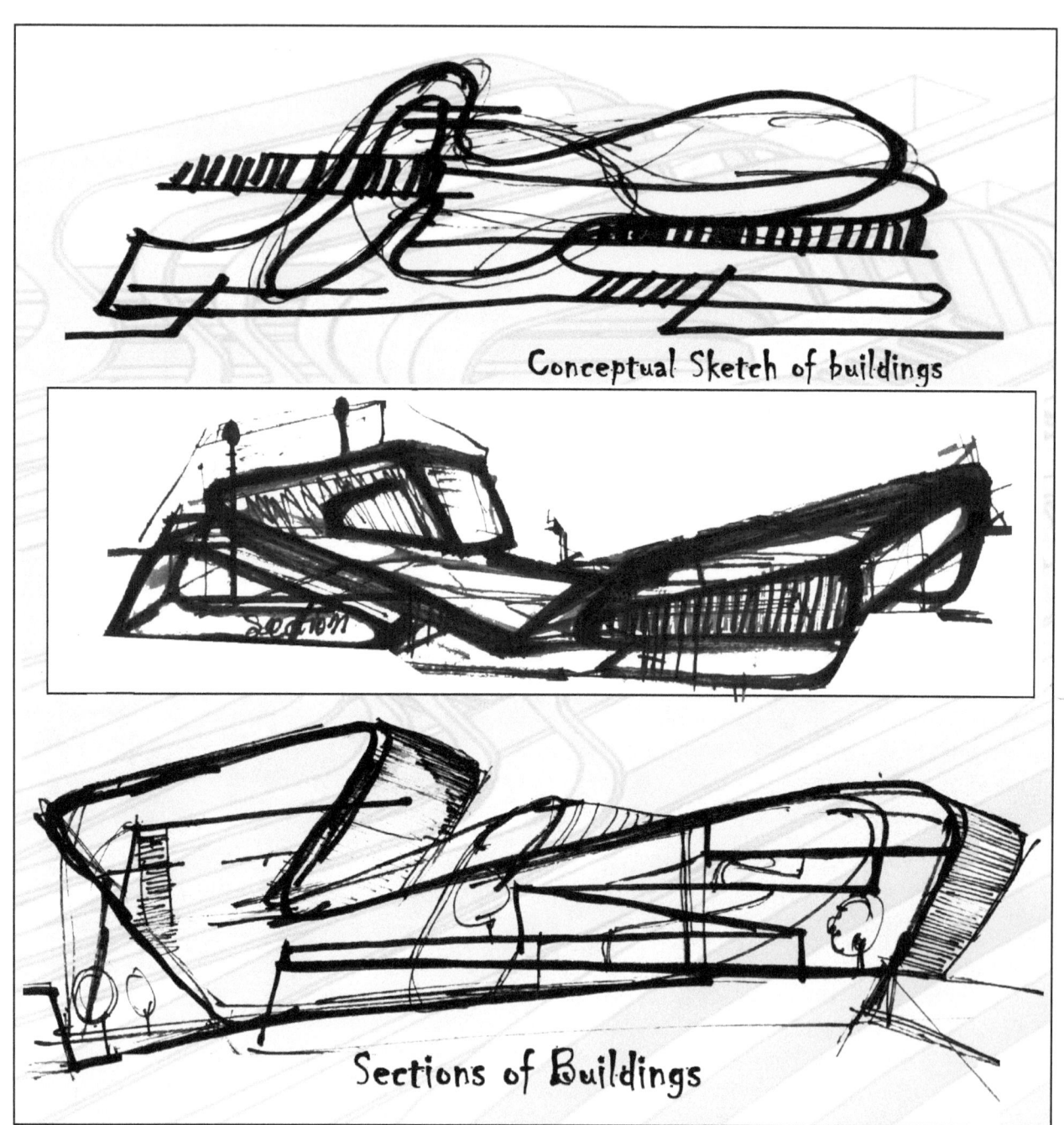

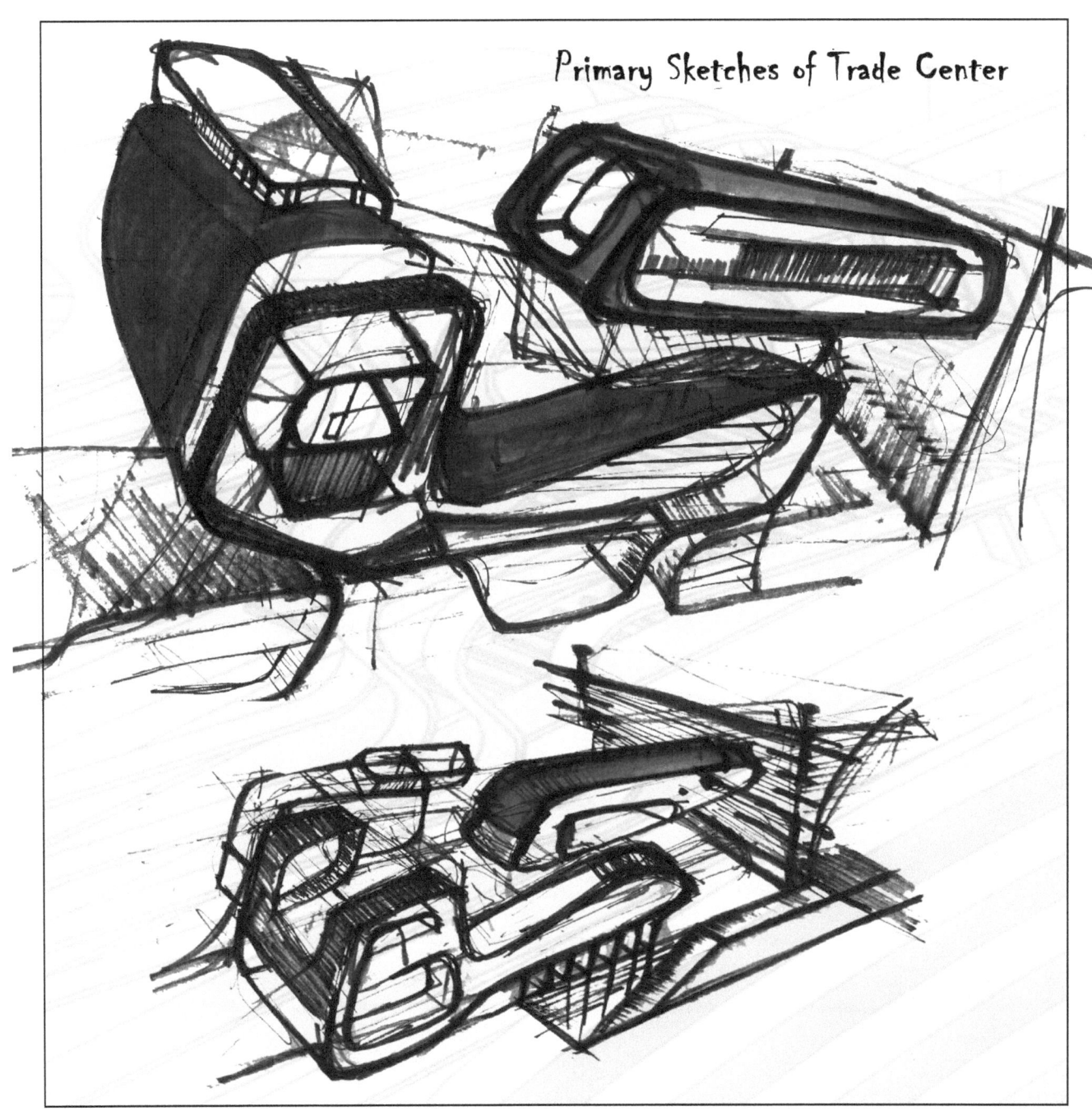

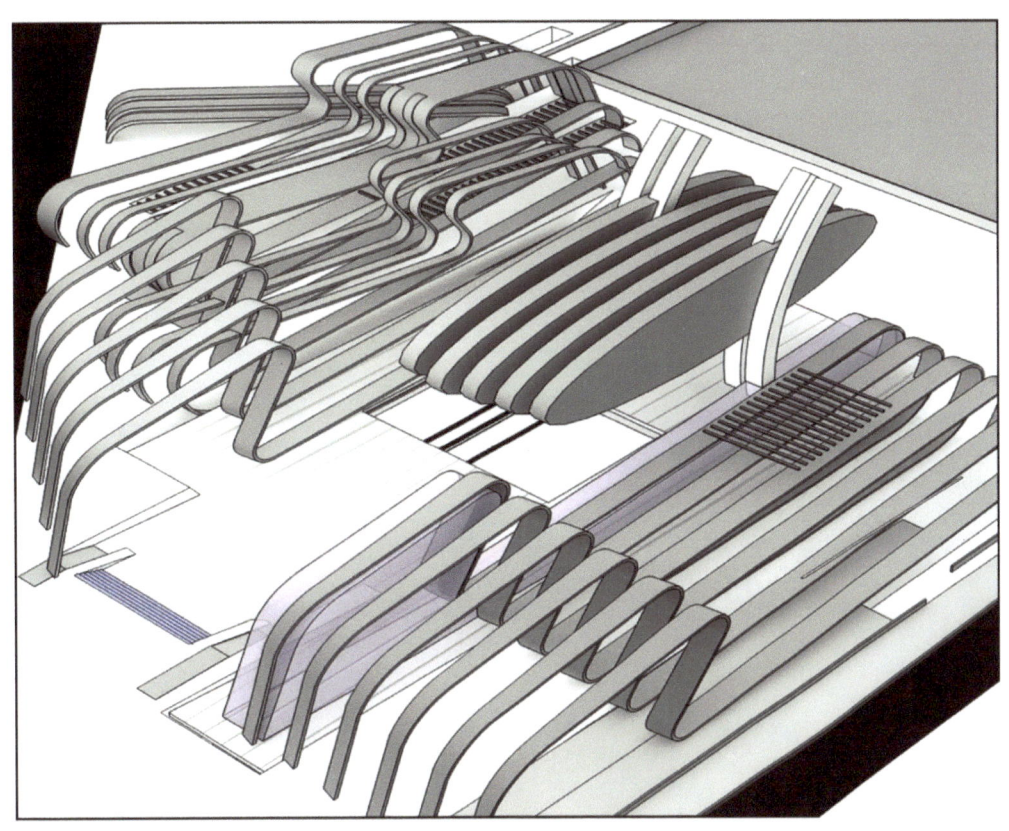

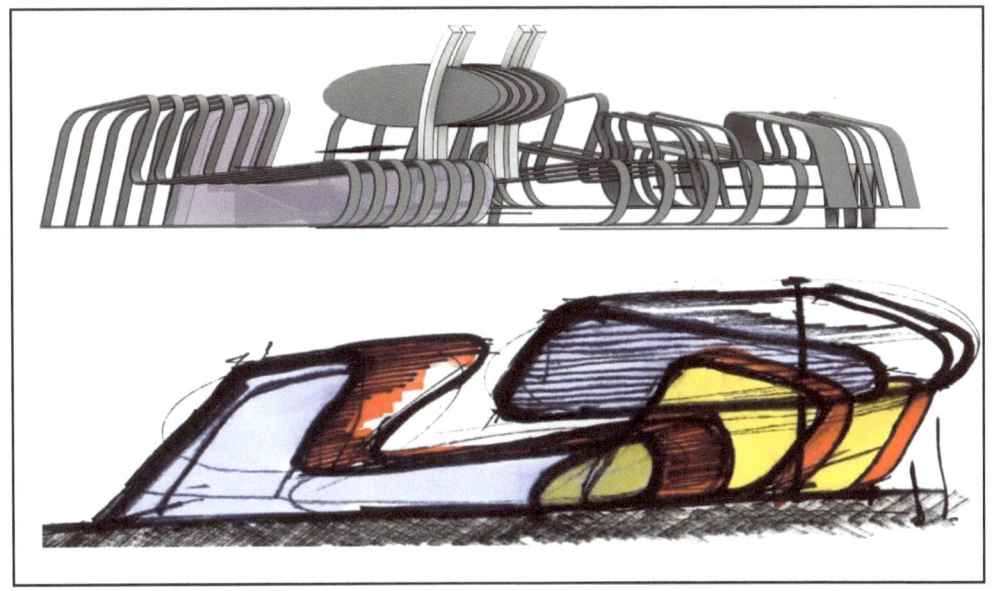

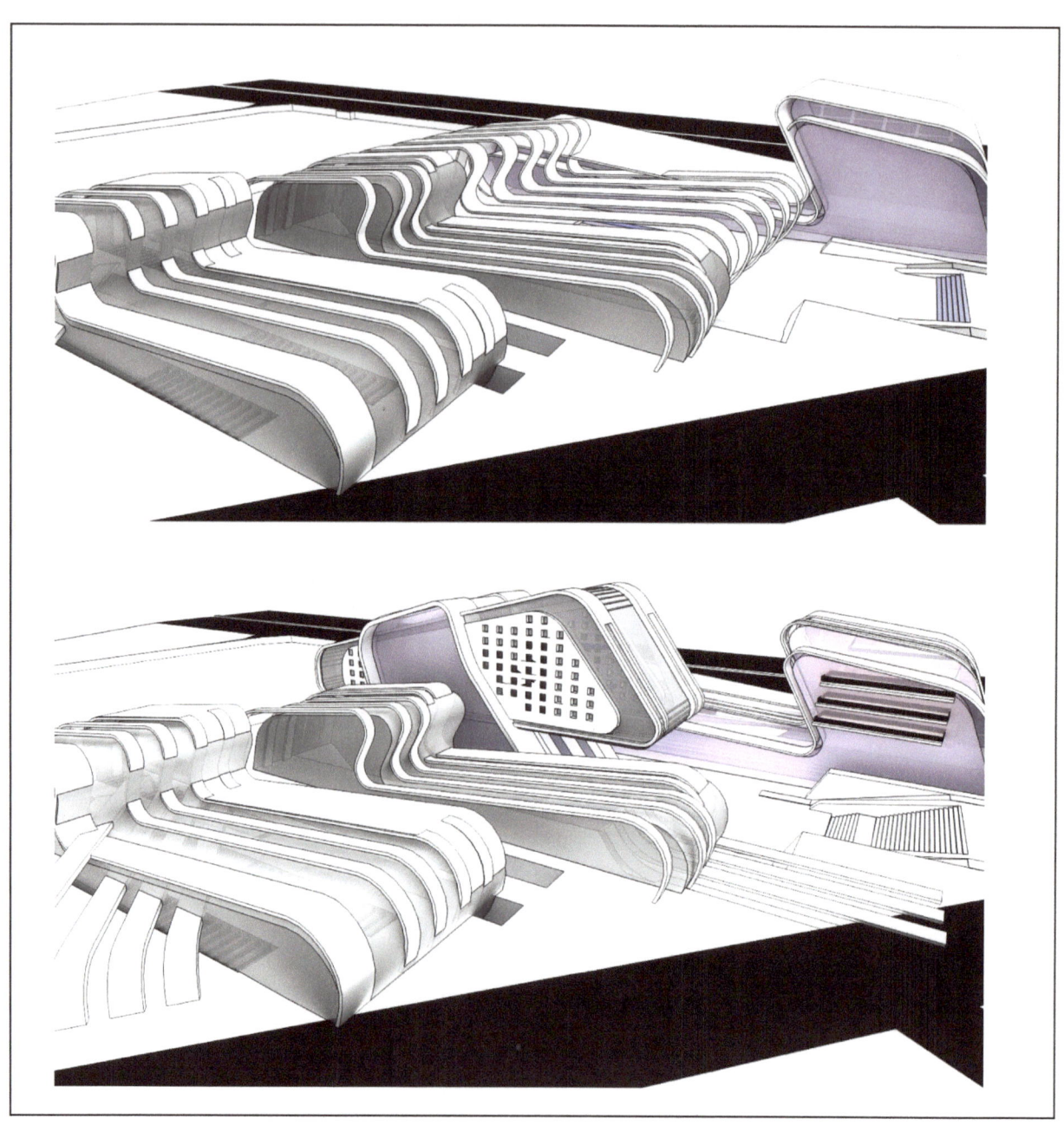

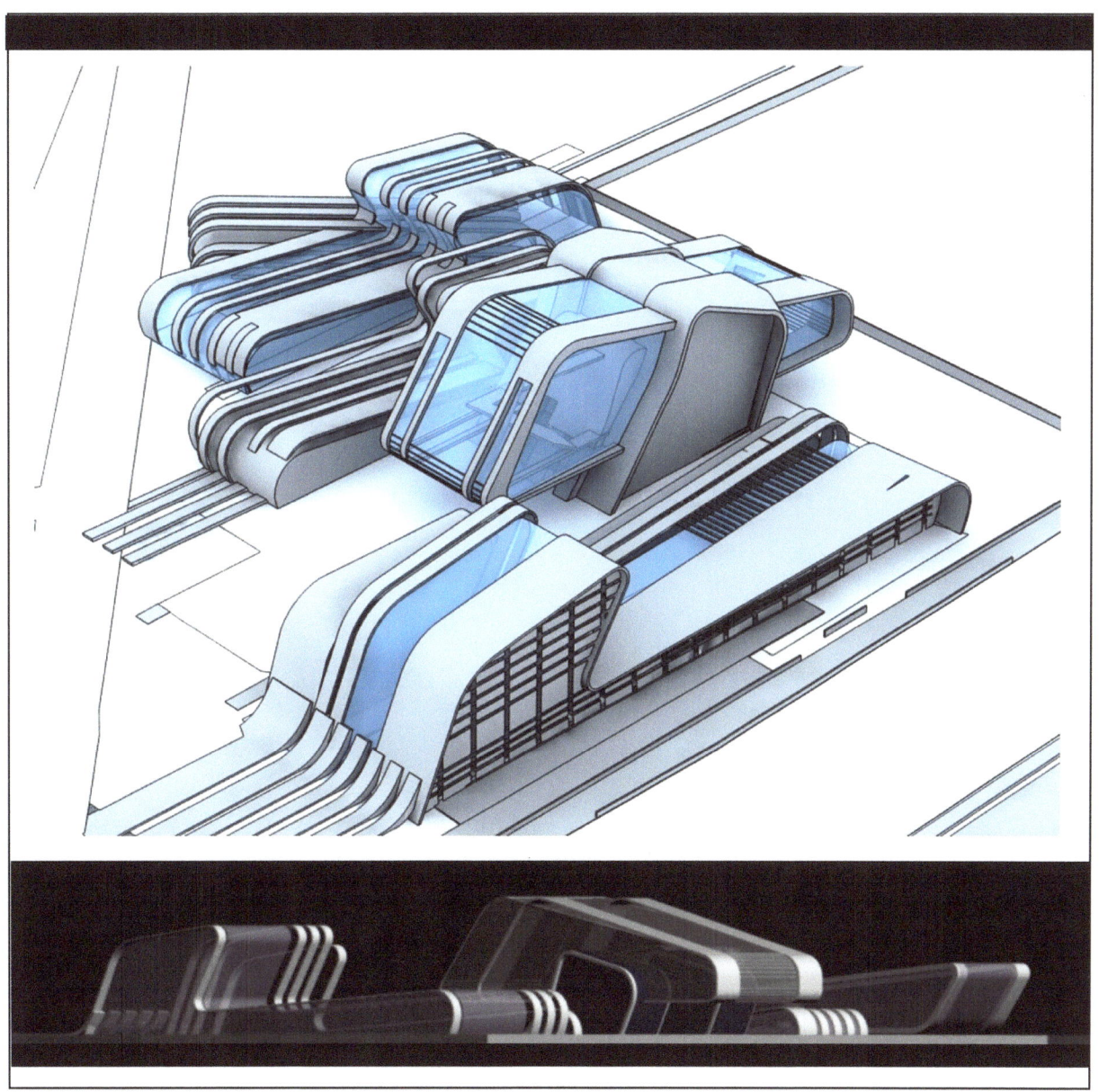

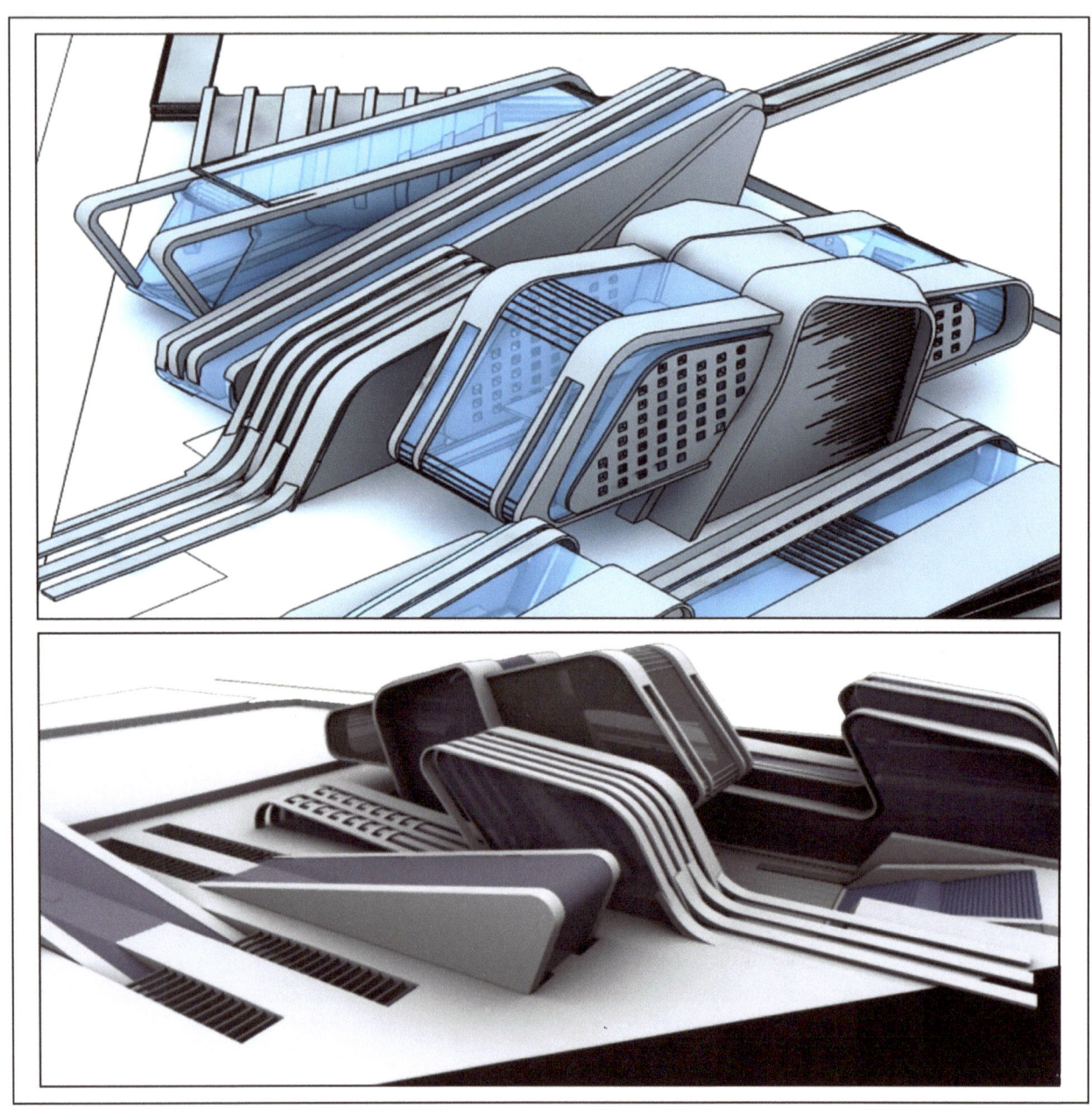

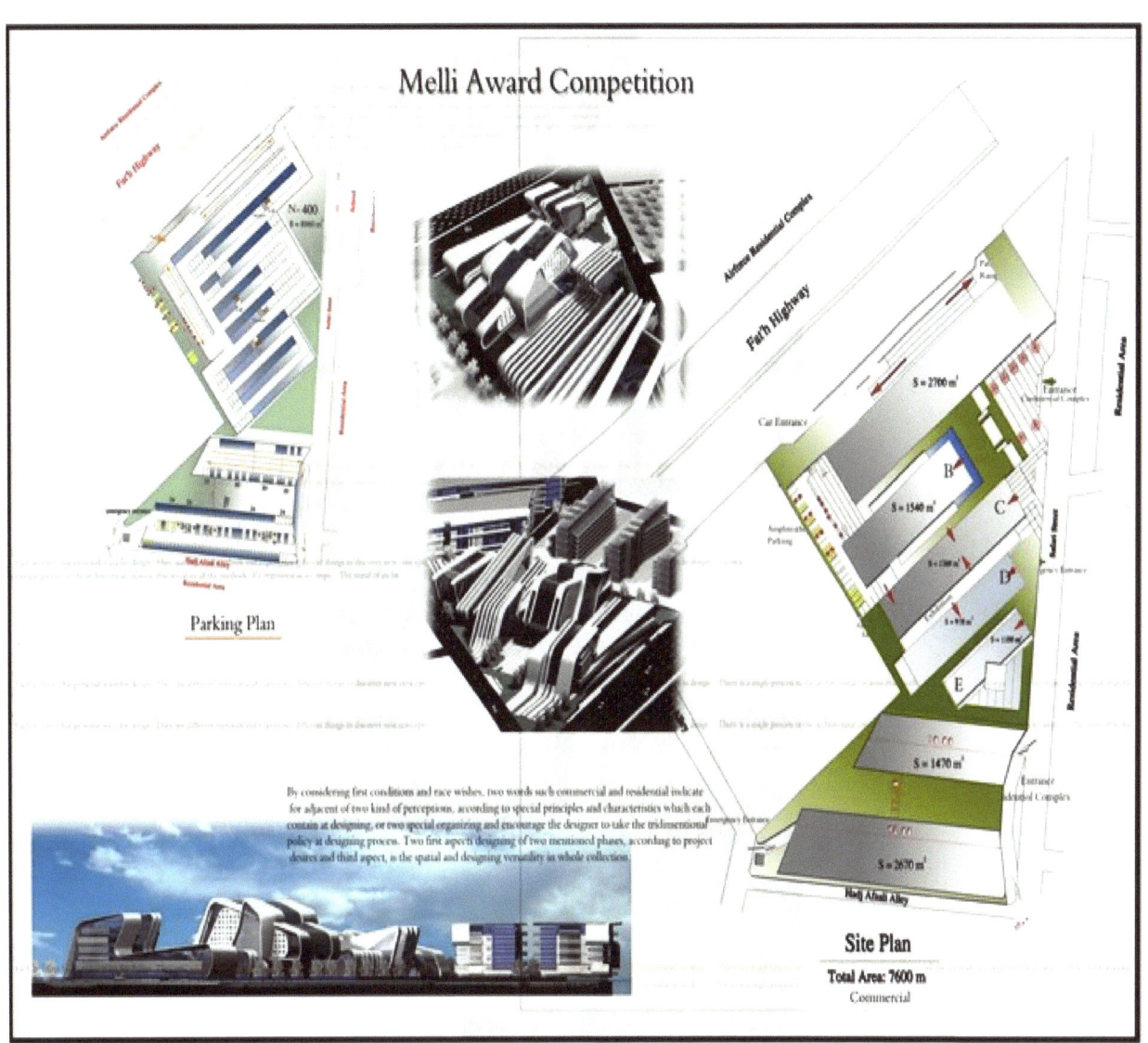

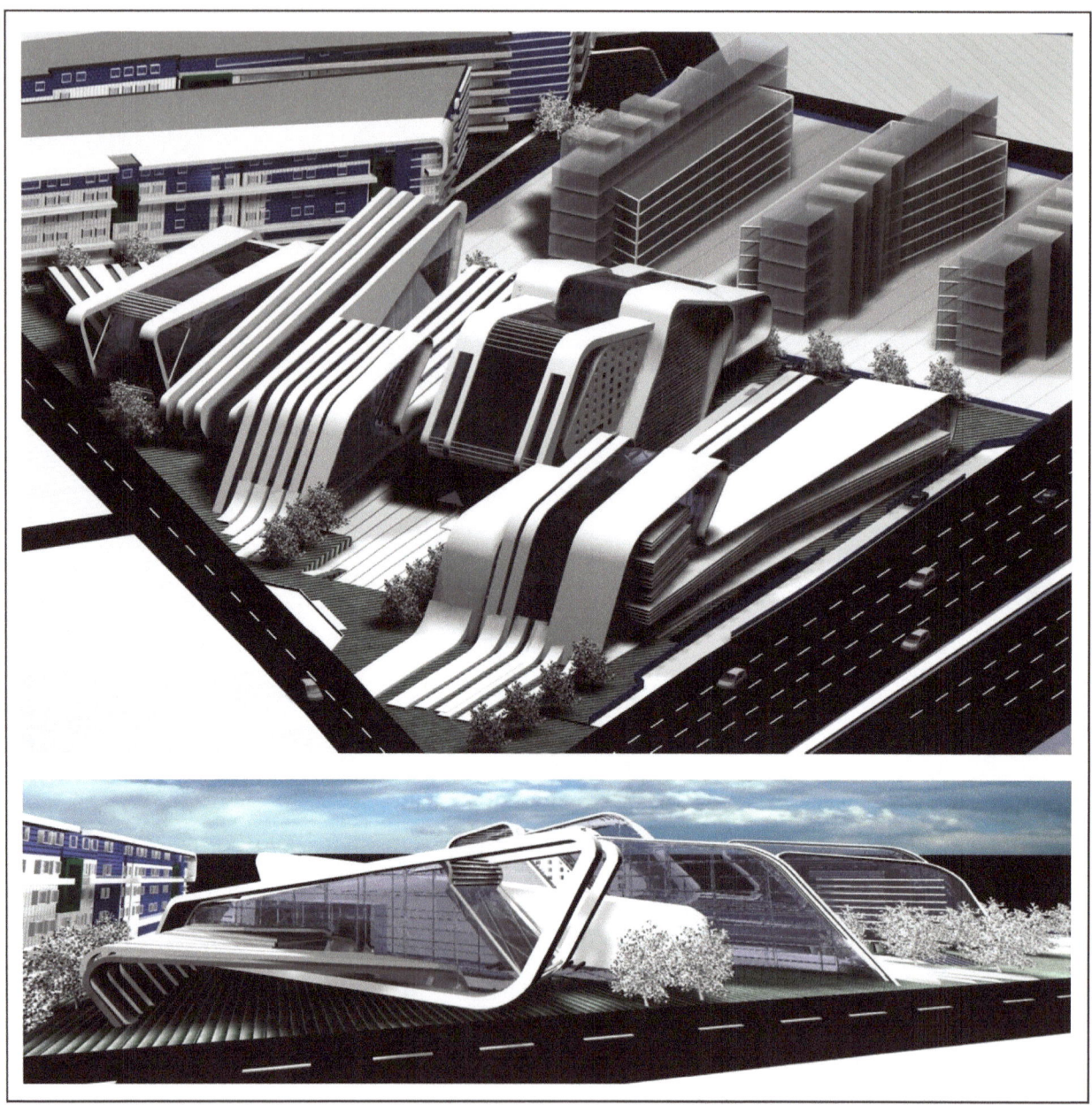

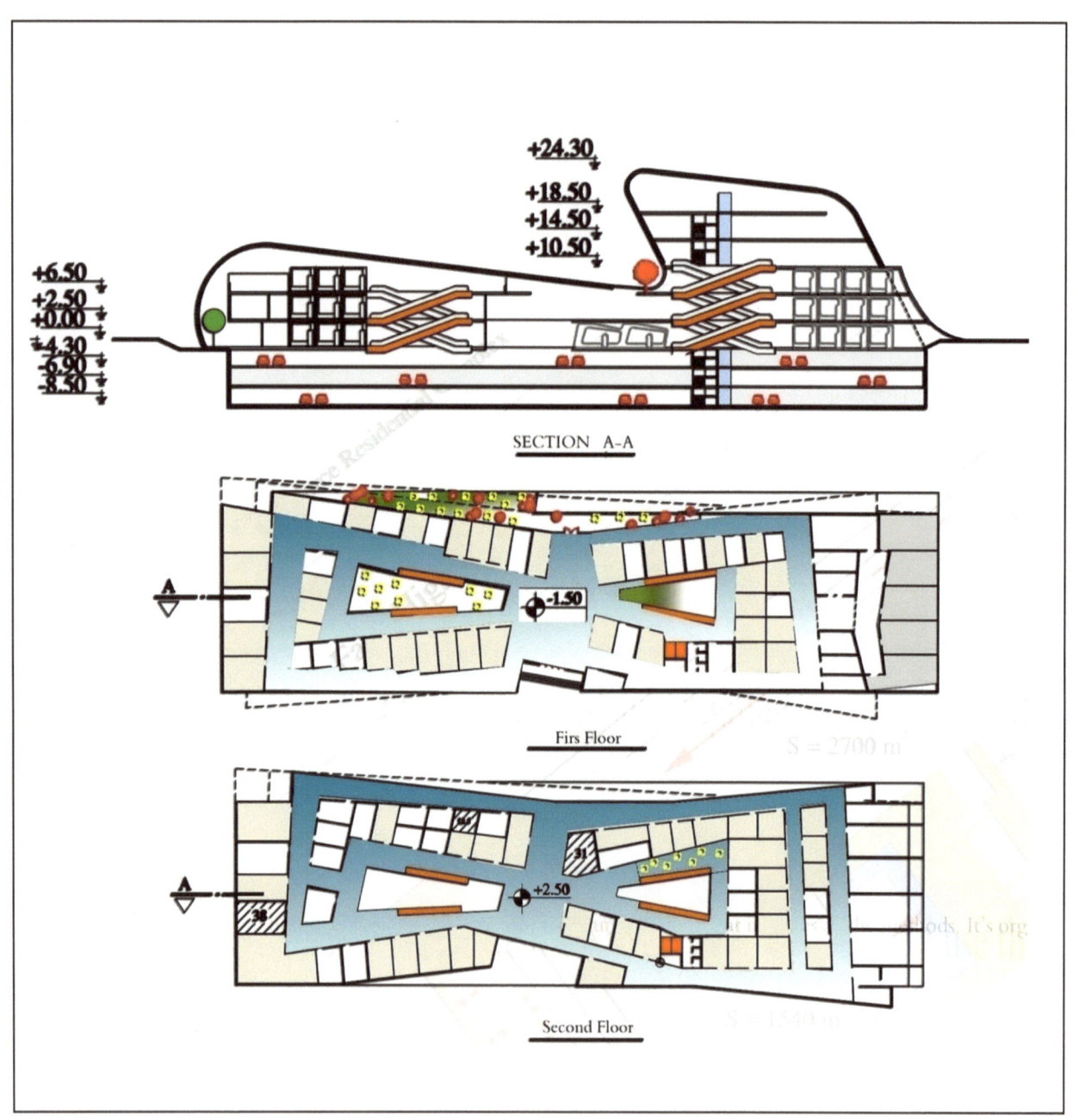

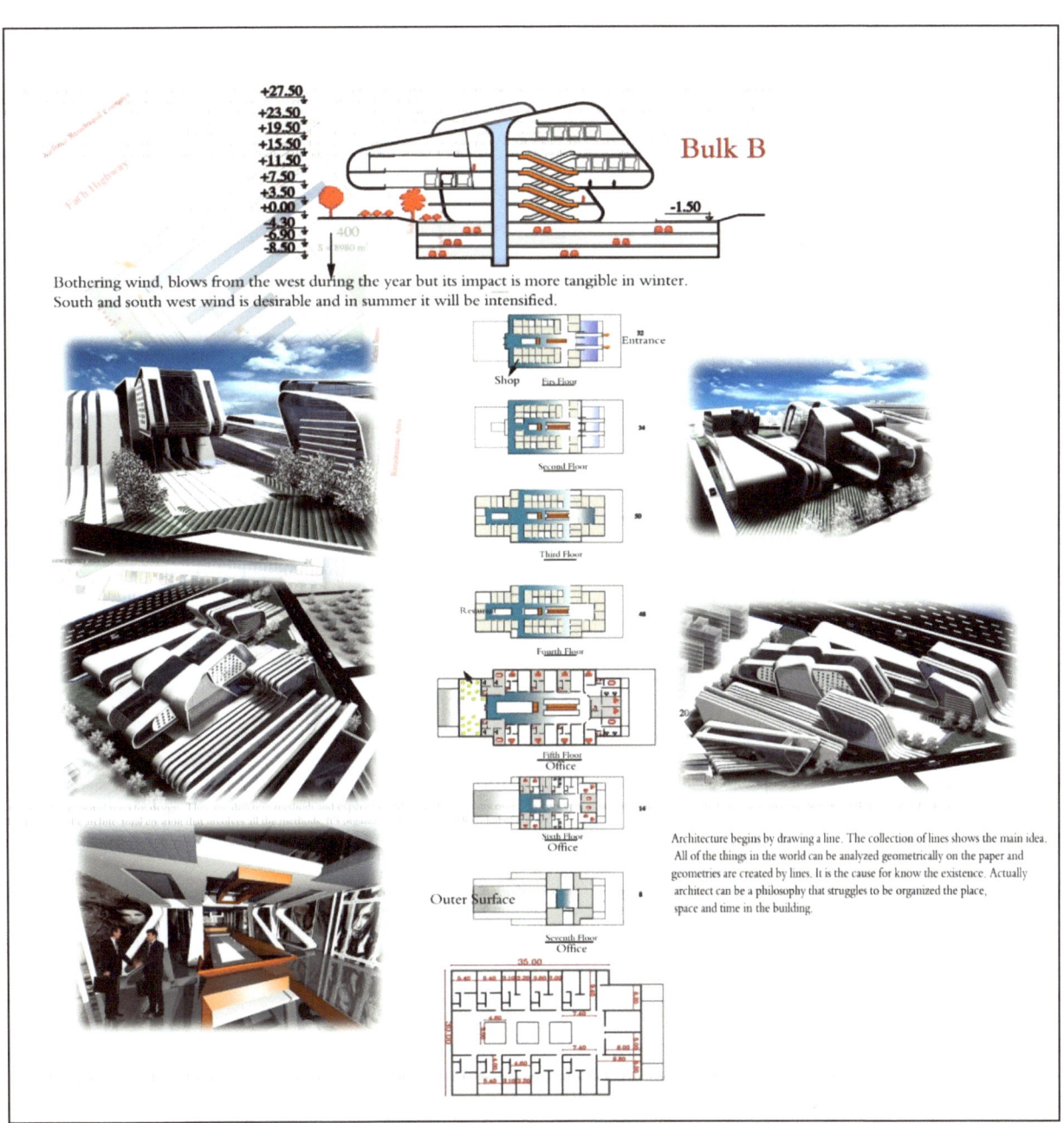

Bothering wind, blows from the west during the year but its impact is more tangible in winter. South and south west wind is desirable and in summer it will be intensified.

Architecture begins by drawing a line. The collection of lines shows the main idea. All of the things in the world can be analyzed geometrically on the paper and geometries are created by lines. It is the cause for know the existence. Actually architect can be a philosophy that struggles to be organized the place, space and time in the building.

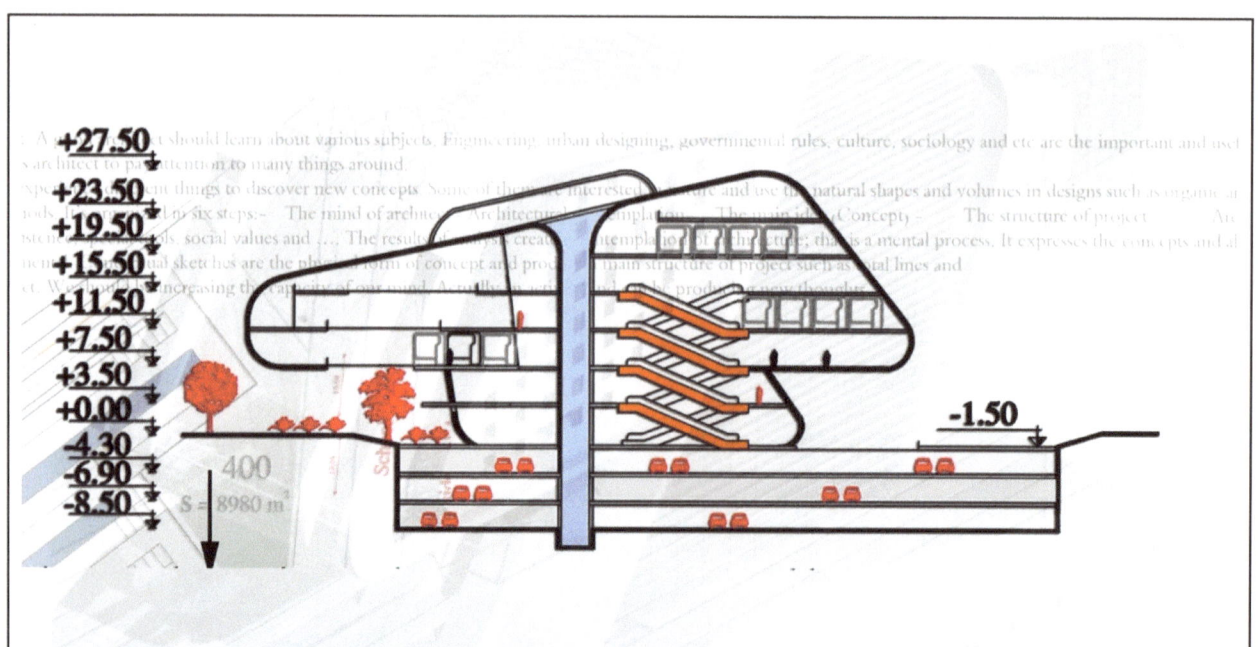

122

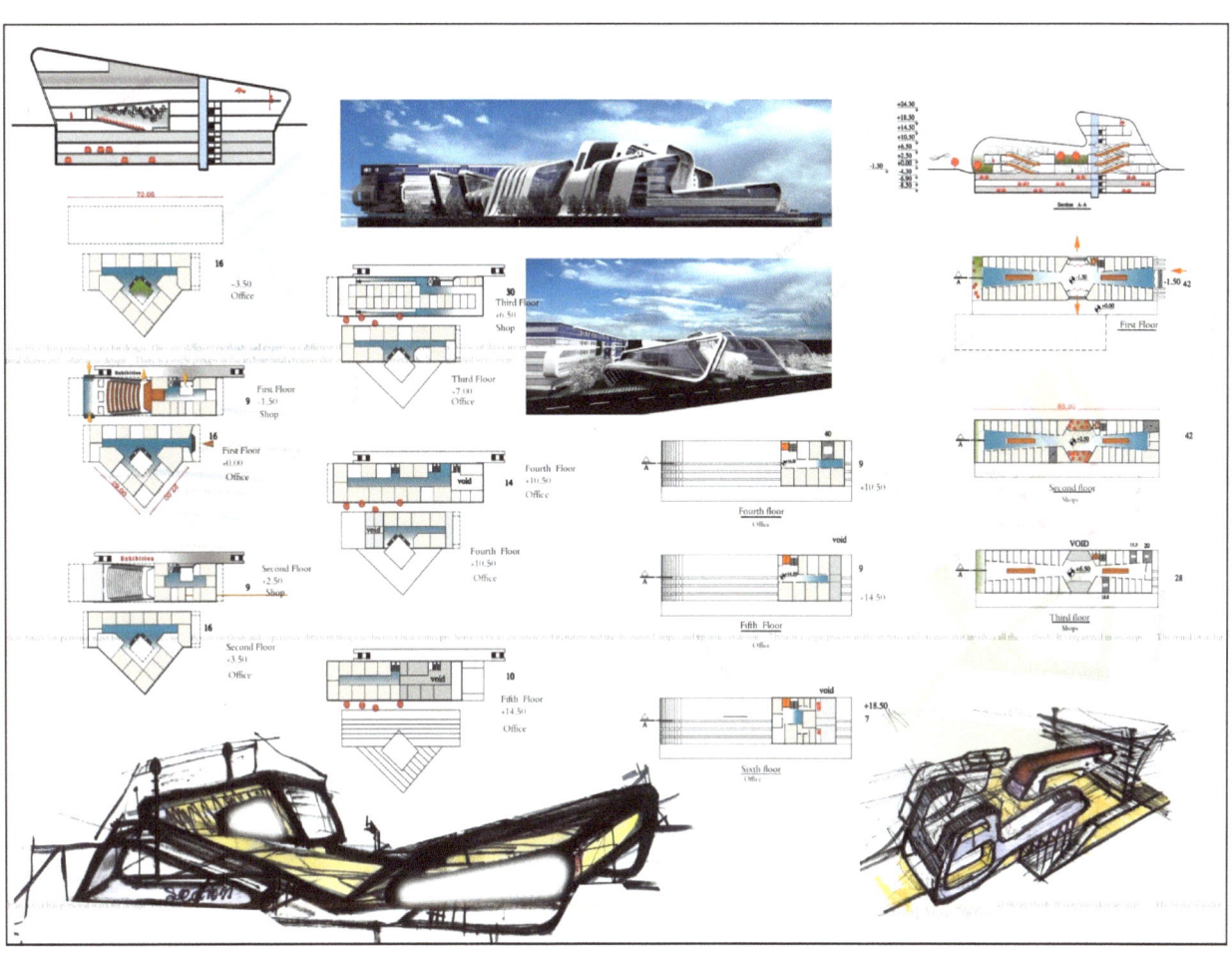

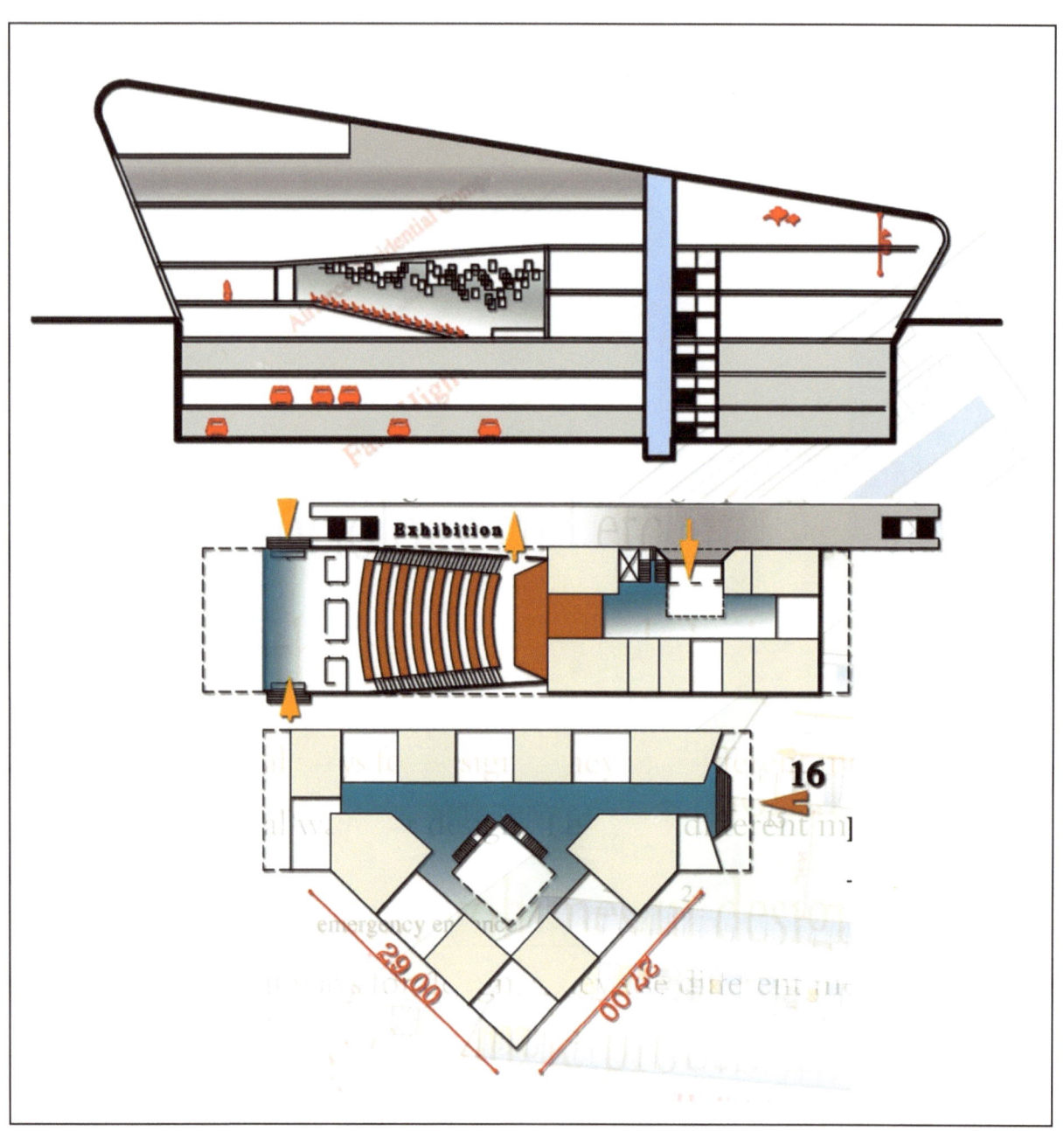

Sustainable house in Iran's desert

The buildings in the Iranian desert regions are constructed according to the specific climatic conditions and differ from those in other climates. Lofty walls, narrow and dry streets, highly elevated air traps, big water reservoirs and arched roofed chambers, are the outstanding features of desert towns in Iran. Hot summer and cold winter which are because of arid environment and also dusty storms, dry and hot and nasty winds have forced human to find a remedy. After thousands years and by gaining experience people has found solutions with diverse shapes for this important case. The desert buildings are equipped with air traps, arched roofed, water reservoirs with arched domes and ice stores for the preservation of ice. Today because of technology development, new techniques have replaced these native solutions. In this study we try to show theoretical topics about issues of stability, climate, green architecture, energy saves and naturalization of architecture in a modern framework and according to aesthetic criteria, which are rarely considered in given issues. Also subjects relating to the materials of buildings and the method of operation of the traditional cooling systems in the cities in the Iranian desert regions are described.

Green House

The concept of sustainable development that as commonly used in the world's scientific communities is termed as one of quality and tends to handle the qualities of life. Its aim is also to enhance the standards of living for the successors. A notion of sustainable development possesses deep contents in three ranges: 1) Environmental sustainability, 2) Economic sustainability, 3) Social sustainability. (Bahri)

In order to realize these aims of sustainable development, it is necessary to attach much importance to it if it is interacted to architecture. It is obvious that the ecological problems have made the architects find a remedy to prevent the threats of these problems from endangering man s future. The notion of a sustainable environment is to sustain the earth to the coming generations in its best form. According to this definition, the human practices can be sustained only when they would be carried out without any loss or diminution of natural resources or degraded environment. The aims behind sustainability of environment are the minimum consumption of energy sources; use of recycled materials; entirely recycled material wasted; protection and supply of energy and recycling it without creating pollutions. Given the points mentioned above, a sustainable building that has the least adverse effect on the natural structure and environment over its life cycle and as long as it is locally and internationally located and well- established. A number of principles should be observed and obeyed while we plan a building in a sustainable way: 1- recognition of location: a sustainable planning is contingent upon a location that can be identified because if we show sensitivity to local nuanced issues, we can occupy it without destroying it. This identification or recognition contributes significantly and can occupy to the development of architecture up to sustainability both given its performance features and given climatic and weather considerations. 2- The relationship between architecture and nature: this relationship can be followed by the recovered environmental life and an encouragement to revert to this mode of living. 3- Gaining good knowledge of environmental effects: their negative affects can be minimized by drawing upon technology and architectural strategies. (Barrnet, 1995)

The consistency and harmonization of a building with a climate constitute is an important principle of a sustainable architecture. One more thing observable in this mode of architecture is that the use of fossilized fuel reserves has been minimized by virtue of appropriate designing of building and the requirements are so parsed that no damage would be laid on the resources belonging to the coming generations. It may be said that the newly- initiated strategies for supplying emerging to the building are likely the variously important parameters that help achieve the aims to establish a sustainable development (Donald, 1999). In this design first we will review and discuss all local ecological feature and designing principles in our target environment where is hot and dry climate in Iran's desert residential places. Then we will purpose our design for a modern house by applying numbers of local designing principles to achieve a sustainable house based on renewable energy sources. The designing processes are done using 3D-Max and VERAY software which common in architectures design.

Climatic designing

A climatic designing is an approach to the ways and means by which we would be able to take any necessary measures to achieve sustainable development and environment sustainability aims (Seyed Almasi, 2004). In a climatic designing process, first and foremost the type of local or regional climate, atmospheric conditions and local weather where building are typically taken in to account; than the bad condition of unfavorable local climate, introduced in this paper a climatic indicator, are identified and finally a consideration is taken in to account how to provide strategies to moderate them so that a good comfort would be provided in designing spaces. Meanwhile, the main aim of climatic designing is to adopt the best approach to designing for the erosion of needs for heat and cooling of a building by substituting natural energies instead of fossilized and electrical energies. This designing process dates back to native architecture of different regions in the world including Iran. They, however, fell in to oblivion with the advent of modern architecture. Therefore, in the exercises of climatic designing the consideration of ways in which the old visions of climatic designing can prove useful. Nowadays, this type of designing has made progress so far that warm water and light in the building can be supplied without using fossilized energies. The use of resources and renewable energies technology is one of key principles in sustainable development. There are three main reasons for this allegation: 1. these new sources affect the environment much less than other energy sources. 2. These sources are renewable and are not depleted like fossilized fuels. 3. The energy required for small communities would be supplied in a cost effective way.

Strategies to REDUCE the effects placed by heat

This climate when the weather is hot, the level of humidity and air temperature rise to some extent that it would be impossible to cool the air by using evaporated frigidity ascended from the surfaces of water and plant. Thus, some other means should take in to account.

Creation of shade

The first strategy to develop shade is to create projections and having a recessing system in the plan of exterior walls. In more than one story build, if upper stories are more projected than the ground floor, it will both create a shade on the lower story view, and avoid positioning under drops of rain. In preparing or devising a plan, also, if both eaves and retreat taken in to account, some parts of a building will cast shadows on other parts in some periods of a day and thus satisfy our needs. Since the building must be safe from not only the immediate radiation of sun but also the reflected rays of it, one strategy to follow here is that a measure should be taken to encircle the open space of the yard with high walls so that a good shadow Casting would be provided there. Meanwhile, a possibility would be provided to plan and construct the yard deeper that we can plan and construct the intended building.

Decreasing the contact surface of external walls to avoid sunrays.

In hot climate, if there are much heightened spaces, they be come hot a littlie later and thus comfort heat would be supplied in this way. In winter, however, the increase height of rooms causes them to become hot in a more lagged way. It, therefore, a consideration should be taken to build a more heightened spaces in architectural designs and develop a suspended ceiling that can be condensed and extend like an accordion, the problem can be solved without fail. In summer when the significantly high rooms supply better the frigidity requirements, the suspended ceiling can be removed and in winter to reinstall it to warm the space during a less period of time. Meanwhile the design of this suspended ceiling and the details used and obeyed in its fitting can also contribute to the beauty of spaces.

Strategies for lowering the undesirable effects of heat on man's comfort

Like shadow and shad provision, ventilation is one of the most important factors for the preventing of unwanted energy in summer. Ventilation not only reduced the thermal energy effect but also decrease its undesirable effect by evaporating the dampness of building. From psychological point of view, air current can directly and immediately influence our sense of cold even in temperatures not more that 34c. The more extended speed of wind contributes to the rate increase of continuous perspiration and there fore the undesirable sense of heat and continuous perspiration begin to recede (Khorami , 2004).

Walled ventilation in a building

1.1.1. Facade ventilation

Use of two-walled layer: In the event an external wall is made laminated (two-ply) and the 10 centimeters wall of facade or frontal is made within a radius of 10 centimeters of the main wall, we can develop a string crevice all over the frontal within a minimum of 30 centimeters of the ceiling. Then, it will be made possible for the wind current to flow out of the bottom of the wall in to the trough of the two layers of wall and finally flows out of upper gap. Air current, if a remains on, considerably contributes to the evaporation of dampness. Besides, sunrays do not radiate directly on the main walls and prevent the temperature from rising. A canopy is also developed to avoid raindrops influence in to the pares of the walls. In addition, it is recommended to fix screen on these openers to prevent entering of unwanted bodied, animals and insects (Fig.1).

1.1.2. Floor and ceiling

- If the building is placed or located on a pilot, the air current will flow from under it (the pilot) which facilitates to create comfort. In the meantime, in areas A where ground water has a higher level, localizing the structure on the pilot minimizes the absorption of moistures from the floor. (Fig.2) - Developing a grid shelter helps create an air current to flow on the roof because if we have solid wall for the parapet wall, no air current would be allowed to flow on the roof. (Fig.3)

Ventilation by taking advantage of thermal run-off

One more option to apply a natural ventilation system in modern building is to take advantage of thermal run-off. A thermal run-off is based on a varied vertical pressure (vertical pressure difference) which is developed in a vertical canal: if the sun s heat or other thermal sources warm air of the lower part of canal in the terminating section of canal and in the most bottom surface, then the vertical pressure difference is created by the heated air lower canal and a current also begin to flow towards the upper side of canal (Baker)

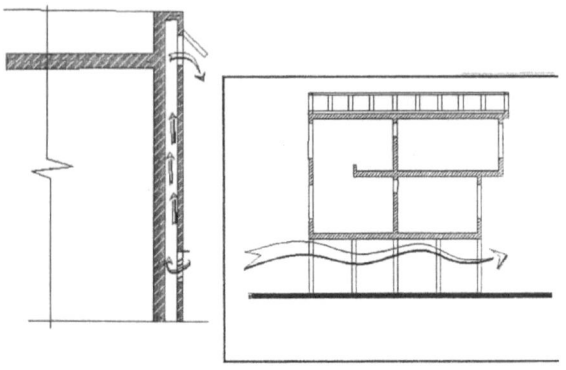

Fig.1. A schematic use of two-walled layer for ventilation.

Fig.2. A schematic of floor ventilation.

A canal can be set up in one side of a building to create a thermal heating in a such a way as from the spaces of the building there can open a compartment like a cooler part to this canal. If there may opener in other sides of the spaces to allow the wind to blow in to the spaces through them, the in blown wind enters the canal through the ports and then is driven out (conducted out) together with canal air current by means of canal thermal run-off.

The thermal run-off developed in the canal leads to a situation where the air inside the rooms is suctioned to the canal direction through the compartment (Fig.4). The more the height of canal is in proportion to its length and width, the better the thermal run-off takes places because according to "Bernoli Effect", through the narrower section The air flows, the more speed it flows. (Mahmoudi 2004).

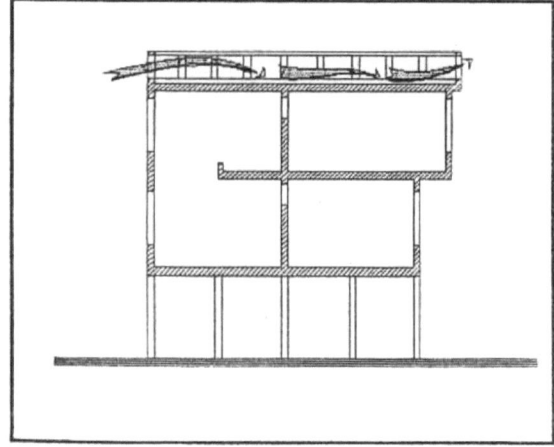

Fig.3. A schematic ceiling ventilation

Using stair box as a suctioning canal and air blower

- If the making of stairs is not materialized with masonries and through would still remain between both steps and if the slabs of the steps are made as porous, we can heighten the sharp roof (range) and make the desirable wind or breeze from in to the building by developing openers on the range, that is to use the same approach by which an air-trap used in hot and humid regions creates natural ventilation by utilizing appropriately the wind. This can also be used in modern building. For residential flats the stair box of which is not directly connected to main spaces and the gates of which are impediments to the entry of wind within the flats, we can let the natural airflow in to the building by developing some openers over the entrances of apartments. - as for trade and office and cultural building in which the various spaces can be partitioned only by one partition, all parts can be so designed as air current could flow up in all parts of under- the- ceiling spaces. Thus, we can position the stairs in the center of building as already mentioned and we can make an overhead trap door above it unit vertical ventilation develops. The most important governing rule on building vertical ventilation is the varied air pressure in lower and upper parts of the building and a concurrent flow of heat towards the upper part (Khorami, 2004). The air current that flows in to the building through the opening windows around it move throughout the construction and flows out of the upper part of the central space. If the force of natural current of air is inappropriate of there appears an unwanted audio problem or that of safety after the windows open, one can use simultaneously both artificial and natural currents. In this situation, the use of fixed or mobile blowers can increase the speed of internal air in addition, alluvium exchange provides good comfort.

Ventilation reveled by Shovadan

In regions where there is a hot climate and the level of ground water is not high such as Dezfol region in Iran, one can be reveled by what exists in the traditional architecture of this city to create natural coldness. Shovadan consists of rooms that are built about 6-7 maters below the surface of yard. The temperatures of these rooms are equal to the average temperatures over a yard. In this way is about 22c all over the year (Ghobadian, 2007). Today designing can benefit both from rooms with function of storage within 6-7 meter deep in the ground and direct the wind in to the Shovadan by constructing a duct against the dominant wind. Meanwhile, this duct can be to steps or stair type that provides the way to gain access to Shovadan with the difference that it is not made of any masonry. One must provide a vertical duct against the duct directing the dominant wind in order to be conducted from Shovadan to the space that is designed to be used. This duct, like that of cooler, can have an opener in rooms and conduct the air in Shovadan rooms. In general, ventilation whit this system is done in such a way that the air conducted in to the Shovadan loses its temperature by cooling with the walls and cold air of Shovadan and then flows through the second duct to the residential spaces. The force of the wind behind the entered wind causes an amount of air inside the Shovadan to exit out through the canal (Fig.5).

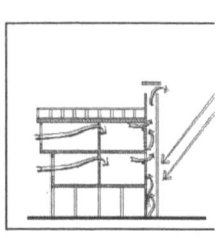 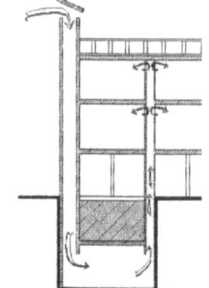

Fig.4. A schematic of ventilation by taking advantage of thermal run-off system.

Fig.5. A schematic of ventilation in Shovadan.

Designing the sustainable house

Our design is based on the following limitations:

Ecological features: high sun radiation, high latitude, low humidity, low raining, cold winter, very hot summer, high fluctuation of temperature during night and day, low plant coverage, dusty weather. **Common house features of the area:** Building volume: extended cuboids, Building form: extended rectangle (plan), Building roof: Dom-shaped, Air-conditioning: increasing height of room's to accelerate outflow of warm air through openings located at top of the dome, Great opening toward central yard-Yard has paved ford and flower bed pit, High and narrow wind wards, Equipped with basement, cistern and cellar to cool the building , Face of the building is coated with shining, light-colored materials, thatch, Thick walls, Materials with high thermal mass.

Urban texture features

Buildings are connected together, compressed urban texture: narrow passages with high walls having elements to porch which function as canopy and used as buttress considering statics. High walls of houses which mostly located at eastern –western direction, Wind wards are located at southern direction. Having secondary yards termed as Narenjestan. Porch is located along vertical or northern axes, Houses are somehow rotated toward west or western south in order to take more light, heat contact level , Houses are inner directed, Buildings are located toward south eastern south. The whole designing process is clearly illustrated in (Fig.6). All steps from first sketches and final results are shown. Details are shown in following figures.

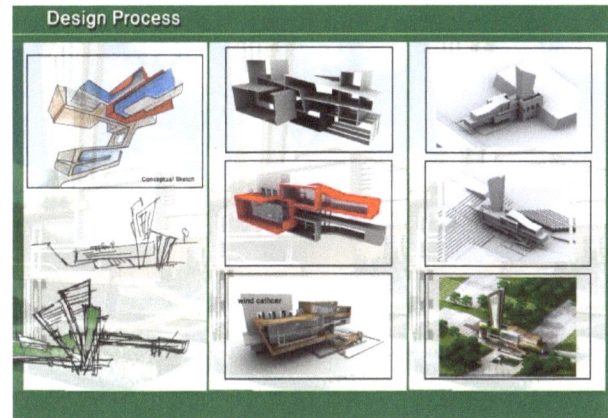

Fig.6. Designing process.

The northern part of house is shown in Fig. 7 and all features of the other parts of house are described in details. Also the balcony of house where is really important in our designing is shown and specification are described. In Fig. 8 we summarize the main plan of the designed house all parts of the house are shown and identified. Building coordination with slope and its position at the heart of earth is shown in the Fig.9. Also the new facilities for building cooling and ventilation and the specific green roof are shown and other climate specifications of building are described in details.

Fig.10 illustrates sun rotation, reasons and causes to have air flow under the building. The position of bright and shadow around the building are identified. In designing of wind catcher, many inactive designs were suggested and researched and then registered in a final design. An inactive vaporization loop has been provided at the base of tower and exactly in the perimeter of water ditch which embodies traditional concept of desert in desert. Key advantage which is provided by this system is the creation of natural air ventilation and lower temperature around internal building in comparison with outside air which under normal conditions needs the reduction of temperature that necessitates further and certain pressure in energy consumption of building. Air which is cooled by passing on water, enter into collection by openings or ventilation towers provided that ventilation towers are in an area protected against dust and above water level and in shadow. Function of wind catcher is so that they bring into flowing air of outside and water basins which are installed into them make air light and cool and direct it towards inside of home (Fig.11). Hence updating these native solutions and using of them can decrease fuel consumption largely and solve most of environmental problems and prevent polluted and poisonous air enter into home, so also helps to promotion of environment quality. The effect of ceiling slop on the ventilation and interior design of the house is shown in Fig.12.

Fig.7. Description of different parts of house.

Eastern part of building is empty toward surface -300, and Water pools have extended from southern part to north of building. This causes air to be moist and absorb dust although partly.
By rotation of sun always northern part of building will be at shade and southern part will be sunlit or vice versa.
This causes air flow under building.
The height of floors ceiling are high about 3/80
. Specially to be sloping of studio ceil direct heat towards western part of room and there is some windows to balcony.

There are bedrooms and living room in underground floor to use ventilation and water humidity.

Fig.8. The plans of the house.

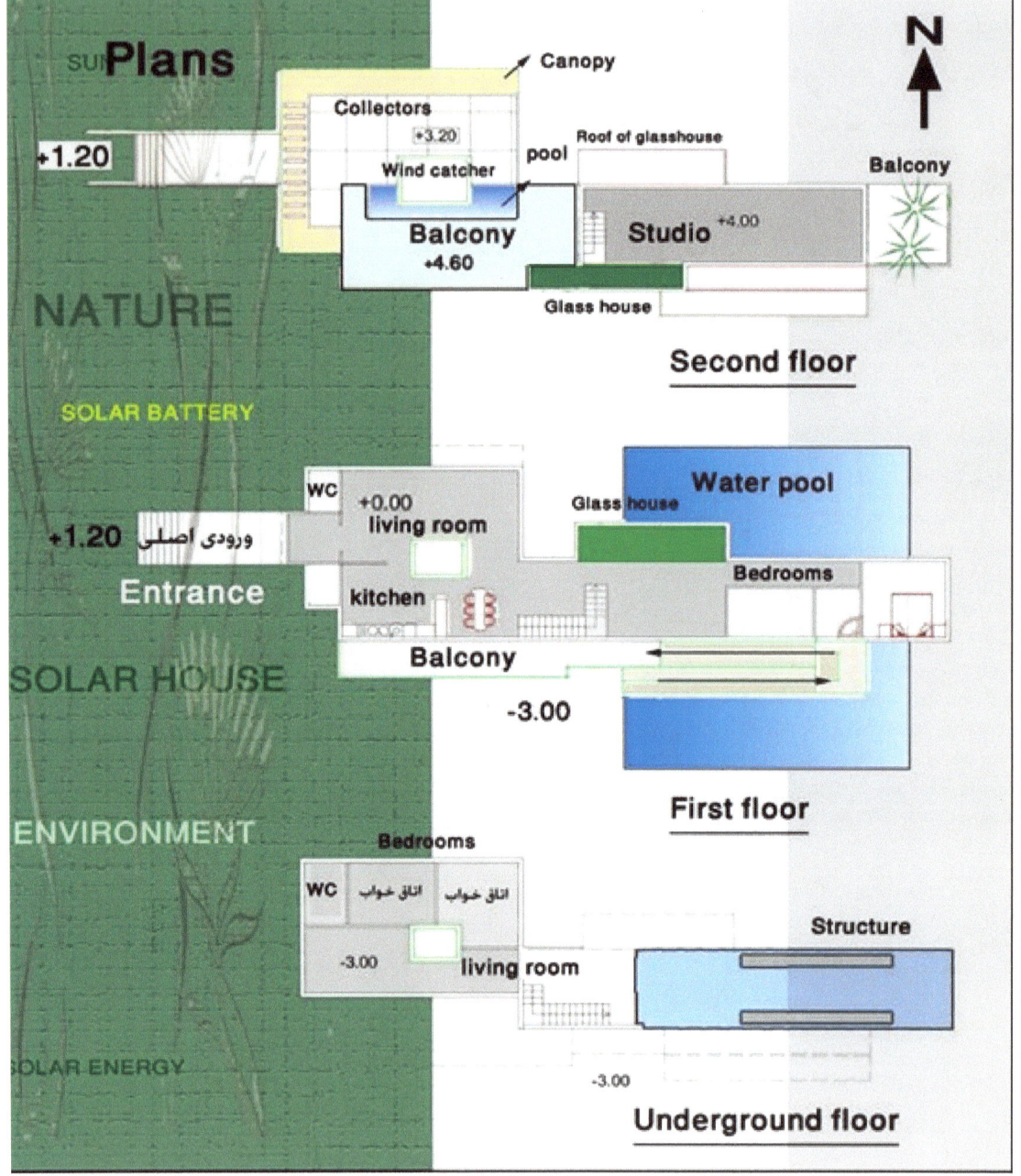

Fig.8. The plan of the house.

Fig.9. Climate specification of building.

Climatic specifications of building:
- Building coordination with site slope and its position at the heart of earth.
- Use of ventilation tower with new facilities for cooling of building.
- Green roof (ground floor ceiling along with water pool which create a suitable space like balcony by shadow making of southern and northern walls)
- Use of three wall and colored glasses in order to prevent dust enter into home.
- Use of at least openings and canopy to control sunlight.
- Most of light of living space in ground floor and design studio in first floor is provided by greenhouses.

Along with moderation of air warmth and exhaustion of hot air, openings of the greenhouse ceiling decrease intensity and energy of sunlight.

Design Process

Conceptual Sketch

wind cathcer

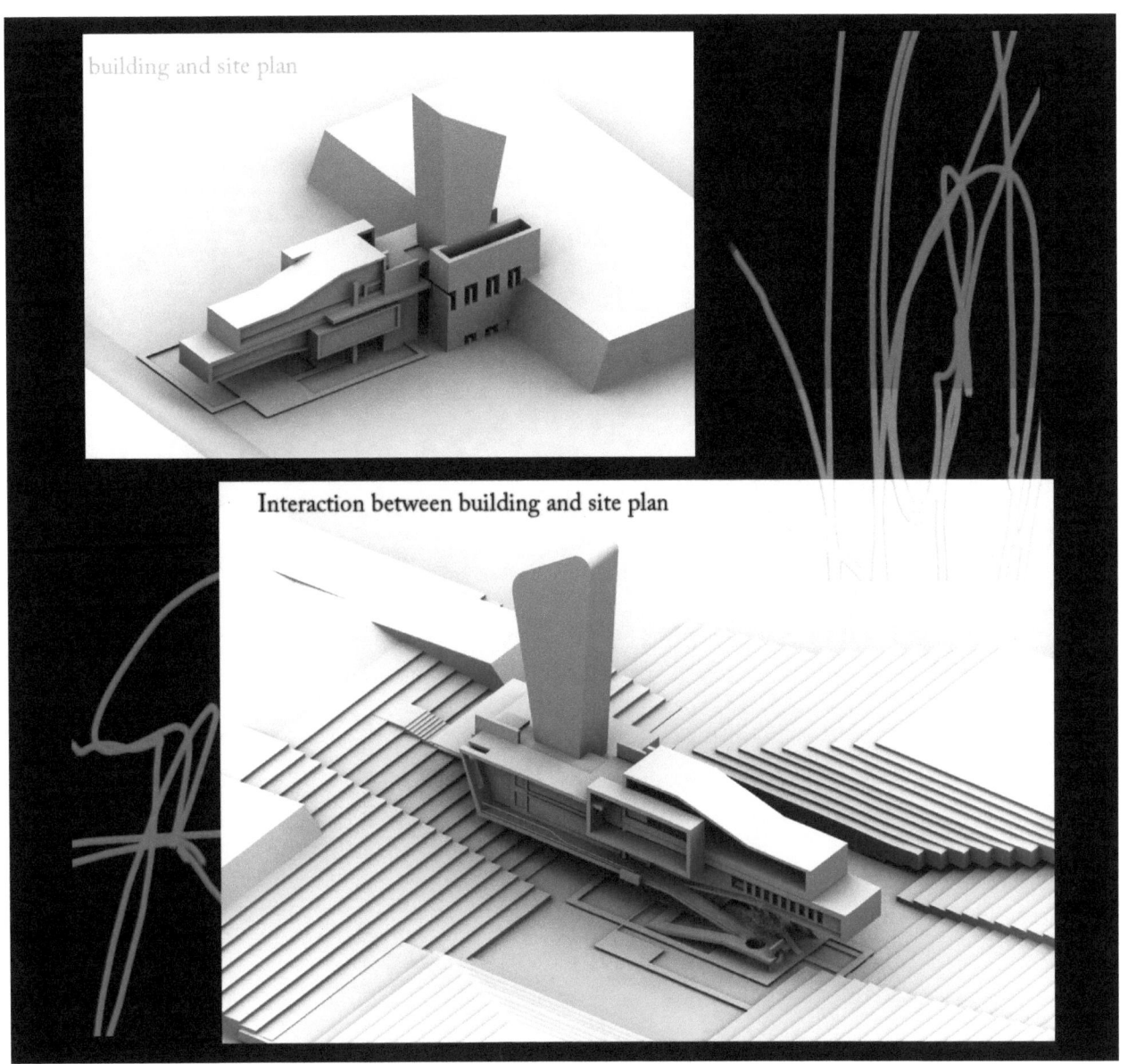

Fig.10. sun rotation and air flow under the building.

Fig.11. Wind Catcher.

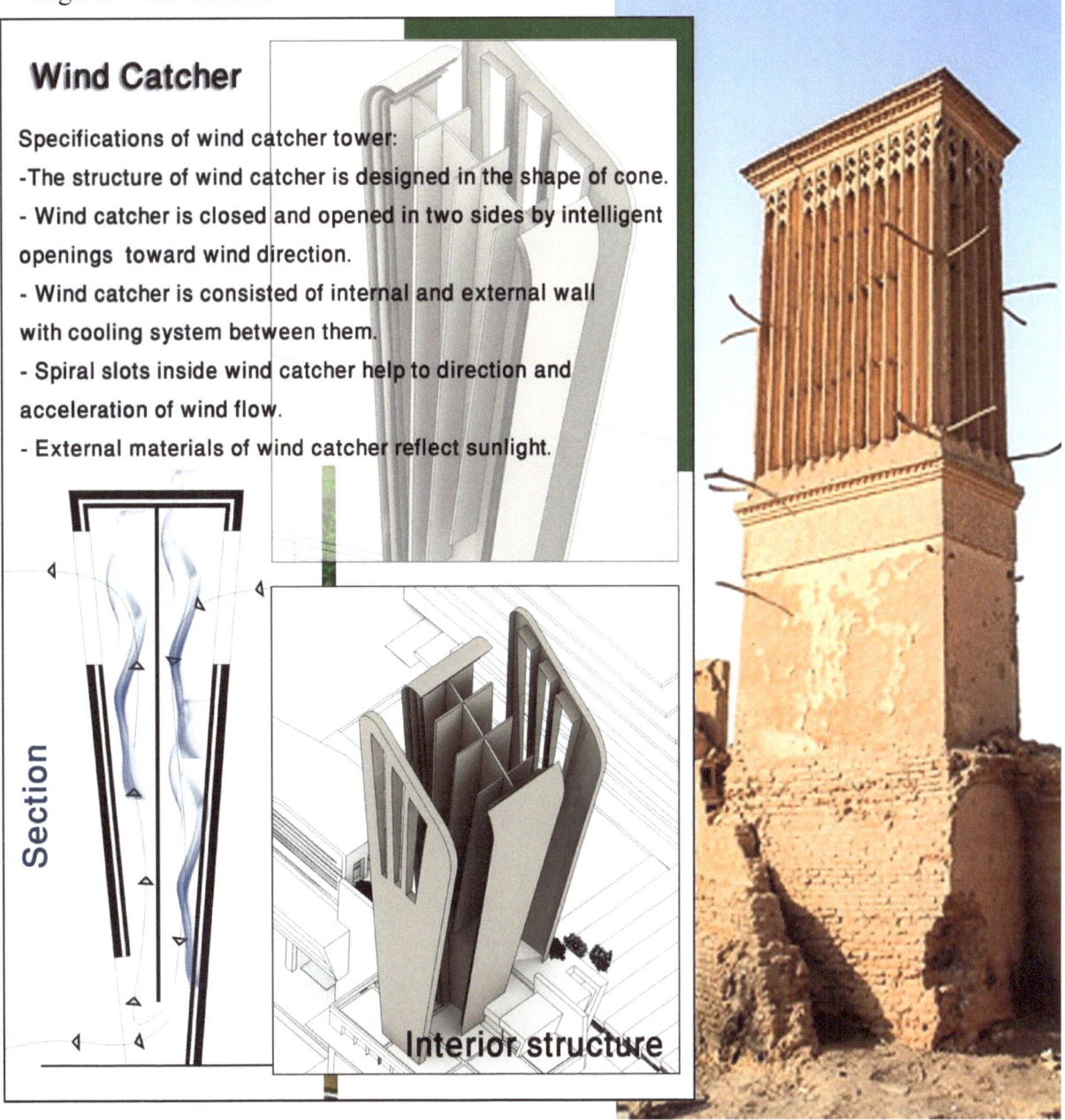

143

Fig.12. The effect of ceiling slop on ventilation.

sloping of studio ceiling direct heat towards western part of room and there is some windows to balcony.

Sketch

When you take a pen to write down your findings as a poem or paintings of line and color on a white paper, you are not aware that nature enthusiastically accompanies you, opens its inspiration horizons in your mind, calls you back for regeneration and involves you mind scope in novel concepts newer than before.

Can you draw what you imagine?

Sketch is a direct, immediate and also more humanistic way to produce ideas. It is more available way to recognize and evaluate space capabilities, embodiment of mental image and swift communication with site and project features.

Frank Gehry states that I think my best skill as an architect relates to finding coordination between eye and hand. I can change to a model what I draw on a paper and the model to a building.

Ability to control the mind and enhancing artist's creativity on one hand and reducing distance of mind to reality on the other hand are two categories should be considered in detail. Close relationship between architect's mind and hand can be very helpful due to quick understanding and embodiment of findings. This is a problem observed in most designers. Non-control of mind and untimely embodiment of mental findings results in disconnection of architect's thoughts and created work and confuses designers in their designing course.

Comments of Charles Jencks, contemporary theoretician and architect, about Le Corbusier designing method is as follow;

"He/she prepared a book for collecting of sketches and a notebook for immediate jotting down of ideas, pictorial imaginations and events. These books exceeding 70 volumes during his/her life are a reason for progress since they changed to new instruments for expression and resources for the next ideas.

Imagine that there are volumes and ideas in your mind and you are interested in exhibiting them as layouts for your project. At this stage, similar to a picture, sketch is a method for material embodiment of ideas. It is similar to taking photograph from door, entrance portal and roof of a building in order to establish a relationship with it. This can be termed endoscopy. Do you know its meaning? It means watching inside.

Certainly, several and different images come to your mind at initial stages and you try that record them by sketches. In fact, they are subjects, volumes and elements should be identified by sketch. You are able to canalize all motivations of free thought, free emotion, form and natural flow in the form of sketches, rough drafts and sculptures.

Santiago Calatrava in an interview with "Architectural Record" journal describes designing and sketching process as follow;

Drawing initial sketches and layouts is an auxiliary instrument for idea embodiment at the next stages and may be the most abstract way to study of morphology and sculpture. A person may draw human body to understand its behavior and motion. Place, landscape and human are very important for me. Their study and scrutinize can be inspiring and define nature of the project.

Finally, problem is not restricted in finding and having an idea; rather clearly expressing of the idea is the main problem. Initial sketches and layouts translated the idea and are very valuable, in my idea.

Henri Matisse, the 20th century French painter and sculptor, emphasizes on importance of sketches and momentary recording of thoughts and elements when he, as a great artist, speaks about his own works. Typically, sketches are communications between you and yourself, a sketch can demonstrate what is in your mind like a letter to the person himself. I think it is an important feature. Sketches become greater and elaborated until you solve the problem fund in a connection or communication, or can interpret it.

What sketches can be effective:
- Strengthening brain right hemisphere (artist mind)
- Empowering thoughts of architect by pencil and paper
- Strengthening imagination faculty
- Recording thoughts

- Recording moments of unconscious mind
- Recording moments of life
- Exciting mind
- Developing, cultivating and understanding of ideas
- Increasing of knowledge from architect and the environment
- Instructing about how to see well
- Sketch plays an important role in creative process and registering of designer's inspirations.
- Sketch activates ideas and passive thoughts.
- Activating of unconscious flow among senses, thoughts, hands, pens and papers (an activity for connecting mind and hand)
- Strengthening of mind and designer's focus on information and increasing their stability
- Demonstrating a lot of information through simple pictures and figures
- Sketch offers kind of meandering search for finding ideas in creative process.
- A sign of a perfect design(Soltanzadeh, 2000)
- Sketching is a way, and maybe the best way, for obtaining information, focusing and strengthening mind for making this treasury. Such a treasury is required in creative designing process.
- Sketching result in participation and development of subject due to cooperative working of students and discussion between instructor and students. These trivial things create a creative process and challenge it.
- Sketching from spaces and buildings teach us how to watch well, consider structures and objects in detail and reveal their discipline and meaning.
- Sketches direct us toward higher levels of environment perception.
- As it has been mentioned, designing is kind of unveiling and dusting of

phenomena. Different ideas and thoughts engage every artist's mind in dealing with subject but in mind structure body, all are abstract rather than real designing. Architect is responsible for determining and expressing these findings in real world. In fact, architect passes through mentality to reality in order to reach the final design and can obtain more information about structure and details of design in each sketch. This is a time consuming effort. Therefore, what an architecture student requires is appropriate and sufficient time .

Design by Foad Bonakdar

Conceptual Sketches or Mental Drawings

(Producing novel ideas and concepts)

Sketches can be discussed from two aspects: 1) there are sketches created for a subject. Initially, a subject is posed and then designer sketches his/her thoughts considering the subject, 2) another kind of sketch termed as "unwanted" is one in which designer does not know the subject beforehand; rather, there are moments with powerful senses of designer such that there is no need for an excuse as order and is manifested in different forms like music, poem or sketch. This is "pure sketch" i.e. designer just thinks for creating sketch and other factors such as paper and subject are not very important. For instance, Abolhassan Saba (great composer and player of Iranian classic music) composed the famous "Camel Bell" music piece in "Segah" apparatus (Persian Melody) on his cigarette box in a bus while travelling to a European country for recording disc. This is a pure music, a pure and spiritual sense without involvement of any order.

Sketch, as the oldest expression method, has always been regarded as the most effective and powerful way in idea production due to direct encounter creates between human and design. Sketches drawn as a result of a person's sensuous understanding and his/her mental structure about outer world, without any thinking, lead to strengthening mental infrastructures and accelerate idea production process. Swift designing of what comes to their mind is a reason for virginity of created forms. At next stages, artist's mental and experimental layers come to operate and change a simple sketch to an architectural design. Different ideas coming gradually to mind create an inspirational space and excite the architect like a poet, challenging with existence, tries to register a concept in a specific and very short time which was typically ignored. An unexpected event bearing deep meanings opens new windows in architect's mind. Architect, like a watchman, waiting for the moment and can reach a supreme understanding through illuminating and encouraging his/her thoughts and senses.(Khiabanian, 2014)

Ambiguous and incomplete sketches are effective in obtaining capability required for extending imaginations. Sketches focus on the most general subjects with the least facilities while constructing architecture main identity. Sense of experimental nature of lines along with transitory sense in some sketches can be helpful.

Typically, at the beginning of designing we ask question about how and from where we can start. We turn over leaves of a book or search in internet to find pictures and lines to be inspired. In this method, we focus on our inner without any question and curiosity in outer world and start our drawing. Your inside architect is wonderfully powerful in understanding and creating of phenomena. It is enough to trust it and begin drawing to prove it. It will provide required instruments including lines and surfaces without your order or expressing your need.

Jackson Polack, a contemporary painter, states that painting has its own life. It is just enough try to show it, believe that there are the best architectural concepts and designs in spiritual world and among galaxies and prepare conditions for their appearing and embodiment.

Be valiant and draw what comes to your mind. Do not afraid of mistakes because there is no mistake. A hunter welcomes danger and enters and dives into sea to find the best pearls. Often, we involve in correcting details and leave the designing aside instead of freely creating and let ourselves to discover mistakes through inspiration and intelligence. Wrong perspective or unparallel lines will act as barriers and divert us from the main route. Do not waste your time for correcting mistakes and just look forward. Most of them will be corrected at next stages and if not, we will finally erase them. Do not let them disturb your mental focus.

Try not to separate pen from paper; solidarity and integrity of lines are important.

Even if you stopped for a moment, do not ask help from your logical mind to complete the design. Do not try to evaluate quality of your sketch before its completion. Nonuse of the left hemisphere will result n more activation of the artist mind.

Believe that creation is a natural phenomenon and creation power can be found in every one's nature. Remember that God is the Great Artist, artists love other peers and He, as creator of all artists, will help us whenever we ask. Trust your inner architect and artists and let them operate freely. It is a mediator between us and great galaxy power which is ready to fulfill our dreams and demands. Conceptual sketches (mental drawings) are just a simple sample of your creative faculty. Such a connection with galaxy understanding will provide you with lots of concepts, ideas and designs.(Khiabanian, 2014)

Henry Matisse, a French painter (1869-1954), describes creation as: "creation is a special task of artists. Where there is no creation, no art will be. It is not correct to attribute creativity power to natural talents. In art field, rue creator is not merely a talented creature; rather, it is a human who was successful in purposefully organizing a wide set of activities result in an artifact. For this reason, creation begins with watching for the artist. Watching well is a creativity act requires more effort."

Michel Shea, contemporary poet and thinker, defines creativity as follow;

"Creativity means seeing what did not exist in advance. You should find out how to call it back to existence and therefore turn to be partner of the existence. We should attend that in architecture designing, architect tries to exhibit new findings from space, form and meaning. Similar to sketching, in writing the students are also asked to take a pen and start writing without stopping and any kind of logical thought. Dominance and control of mind on subject are going to be created will be enhanced through repetition and practicing. A person who writes down every word found in his/her mind will face meaningful sentences after 4 or 5 pages[1].

---

[1] Most colleagues unbelievingly consider conceptual sketches and students usually take pen unwillingly in sketching sessions due to behavior of other instructors. Experiments have shown that at least 4 sessions of practice along with sketching will result in relative productivity and mental flourishing of students which will be deeper during these sessions.

Conceptual sketches of bridge
(Mental drawings)

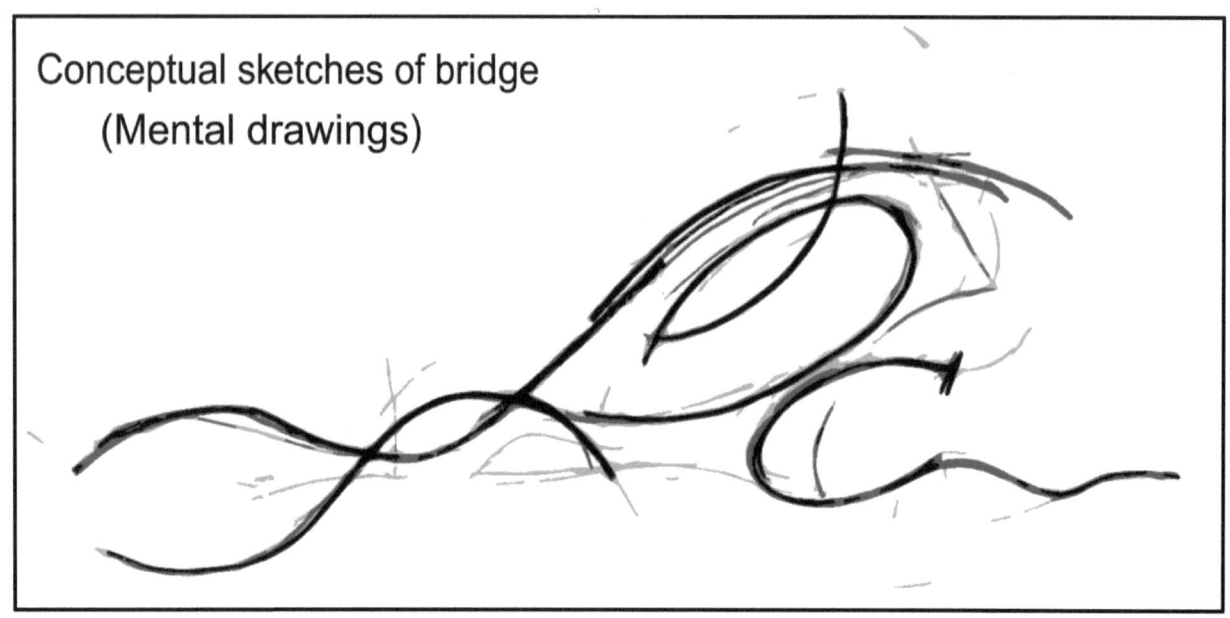

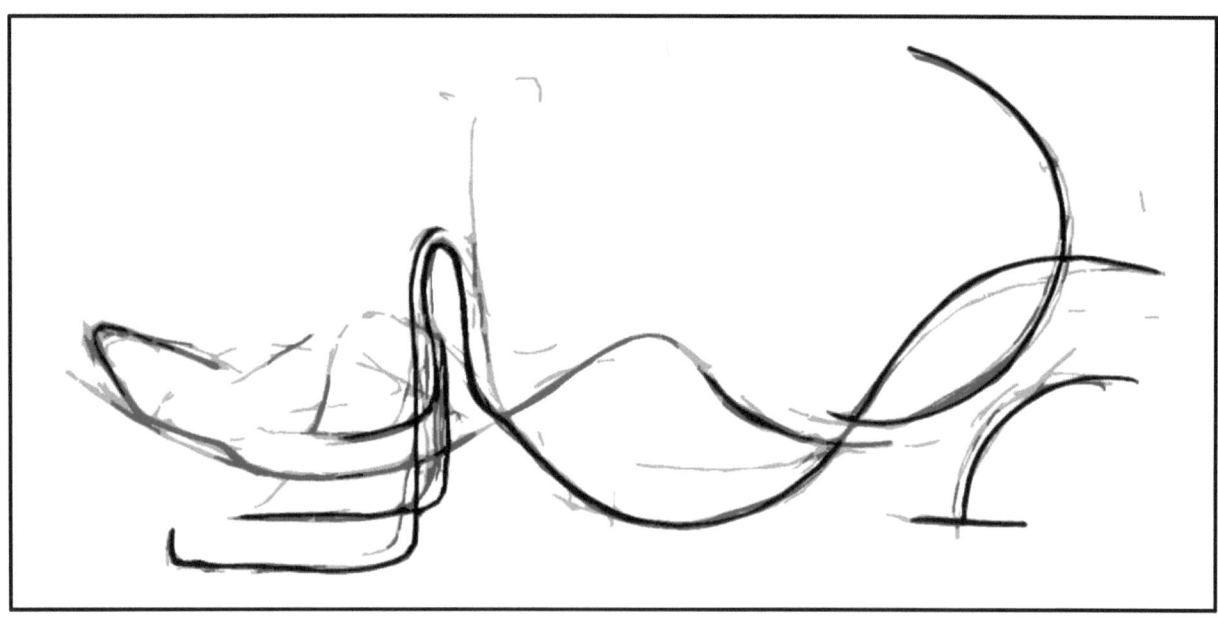

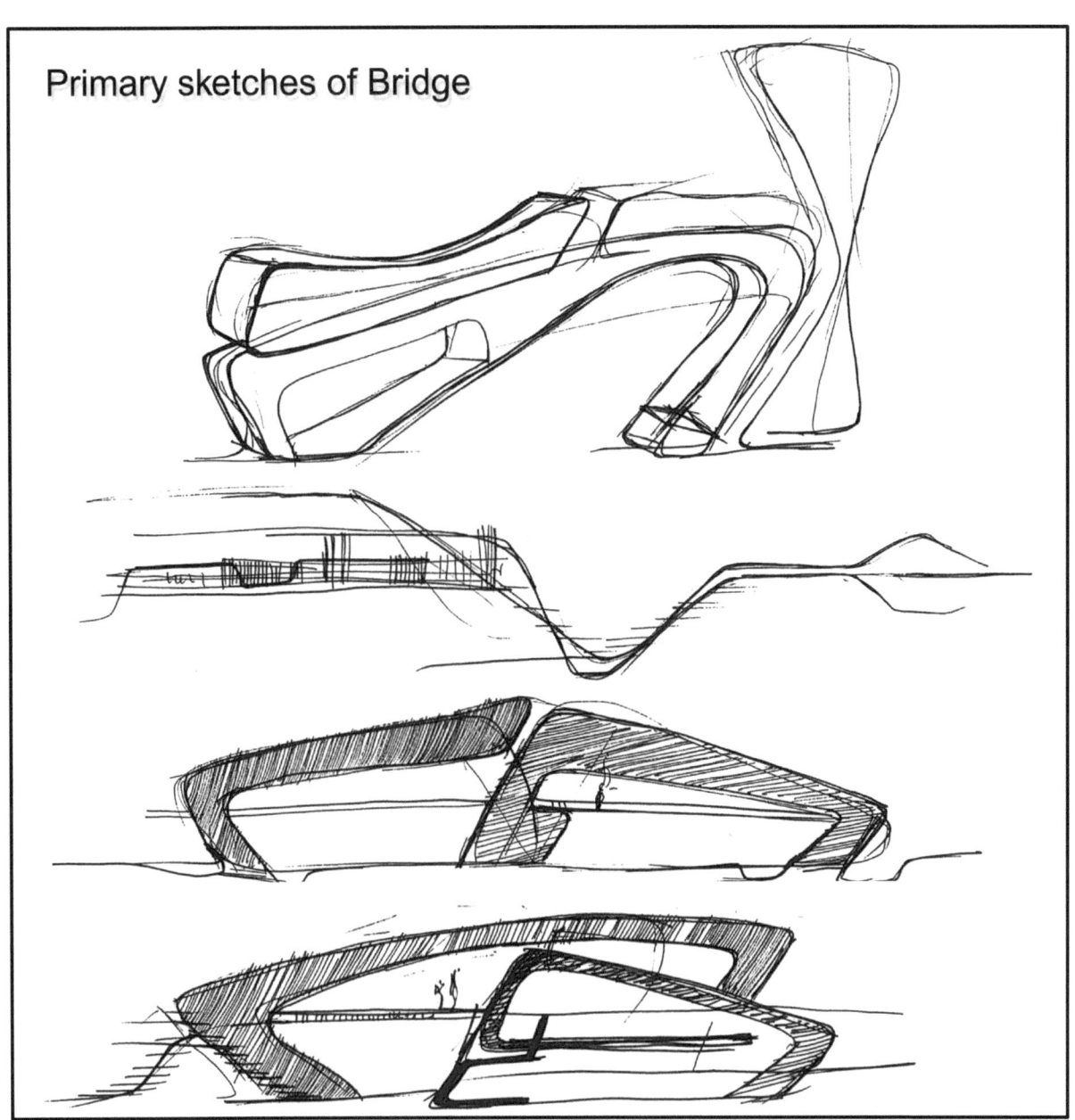

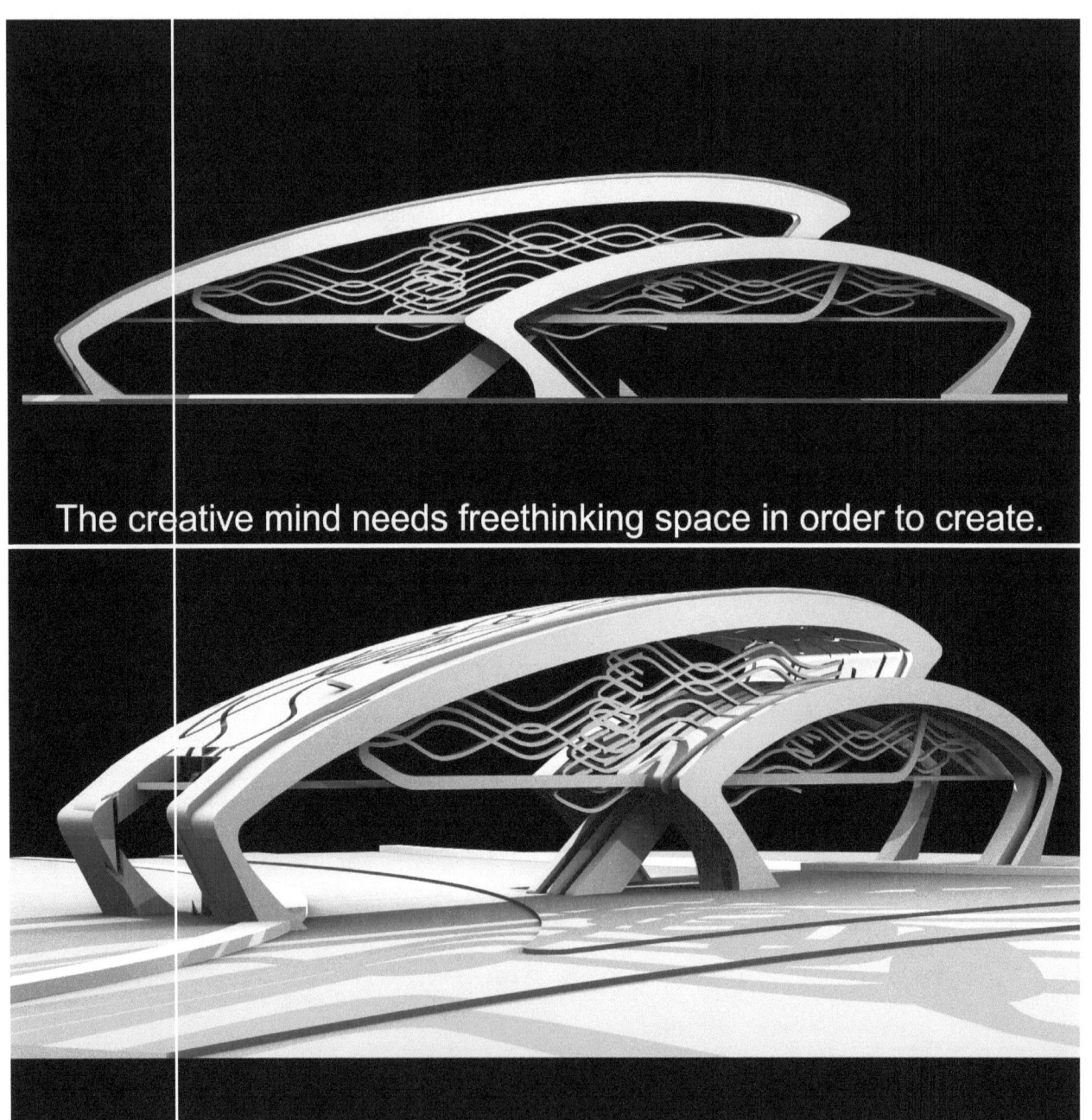

The creative mind needs freethinking space in order to create.

Learning Means Step by Step Movement

Jiddu Krishnamurti, an Indian thinker (1895-1986), believes that repetition and practice are the best teachers because they encourage your inner child to look for more and newer information. These new findings which are more perfect than before considering form and content will act as the best pattern for completing and correcting of your sketches or handwritings.

Unconscious mind or your inner child produces implicit information during sketching without the architect proficiency and knowledge in this regard. Every conceptual sketch includes new ideas, forms and structures in addition to embodying of architect's thoughts and ideas and strengthening his mind and creative faculty. Continual repeating of sketches results in reaching a specific process of designing. (khiabanian, 2014)

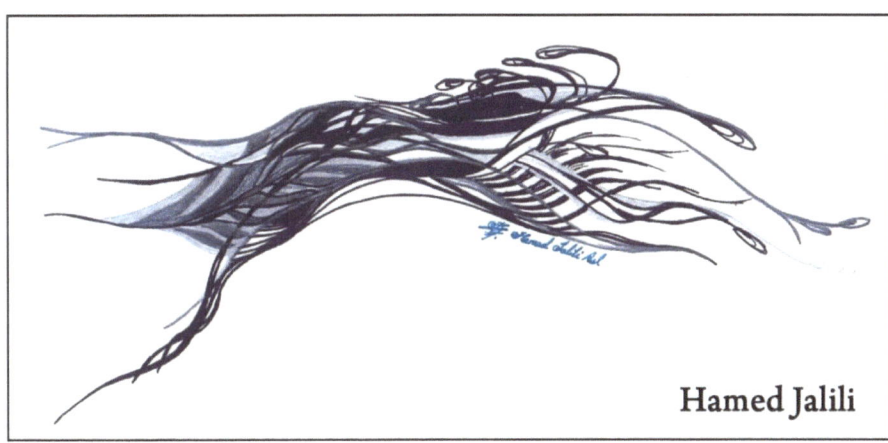

Hamed Jalili

Hamed Jalili

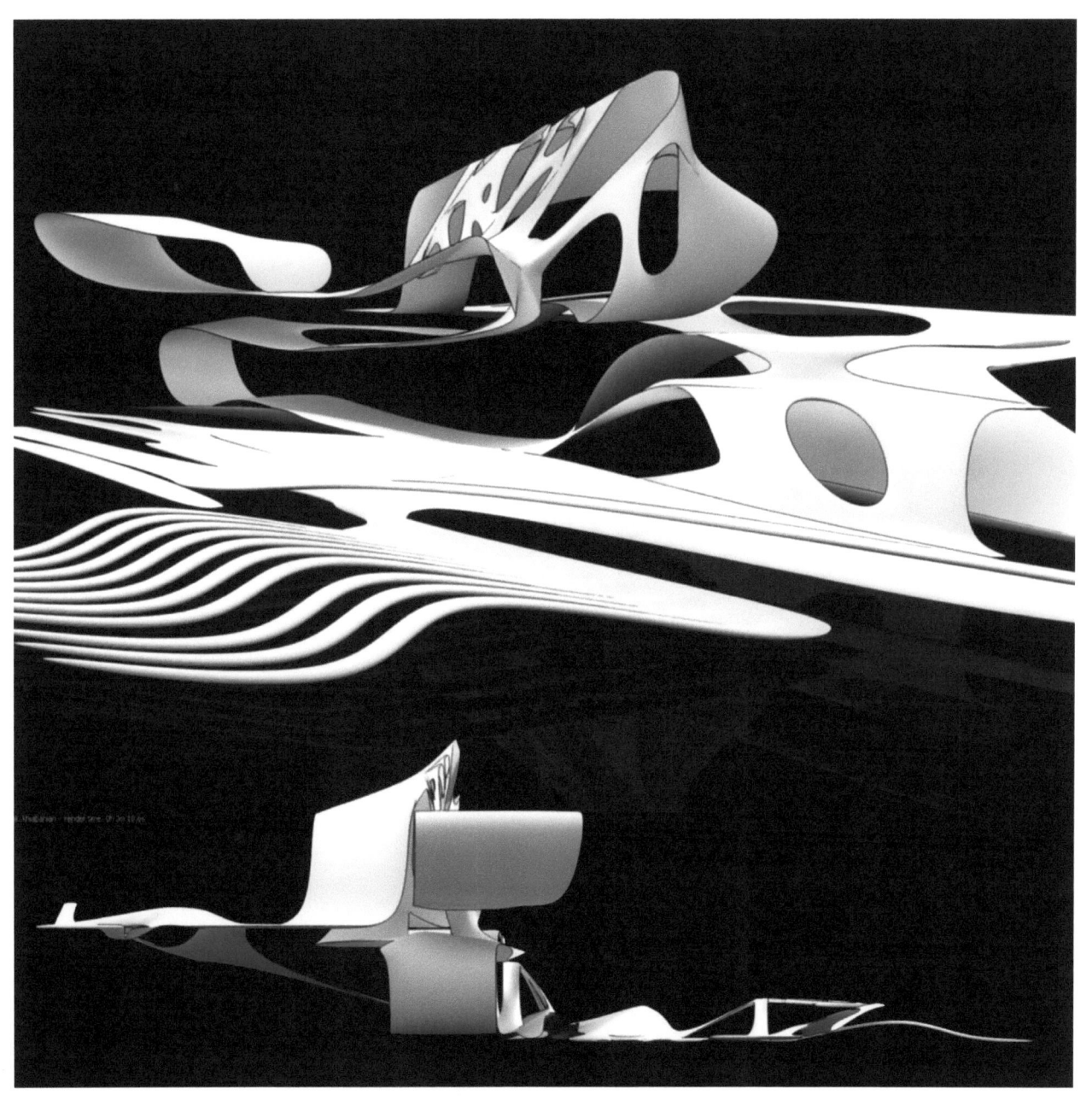

Modeling of Sketches

Looking for some examples of conceptual sketch visualization

Primary Sketches

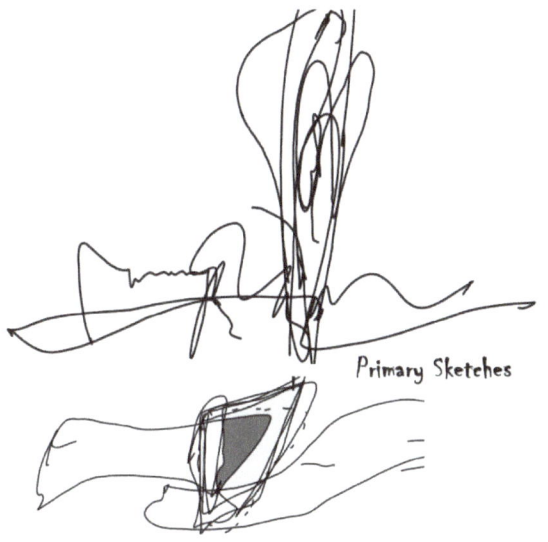

Primary Sketches

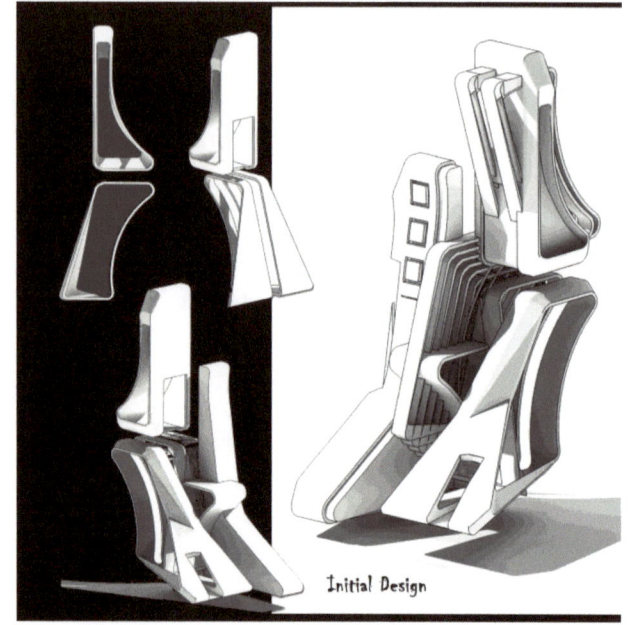

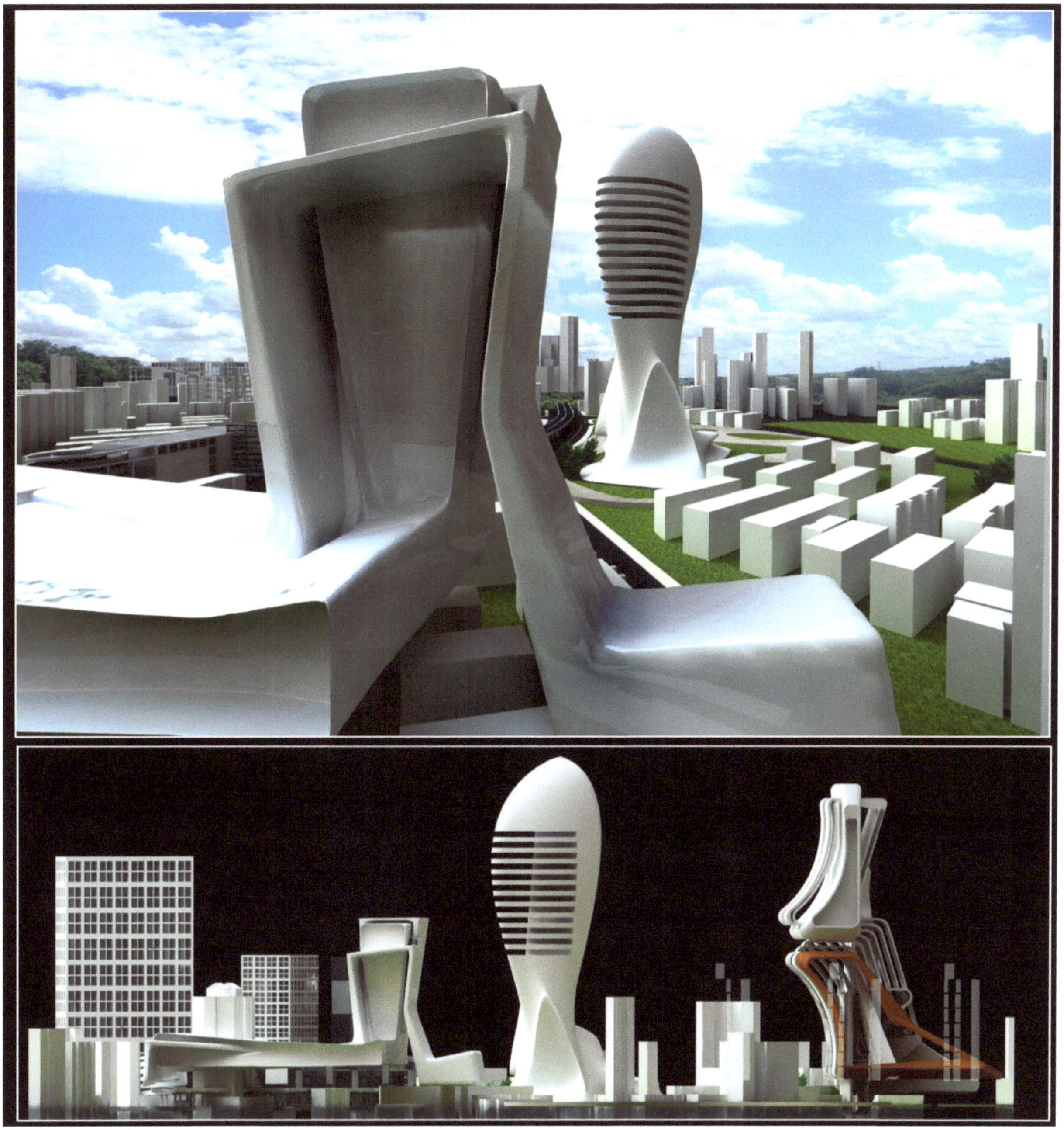

Fundamental Principles in Sketching and Strengthening Creative Faculty

In conceptual sketches or mental drawings, the students are asked to begin drawing free from any thought and without any background of architectural form and space. Stopping of hand is not allowed. Continue your drawing without any judgment about completeness or incompleteness of forms. Do not let samples of previously seen pictures and figures find their way to your sketches. Fly to depths of your inside like a releases bird and let your mind direct you. Such dealing is the most important feature of sketching. Most architecture students deal logically with architecture and look for cause and effect in designing so they distrustfully approach this method at initial stages. Be patient, encourage the students, enhance their self-confidence and direct them through completing and scrutinizing the sketches.

At the next stages of architectural practices, the teacher tries to teach students how relate and coordinate their brain hemispheres. Some of them will be referred.

- In architecture designing, begin with familiar and simple volumes and figures like cube and try to reach a novel and creative structure via practicing and repeating the forms. At initial stages of architectural instruction, focusing on complex computer volumes will result in mind tiredness in spite of their attractiveness.
- Always carry designing instruments with yourself like a fisher who calmly thinks about sea rather than fish.
- I am creative (write down this sentence on top of your paper before sketching).
- No matter where you are. Begin your sketching without any question.
- Avoid any concentration and use your logical mind (periodically, of course)
- Maximum use of artist mind
- We learn through practicing. Acquaintance with pen and paper is

necessary for learning of architecture. Sketching is one of the best and most important ways to learn architecture.
- Leave some places blank for ideas you have not ever had or others' ideas.
- Listening to mind evocation and draw what you are forced to without any loss.
- Use weak and thin lines and thicken them at the next stages.
- Do not confine yourself to descriptive instruments and techniques (it is better to ignore perspective or disturb it!)
- Rout is more important than result. When results direct the route, you are hindered from surrounding events. This is while there are so many cases along the route and you should stop and think about them.
- Draw lines calmly and without considering architectural thoughts and styles.
- Act calmly like a bird flying in wind.
- Be fond of your experiences (as you love your ugly children). Enjoyment will lead to progress and develop. Cultivate freedom of thoughts and actions in doing your tasks as experiences, repetitions, efforts, assays and even fine mistakes.(Mohamad Panah, 2007)
- Hang your sketches for days and weeks where you can see them (office, kitchen…)
- Think about your designs and sketches. Sometimes, a design can involve you for hours (be patient).
- Use warm colors.
- Sketch with high pleasure and motivation.

When individuals are motivated and pleased to do something, maximum of their creativity will be appeared. Creativity is an internal incentive. This creates a strong internal intention to do tasks enthusiastically. (Khiabanian, 2014)

Conceptual Sketches of Neda Mansouri for landscape design

Exercises for Better Understanding of Space and Increasing Designing Potentiality

1- Strengthening Creative Faculty:

In this drill, one of the geometric figures such as square or triangle has been selected. Designer tries to draw it in a new and even different form through use of geometric figures and kinds of lines (straight, broken and curved). There is no limitation in use of lines and number of drawings. Typically, artist's mind starts its activity after 20 sketches and creative and unexpected designs may be observed. This practice increases designer's control on lines and forms and creates novel ideas and thoughts in artist's mind in addition to strengthening creative faculty. At later pages, square and triangle have been selected as the main figures and my respectful colleague, Ata Chokhachian (One of my students), has drawn 45 sketches for each figure each of them includes extent information of line and form synthesis and interaction. At final stages of the practice, a sample of square expression has been selected, developed as a tree-dimensional one and changed to an architectural structure. A valuable experience demonstrates most of unsaid aspects of a designer's creative mind via repetition.

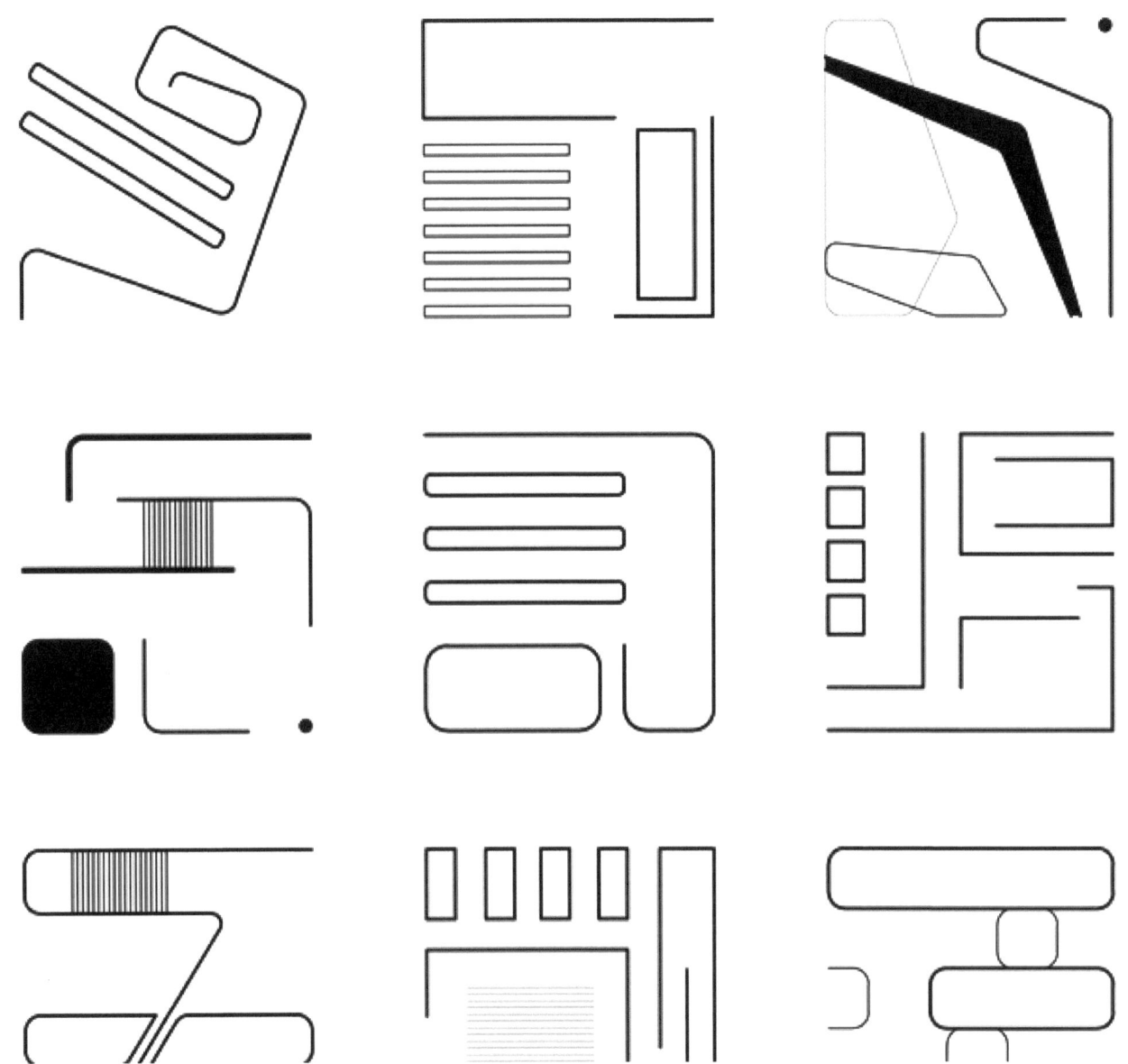

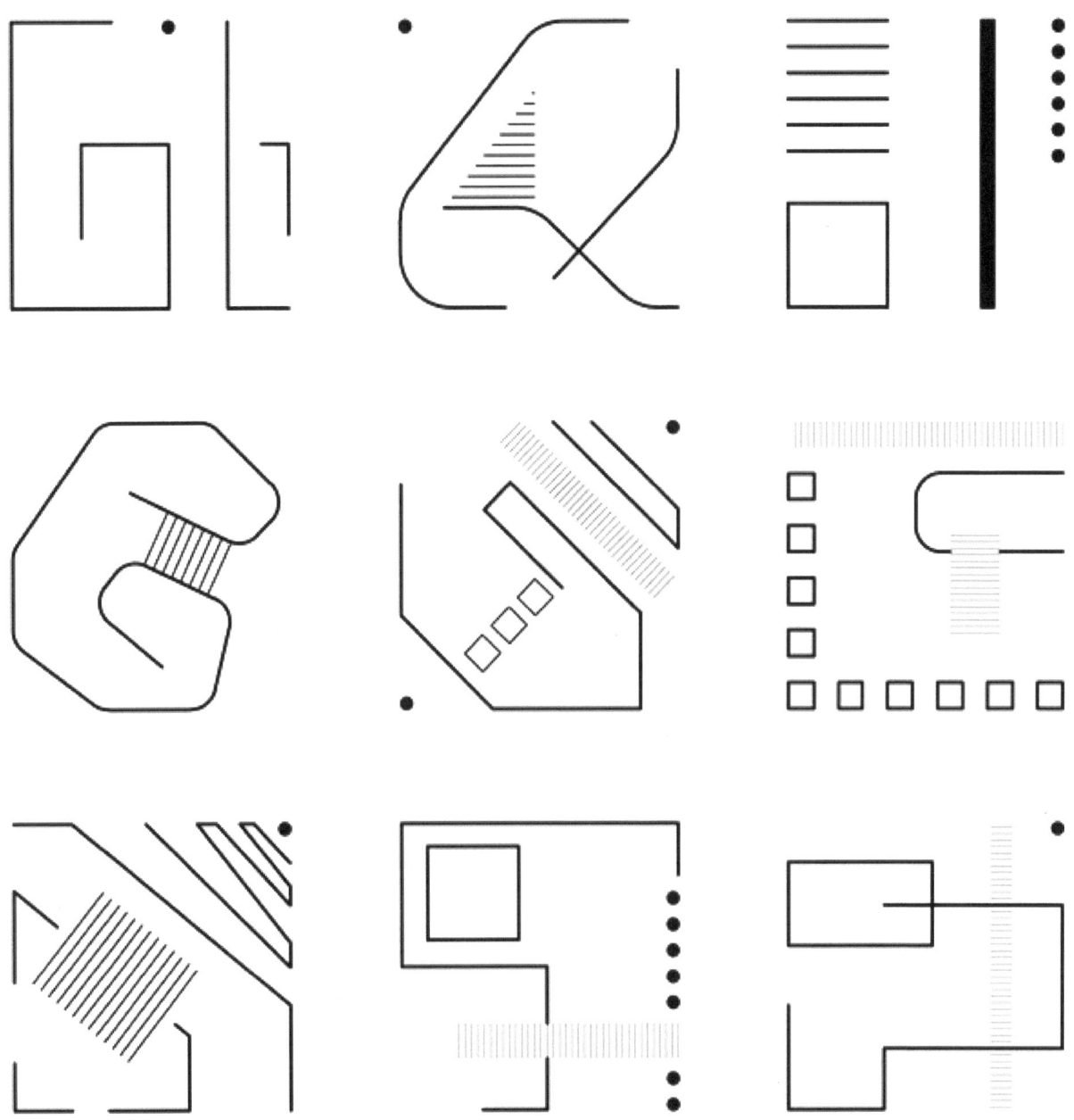

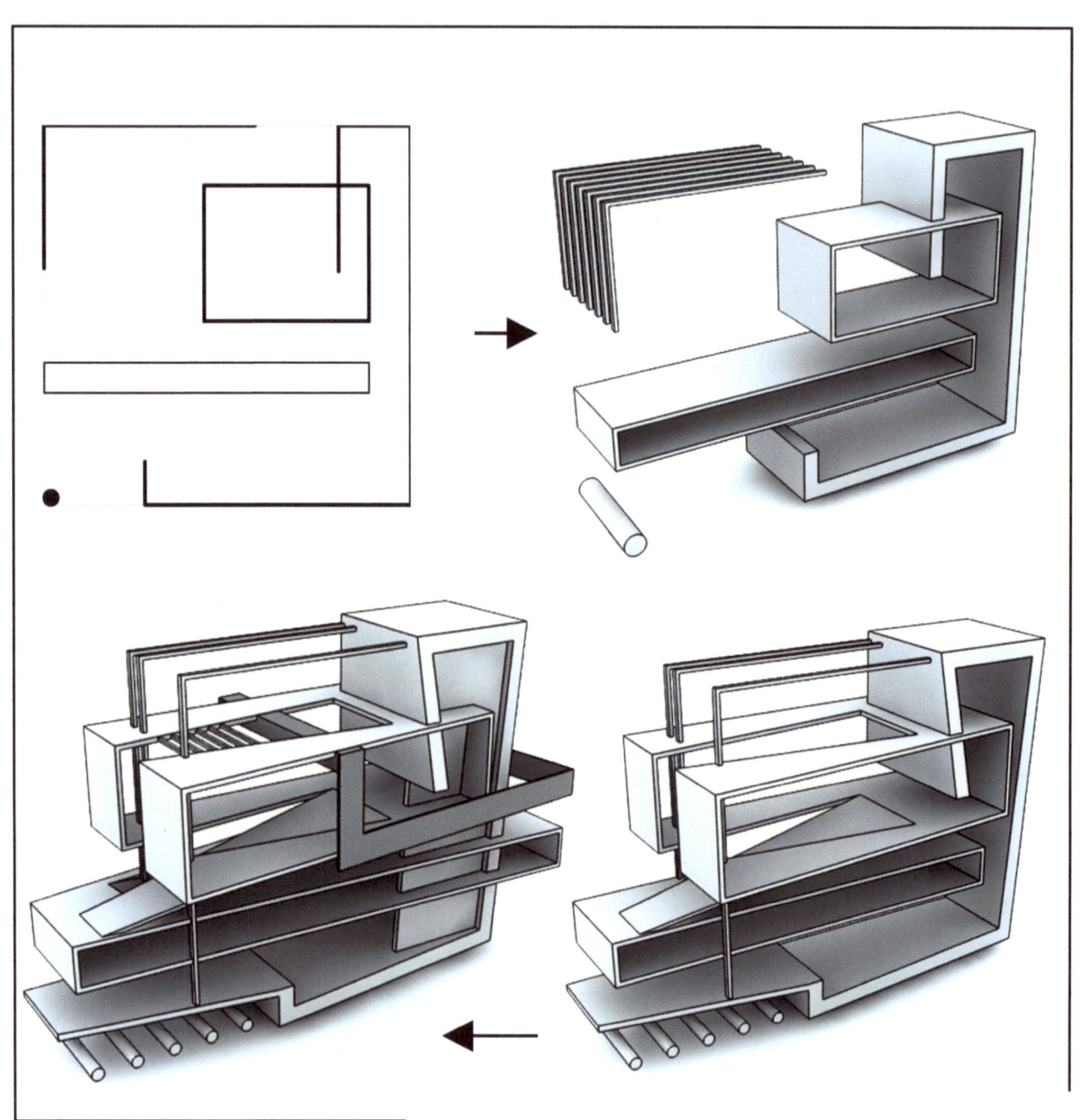

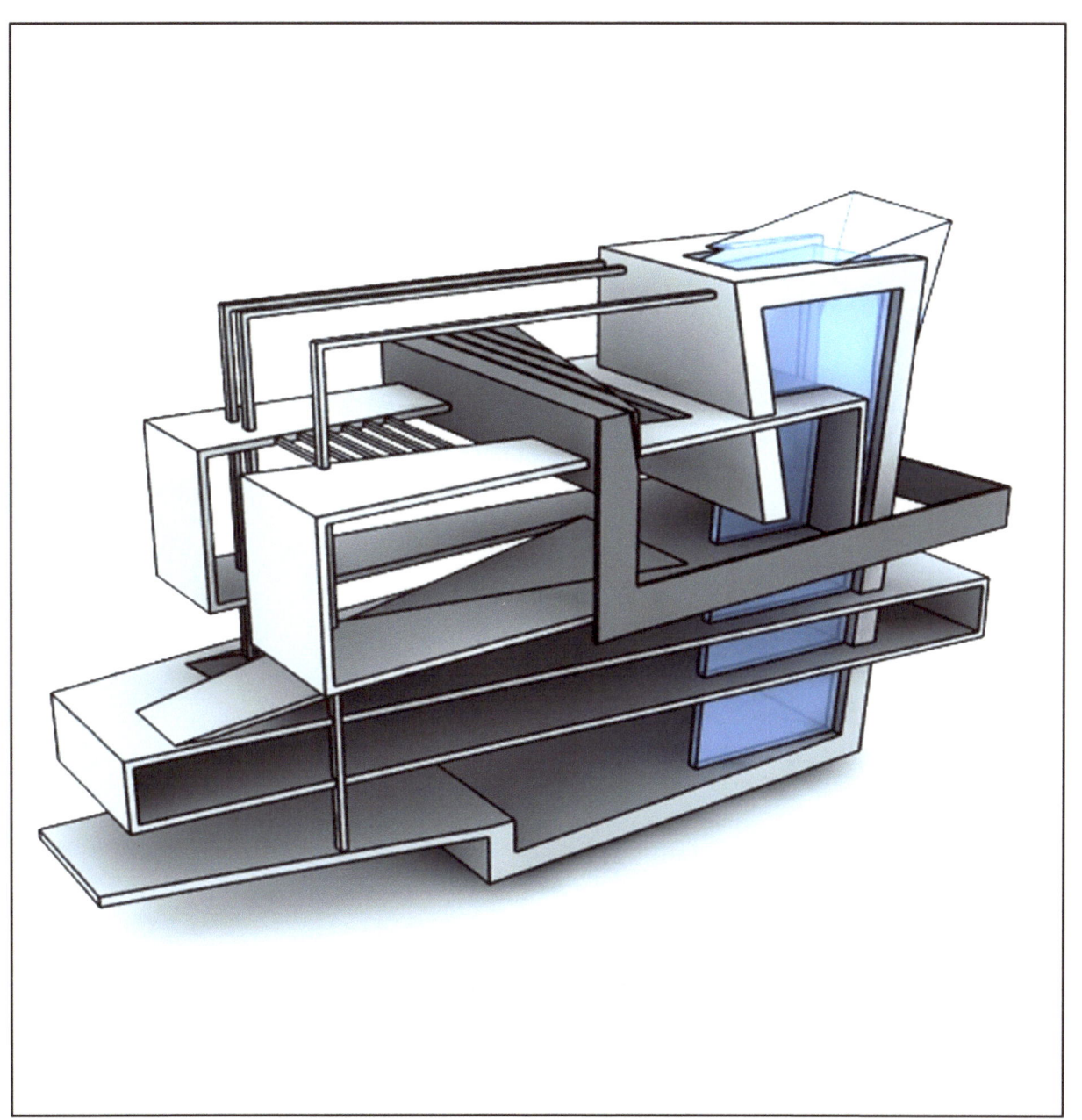

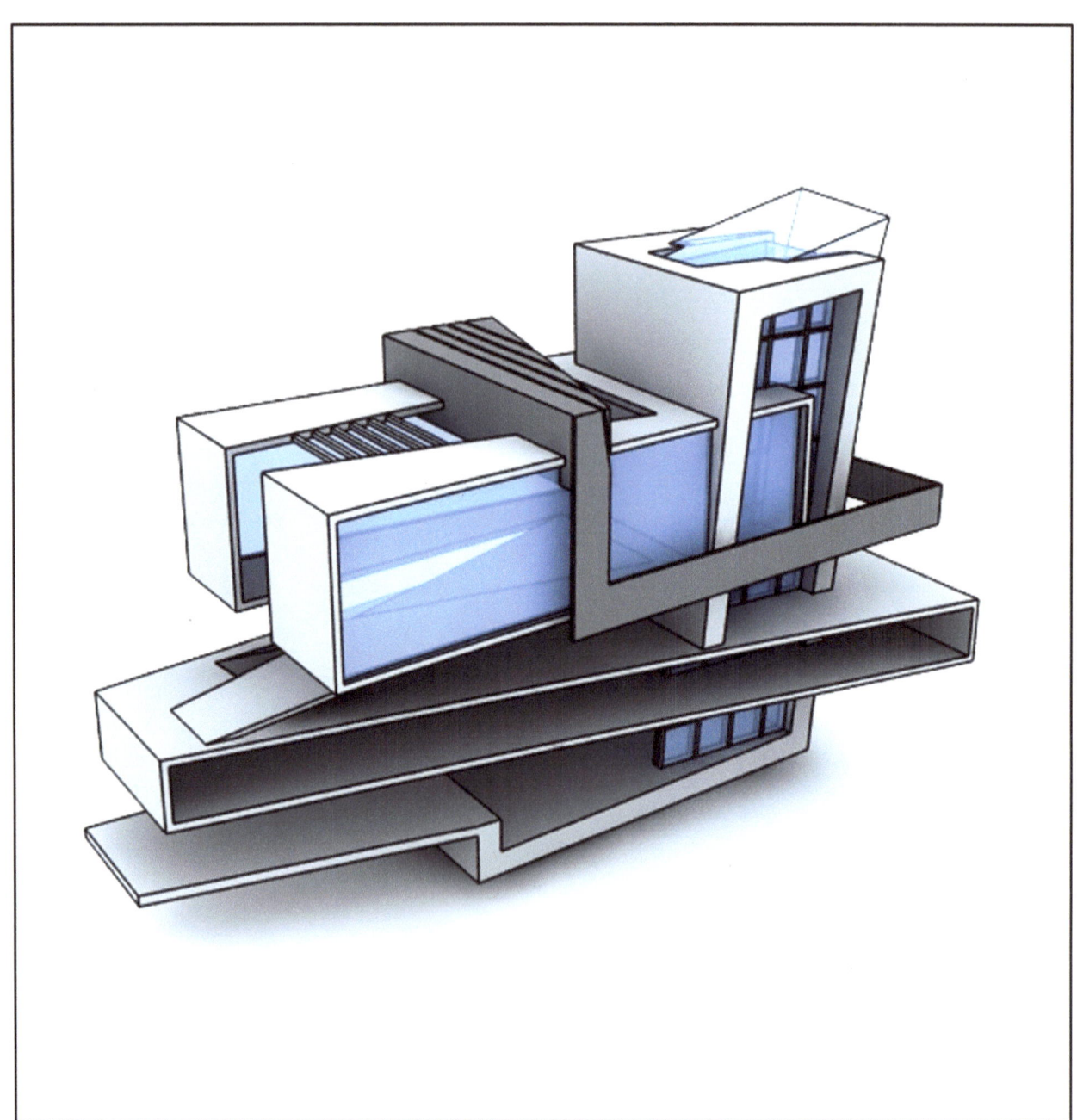

Examples of student projects

Zahra Alaghehmandan

Zahra Alaghehmandan

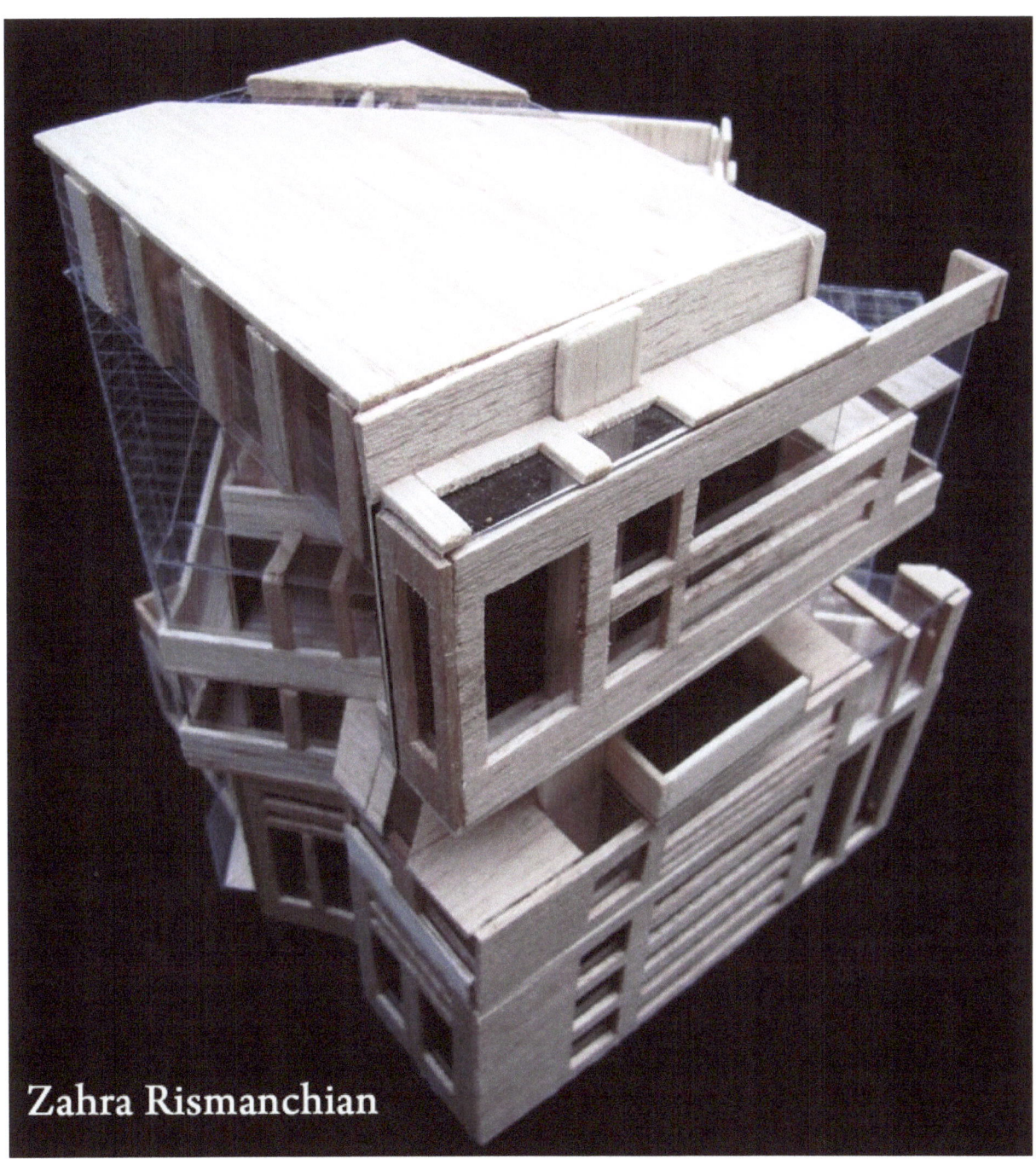

Zahra Rismanchian

Zahra Alaghehmandan

2- Move from whole to details: Analyzing volumes to simple Platonic figures.

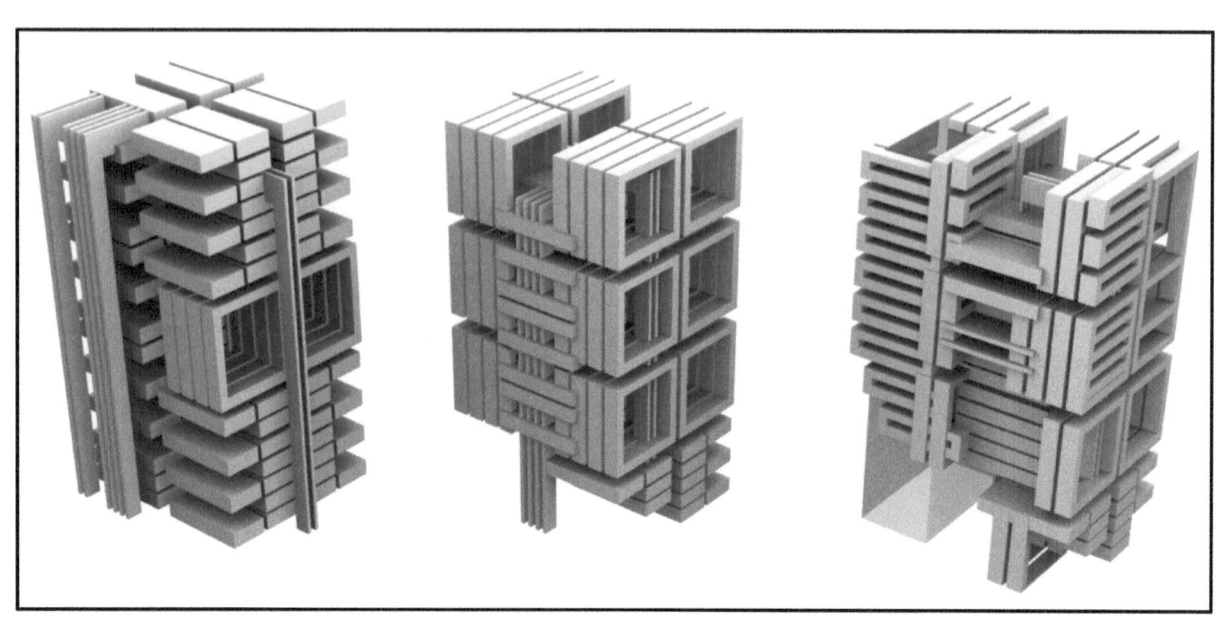
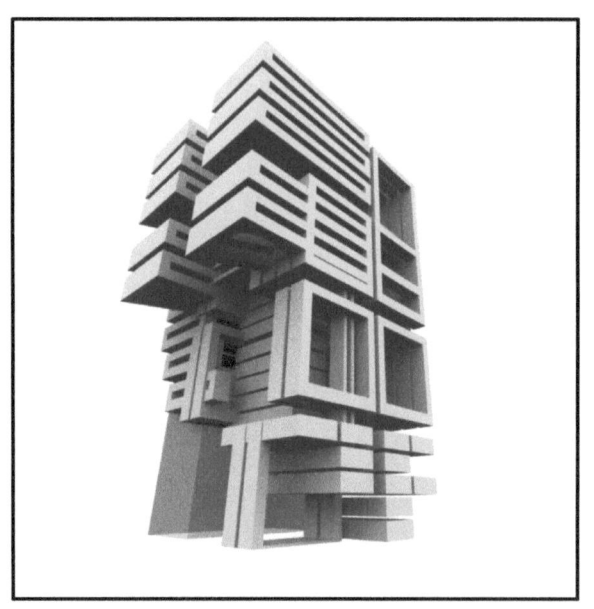

3- Move from details to whole: in volume designing, try to express a volume as a combination of different volumes instead of using a big volume and breaking it down to details.

Following picture demonstrates a creative student who has offered a layout through inspiration of the solar system and an oval center. His ideas include dynamism, motion, central structure and movement of layers on each other. Looking for the nature to find a mediator or concept for embodying ideas, this student has selected the solar system (changing of idea to form). He has analyzed structure and changing capability of the system circuits to architectural structure and finally reached to such a design which, somehow, has been generated by his creative mind. The structure reminds the solar system considering its form

At the second stage, the student begins designing through practice, paying attention to whole- details method and resorting to his/her creativity. Here, he/she uses a transformed oval as a whole and circle as a symbol of planets. Repeating of whole on details, combining of layers, designing and controlling of volumes from different aspects, plan and profile are what used by the student to express his ideas. Although such a method requires practice and experience, the result is far from your expectations and learning. This method is similar to movement of designer from different stages and frequency of volumes. He/she finally reaches figurative and mental purity.

It should be mentioned that this practice mainly focuses on strengthening student's right hemisphere, obtaining full information from volumes considering content, synthesizing and changing, enhancing self-confidence and increasing his/her brave in testing unknowns.

Perspective

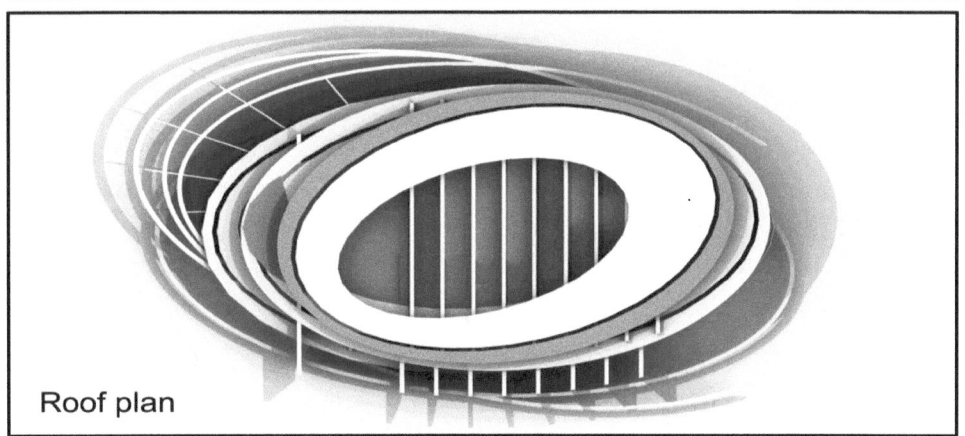
Roof plan

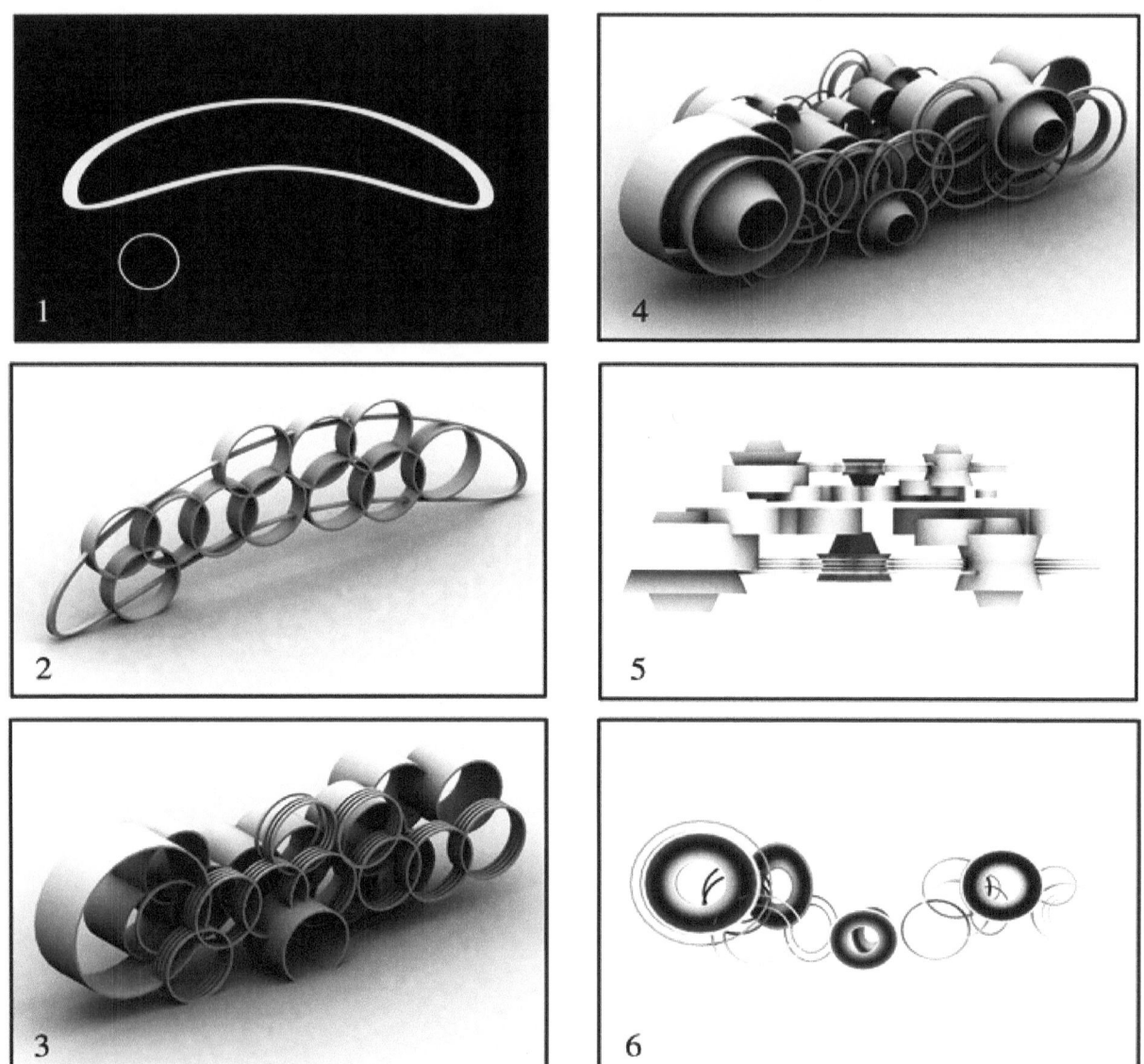

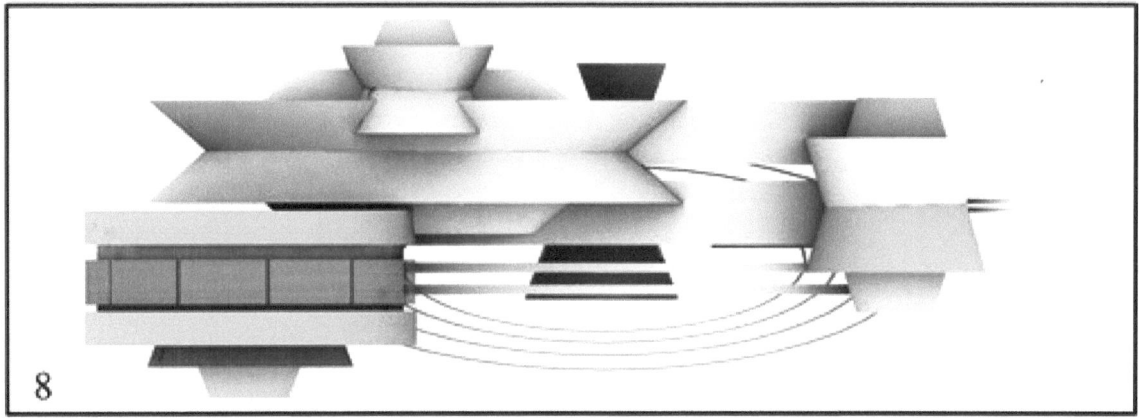

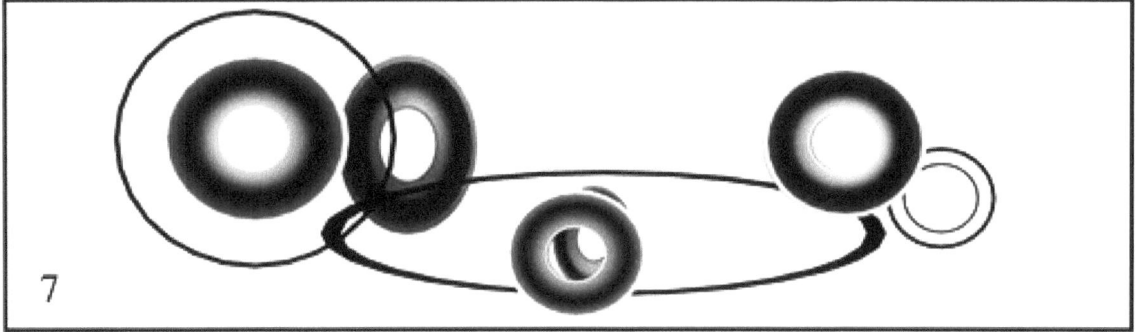

4- Designing of projects as a perspective cut: use perspective cut in initial stages of designing, registering your ideas or extracting structure from concept. Observing internal and external parts can be helpful in unity and spatial interaction of the project. (refer to conceptual sketches in the previous pages)

5- Repeating and changing of form

Trying to use repetitive and symmetrical elements at uniform and harmonious parts of a building such as windows and columns is one way to reach unity in building design. Objects similarity, even partial, is an appropriate way for expressing their union.

6- Concurrency

In designing, architect should concurrently succeed in volume, profile and plan. Volume designing will not lead to accurate results without considering functions and plan designing or vice versa. Internal and external parts of an architectural space should be coordinately and interactively designed considering content and function. Only in special cases- considering specific ideology of the architect or project- such changes or contrasts may be allowed in this kind of dealing.

7- Mind strengthening: creative embodiment

8- Hand strengthening: designing of architectural perspectives and works

9- Enhancing hand and mind relation (conceptual sketches)

10- Analyzing and simplifying architectural works and buildings to geometrical figures (analyzing of architectural works direct us toward thinking about other options of undiscovered patterns and provide new findings for us).

11- Completing incomplete pictures or sketches of architectural works. Offer vague pictures from generality of a building or an incomplete sketch and ask them to complete it based on their own discretions.

12- Connecting masses

this can be done as a two- or three-dimensional exercise at continuation of the previous one. Provide students with several masses of volumes and figures and ask them to connect these figures. Teach students to draw a rectangular landscape (instead of integer designing) and divide it horizontally into two parts and design their volume and landscape through connecting these two elements. Possibility of creativity and dealing with details increases in this method

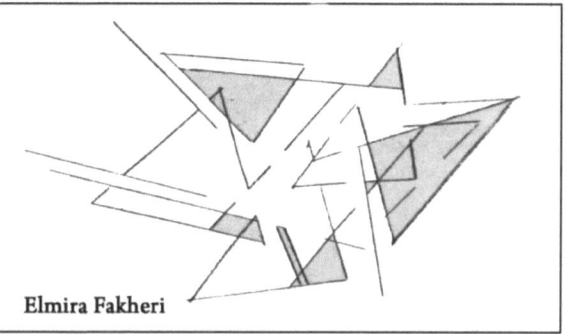

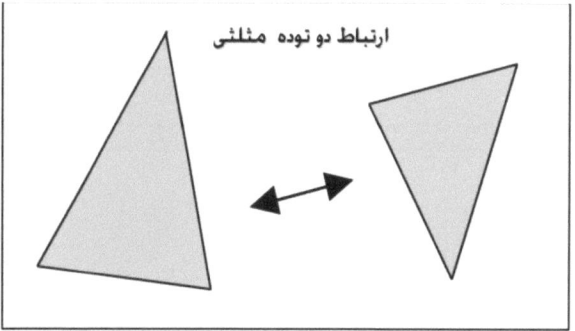

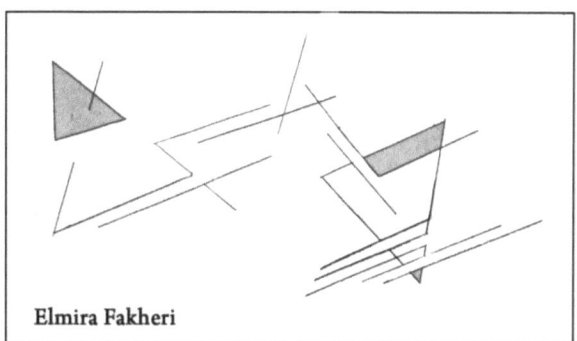

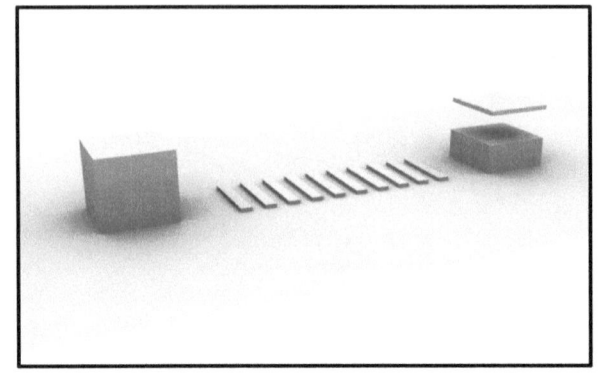
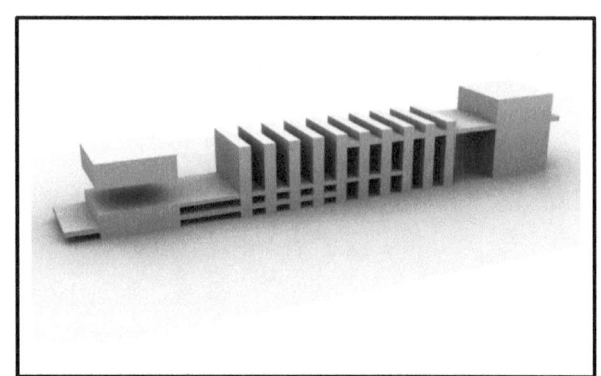
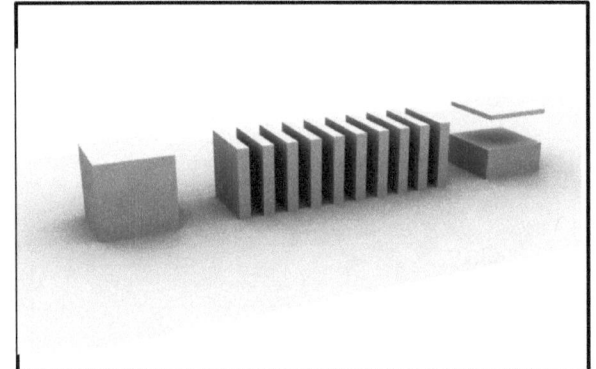
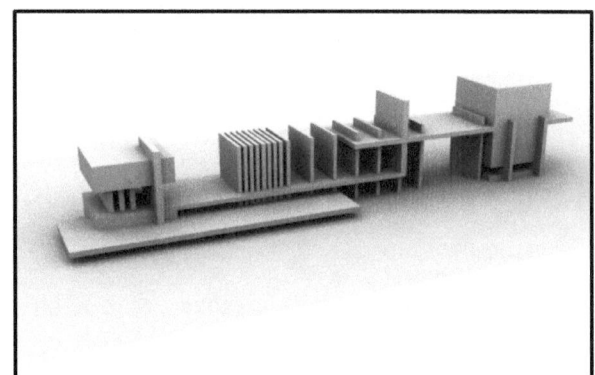
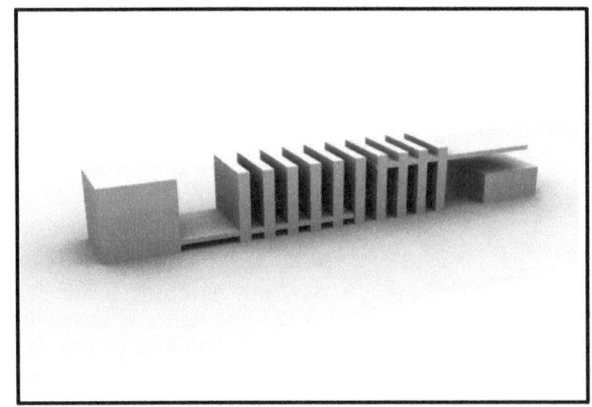
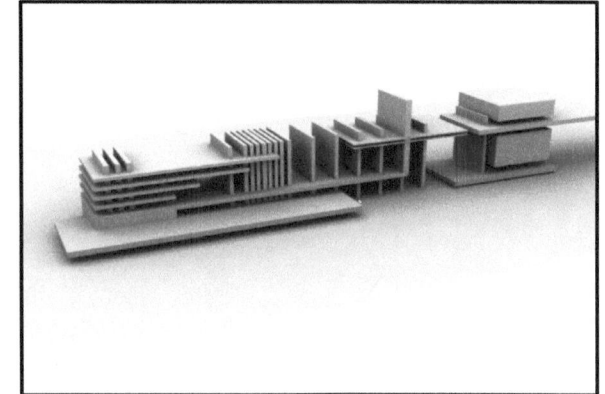

 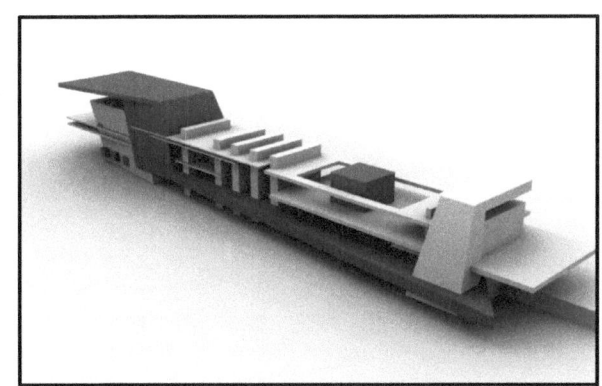
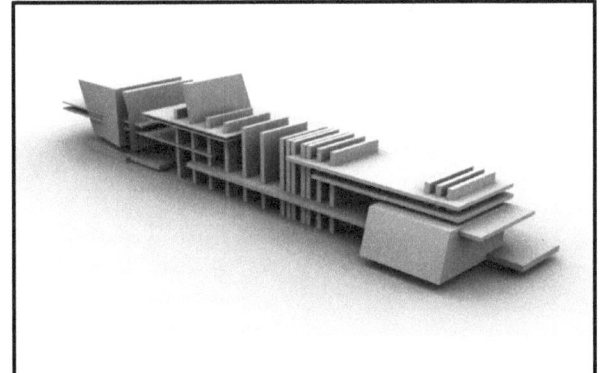 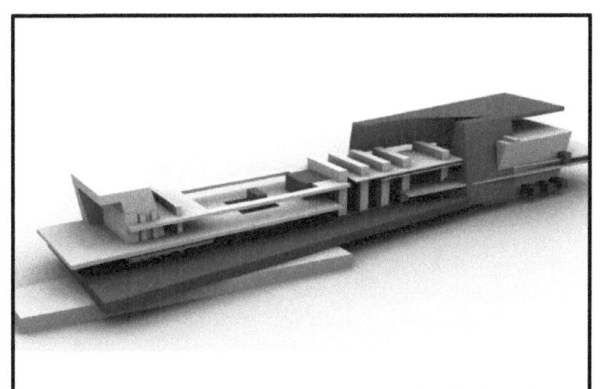
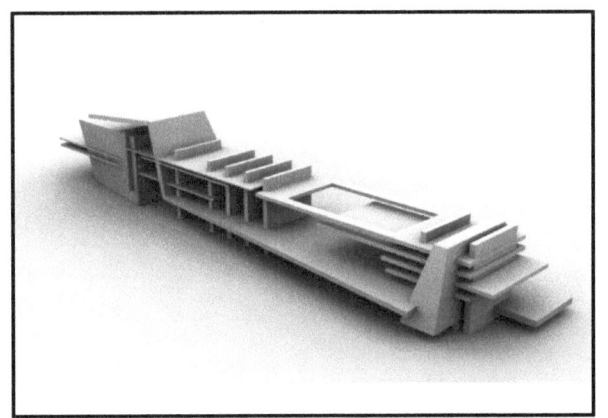 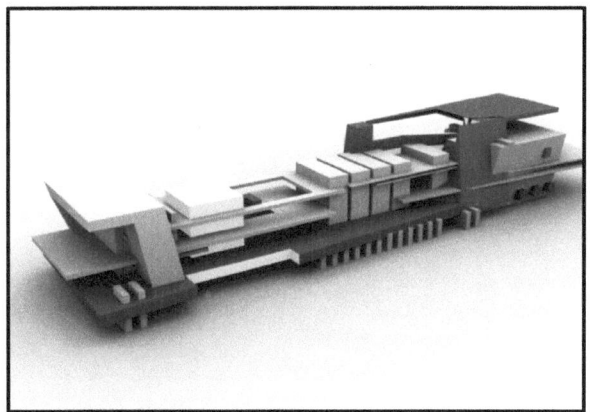

Connecting masses

(Design by Haniye Khalegi)

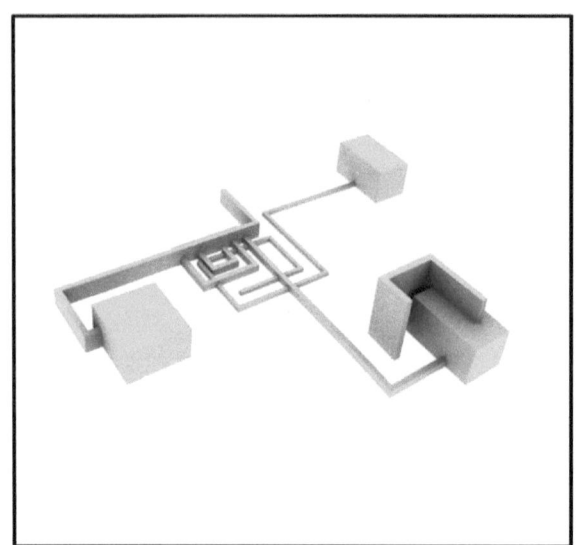
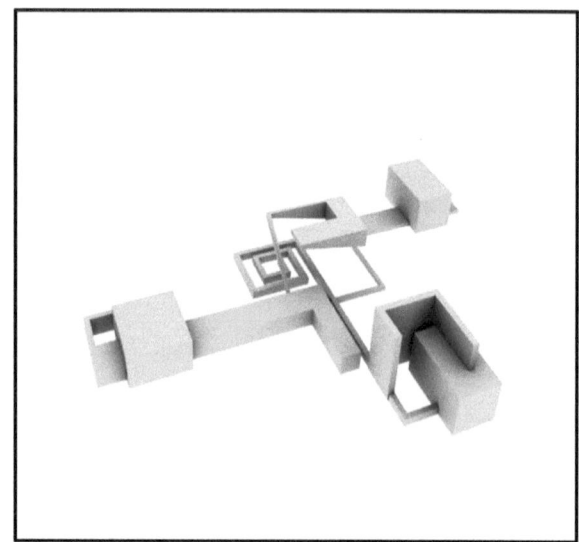
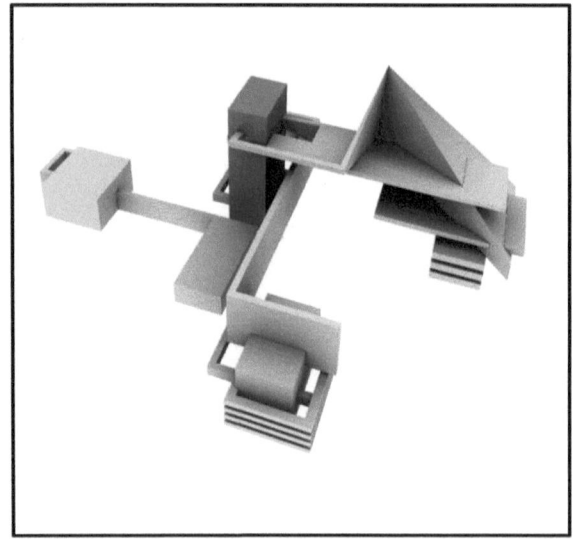
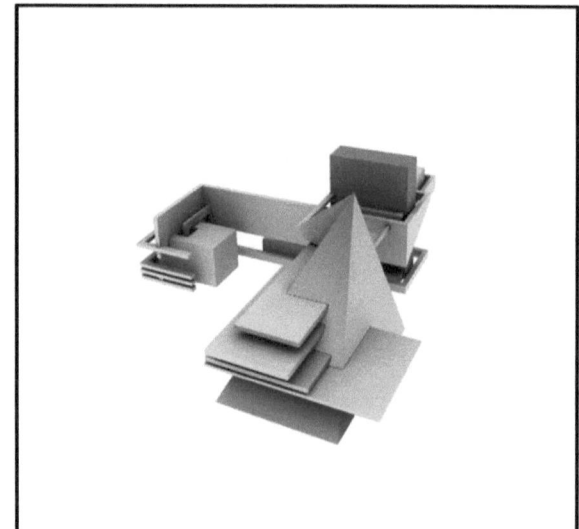

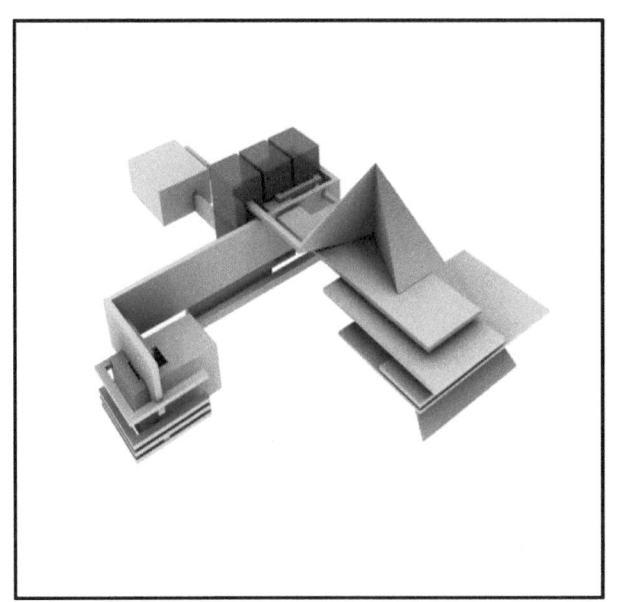
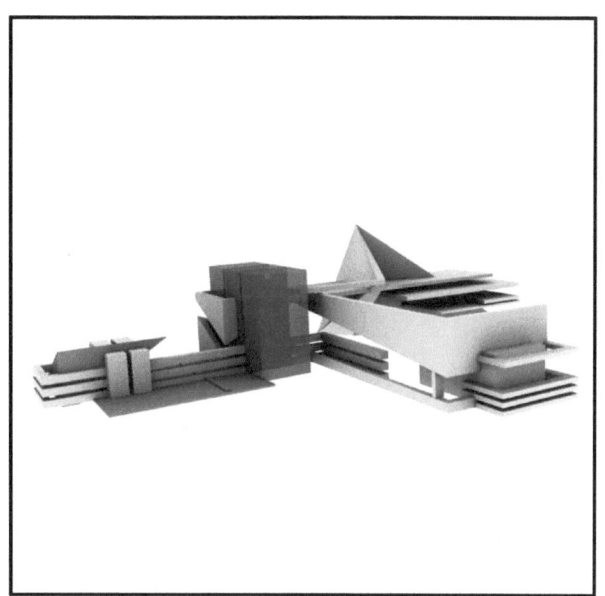
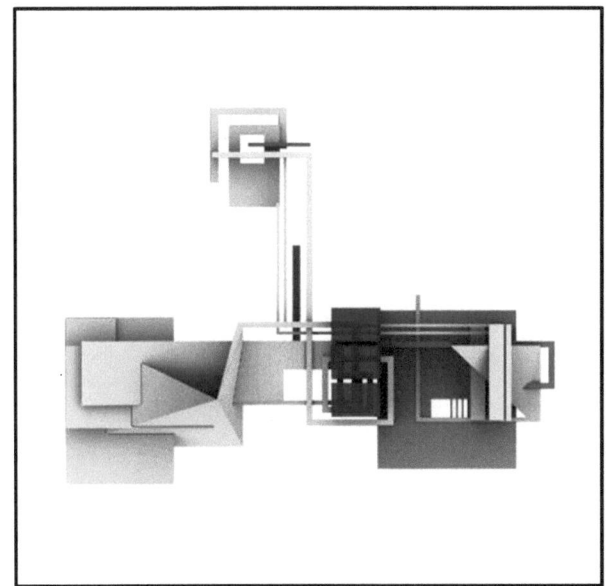
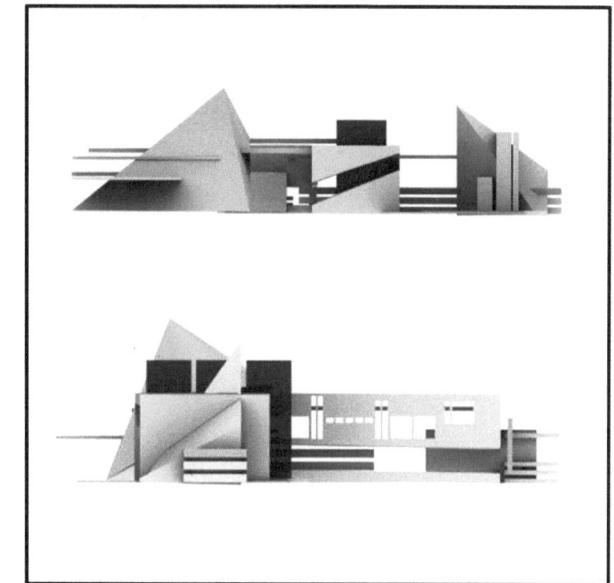

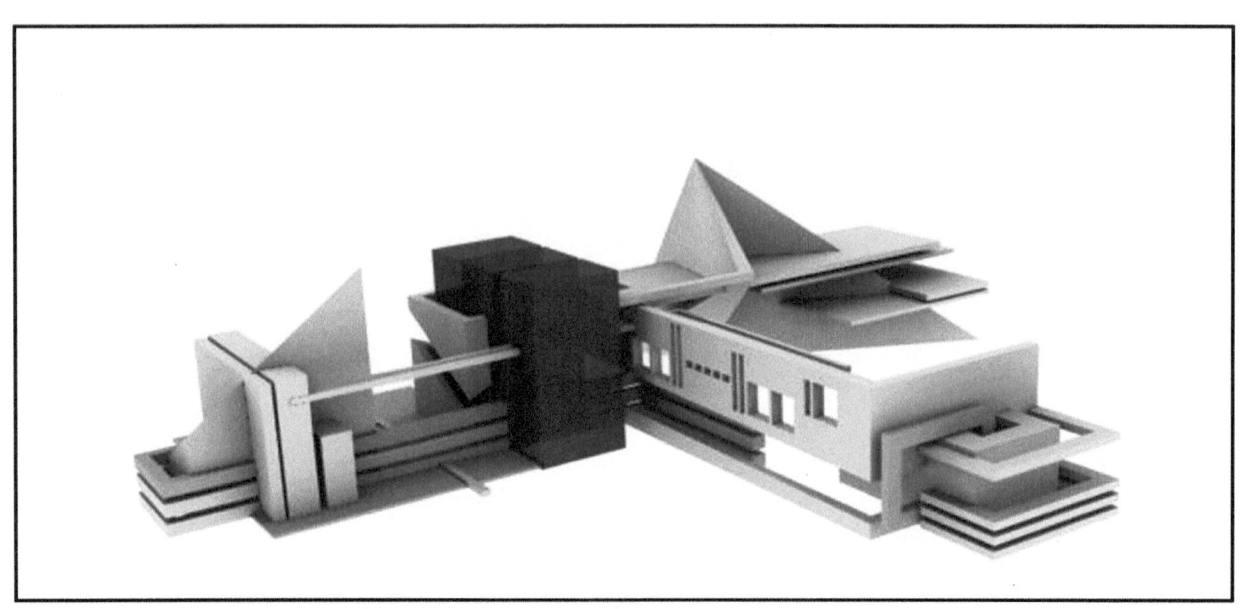
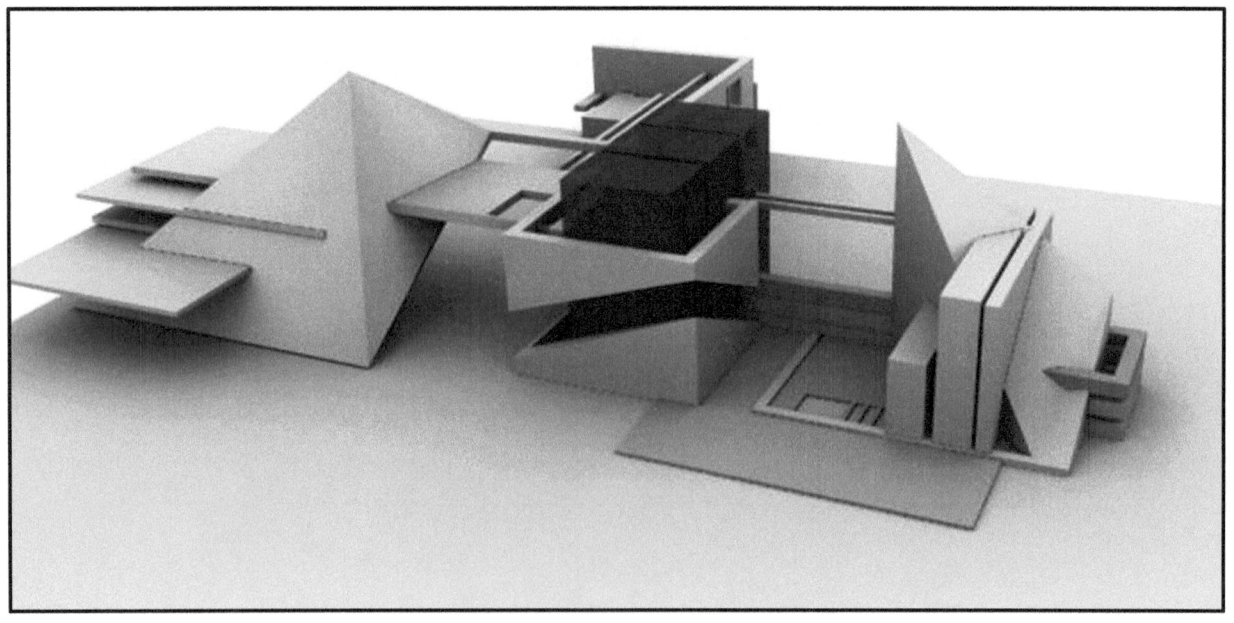

Zahra Alaghehmandan

ارتباط توده ها

Zahra Alaghehmandan
ارتباط توده ها

13- Symmetry, change and repetition

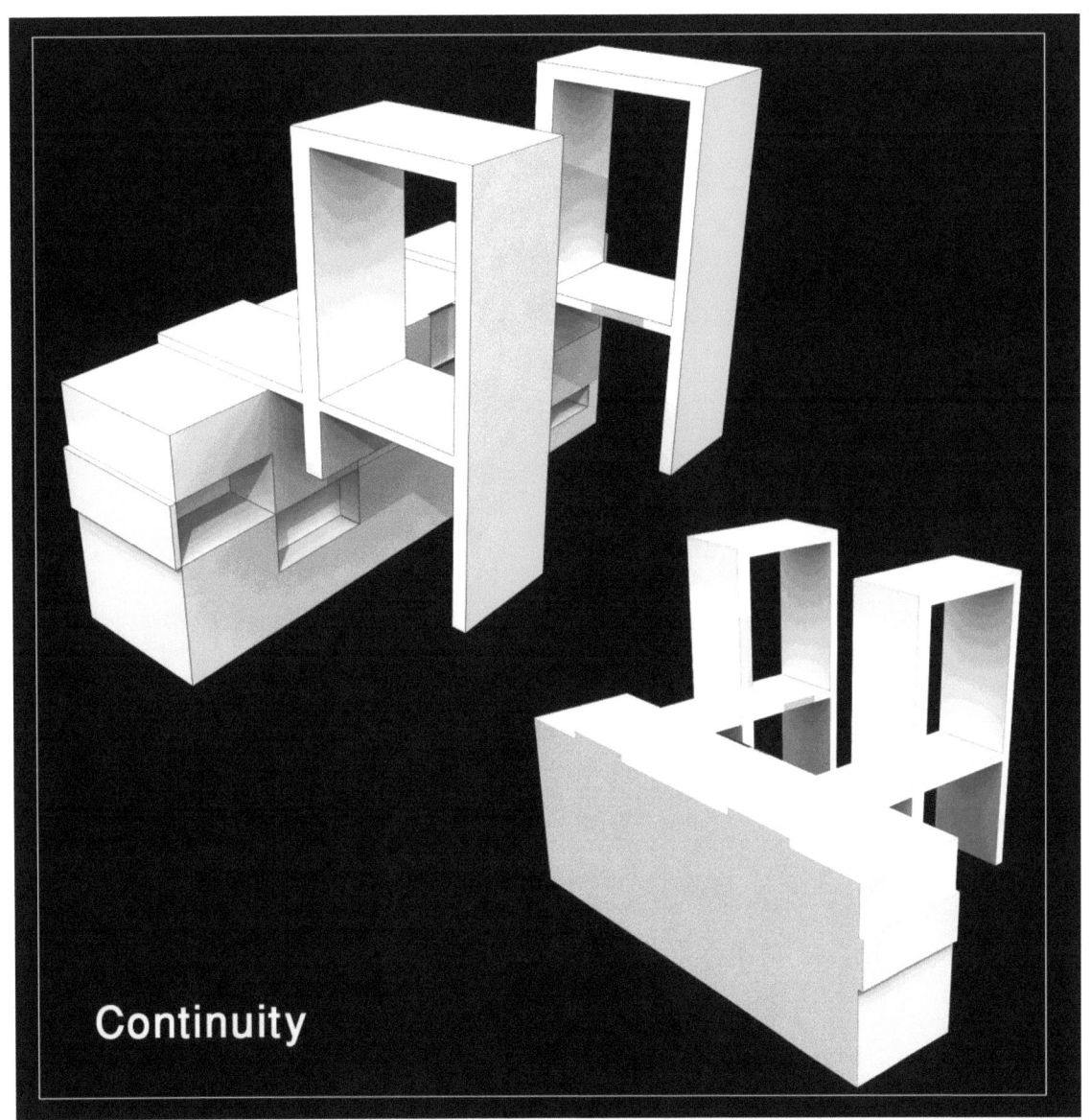

Continuity

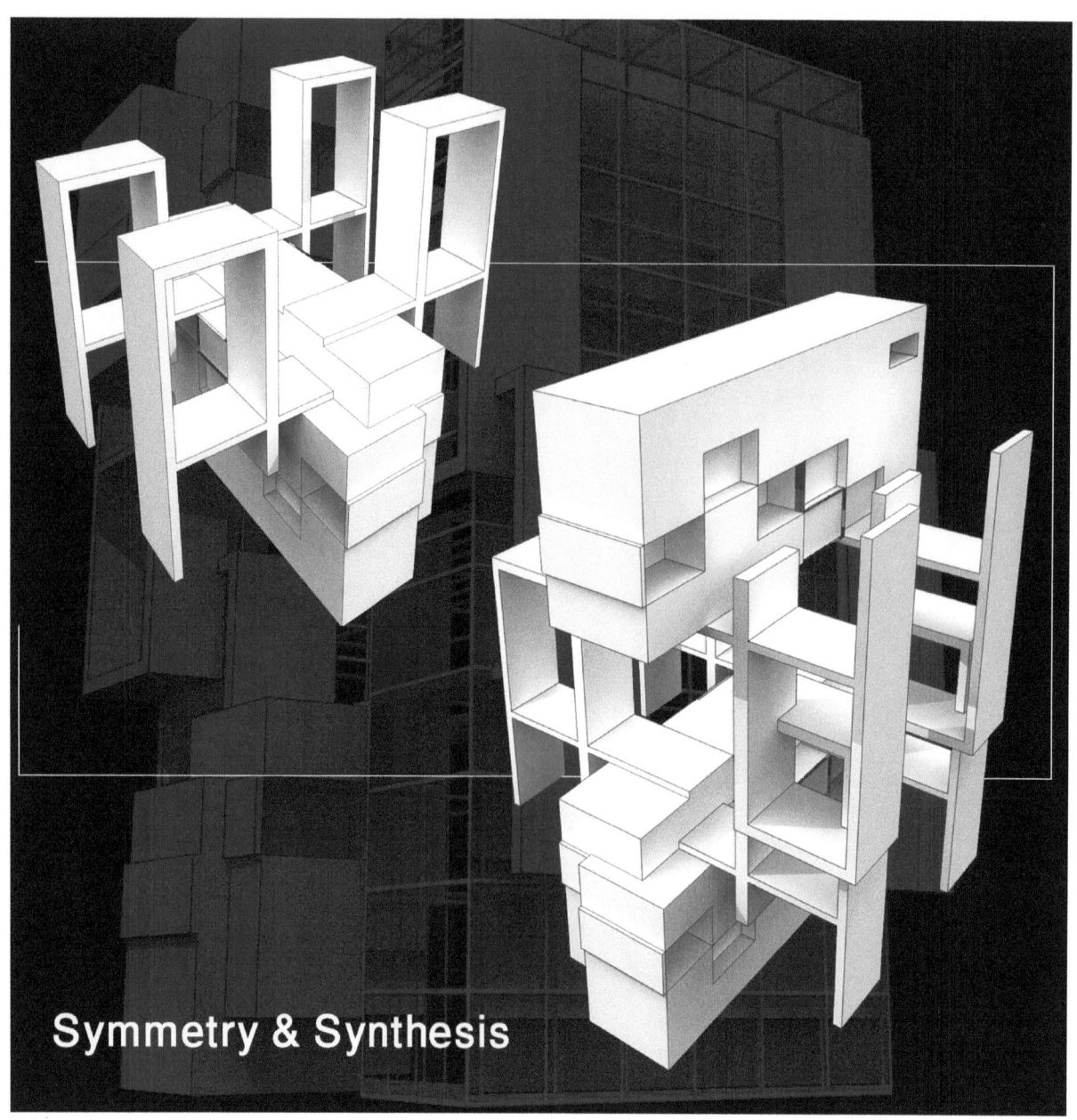

Symmetry & Synthesis

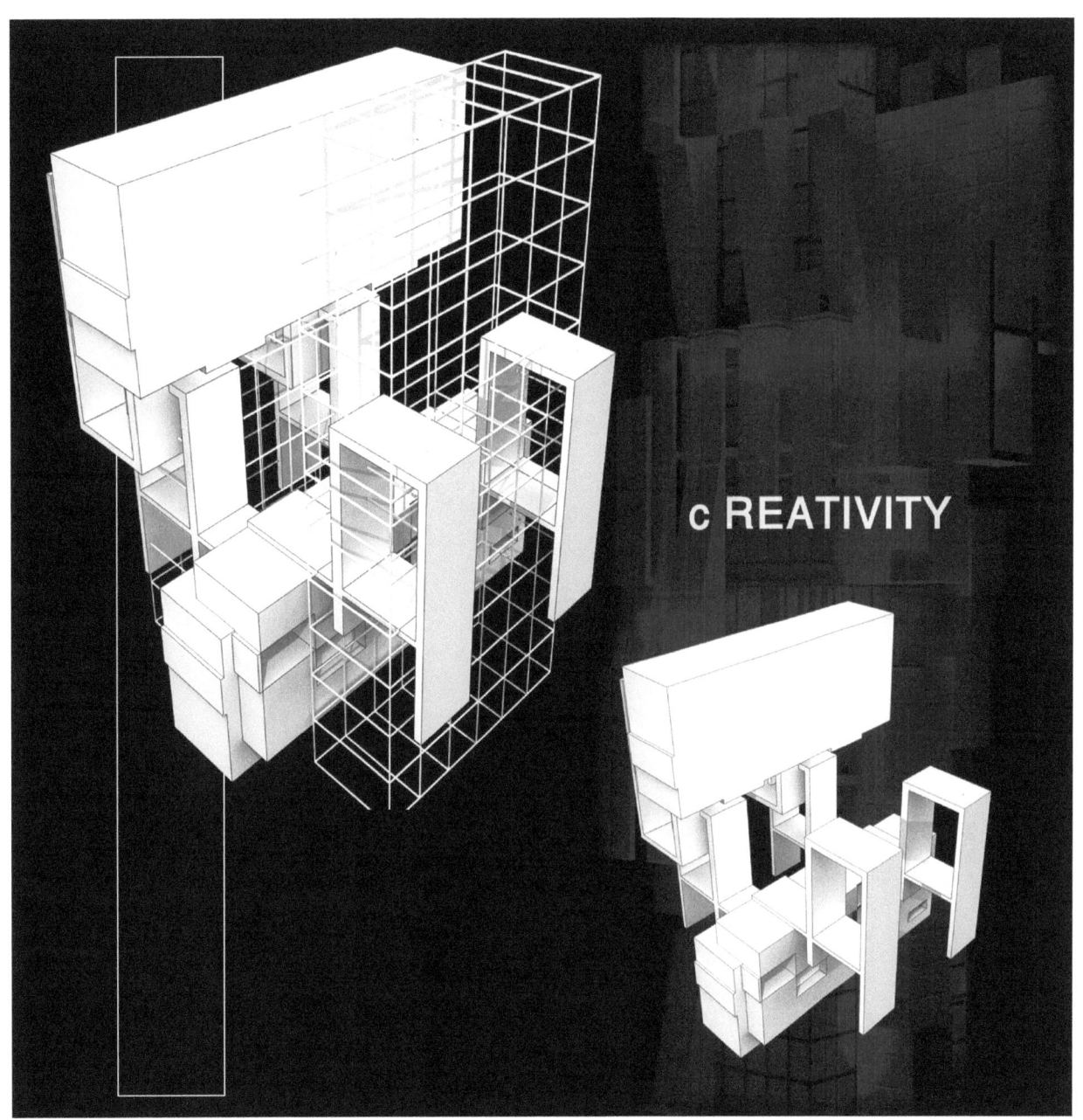

c REATIVITY

Vertical Spread

Three-dimensional design

Architects are proficient in reading and interpreting straight and two-dimensional lines (plan, section, and elevation). However, the best architects are not able to know everything about buildings. In design process, precise one- and two-point perspective sketches of buildings and interior spaces let you learn your expectations about how building and its function and perspective is seemed in real experiences and imagine design opportunities not clear in two-dimensional drawings.

Three-dimensional design let you imagine project design in a coherent whole related to and coordinated with the understudy elements and spaces and design quickly and energetically. Thorough knowledge about combination of volumes, relation of different surfaces of the construction and their arrangement, continuity of windows, height of parapet and form of sky line, difference of stories, continuity of lines and vertical surfaces adds to precise function of plan and provides better conditions to innovation, development, and completion.

Three-dimensional design is lines and sketches moving in three dimensions and make whole. For example, the designer does not design façade separate from other surfaces and facades of the construction rather he/she initially makes generality of the architectural structure and designs every surface and elements in relation with whole and lateral surfaces. In this case, design of façade projections and changes of the plan of stories are specified from beginning and serves as part of construction rather an integration completed at the end of the operation. Importantly, effect and continuity of elevation lines and windows rows may also be observed in lateral surfaces. It adds to coherence of the construction and determines the way to future developments.

Unfortunately, two-dimensional combinations are drawn and the surfaces emerging among lines are made high as dominant design method while three-dimensional design originally challenges with space. Contrary to two-dimensional thoughts trying to divide space into two-dimensional plans or solve vertical relations of construction as different sections, this method deals with space organization, a method setting architect's mind free from length and width of space as well as downward incomplete and two-dimensional perspective to the desired space and guides it directly toward three-dimensional and interior space.

Furnishing houses or offices, some points are taken into account as follows:
- Wardrobes or bookcase are placed and lusters are hanged considering ceiling height
- Height and depth of curtains are adjusted with that of windows and radiators placed in front of window or horizontal bars of the structure, respectively
- Thickness of pillars and their position affect type of decoration and even number of chairs and furniture
- Color of wallpaper affects size, brightness, and even tranquility of space
- Location, color, and appearance of lights are important
- Variety and solidarity of spaces should be considered carefully
- Suspended ceiling of kitchen should correspond with voluminal events of living room

Three-dimensional design is not limited only to design of exterior volume of the construction and its effects on surrounding space; rather it solidly includes interior and exterior spaces with more accuracy and responsibility. It is mainly responsible to organize space, whether interior or exterior. The relation between interior, exterior, and surrounding spaces (spatial-visual effects of the building on the surrounding environment and vice versa) are solidly discussed and designed from beginning. They are not regarded as elements where it is tried to coordinate them or extend continuity of elevation surfaces to inside of the building after designing of the exterior volume.

Samples of computerized three-dimensional designs will be presented in coming pages. Continuity of surfaces from three coordinate directions makes spatial structure interacting interior and exterior spaces.

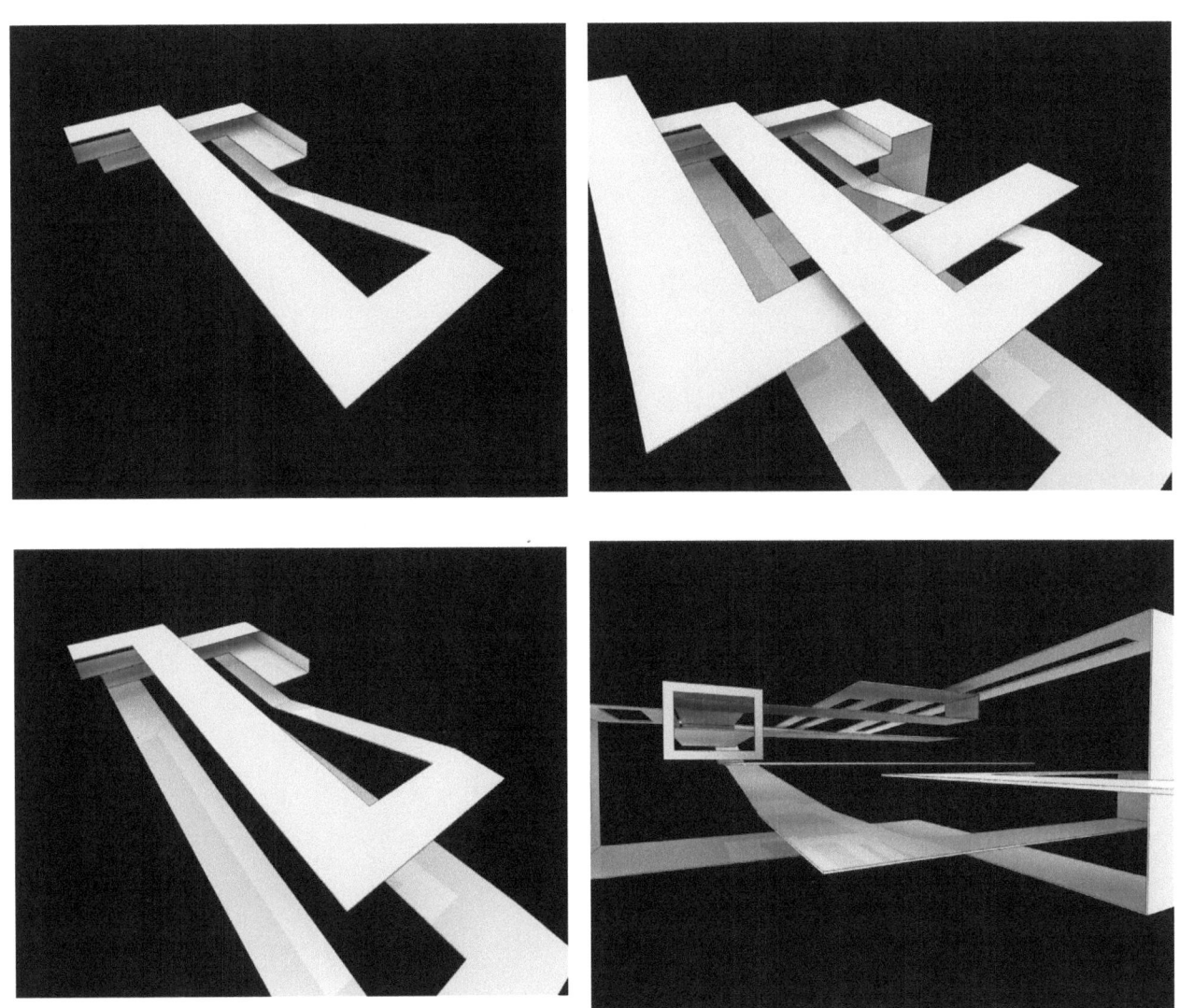

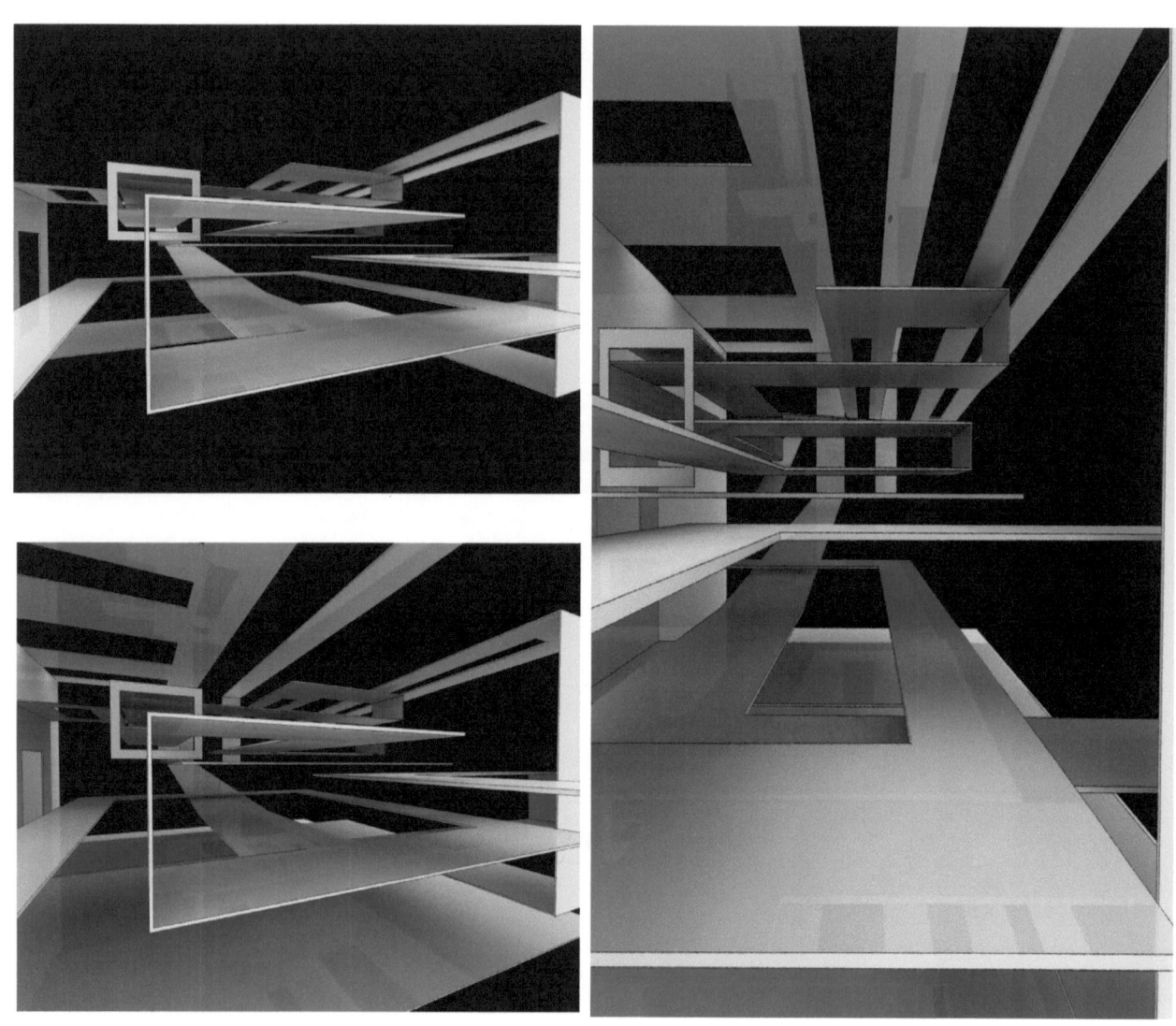

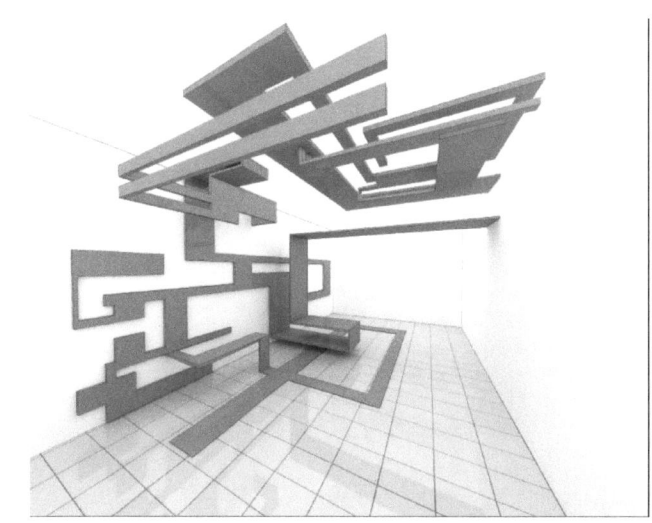

Samples of interior design process

A movement from surface to space design and components such as suspended ceiling, staircases, furniture (tables, shop window, etc.)

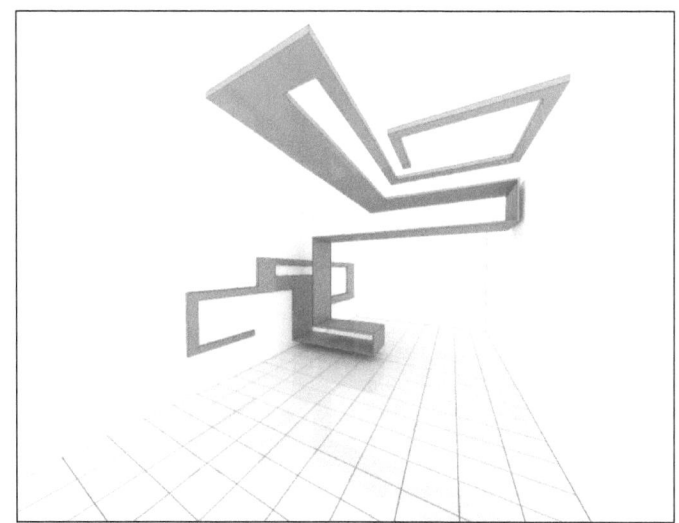

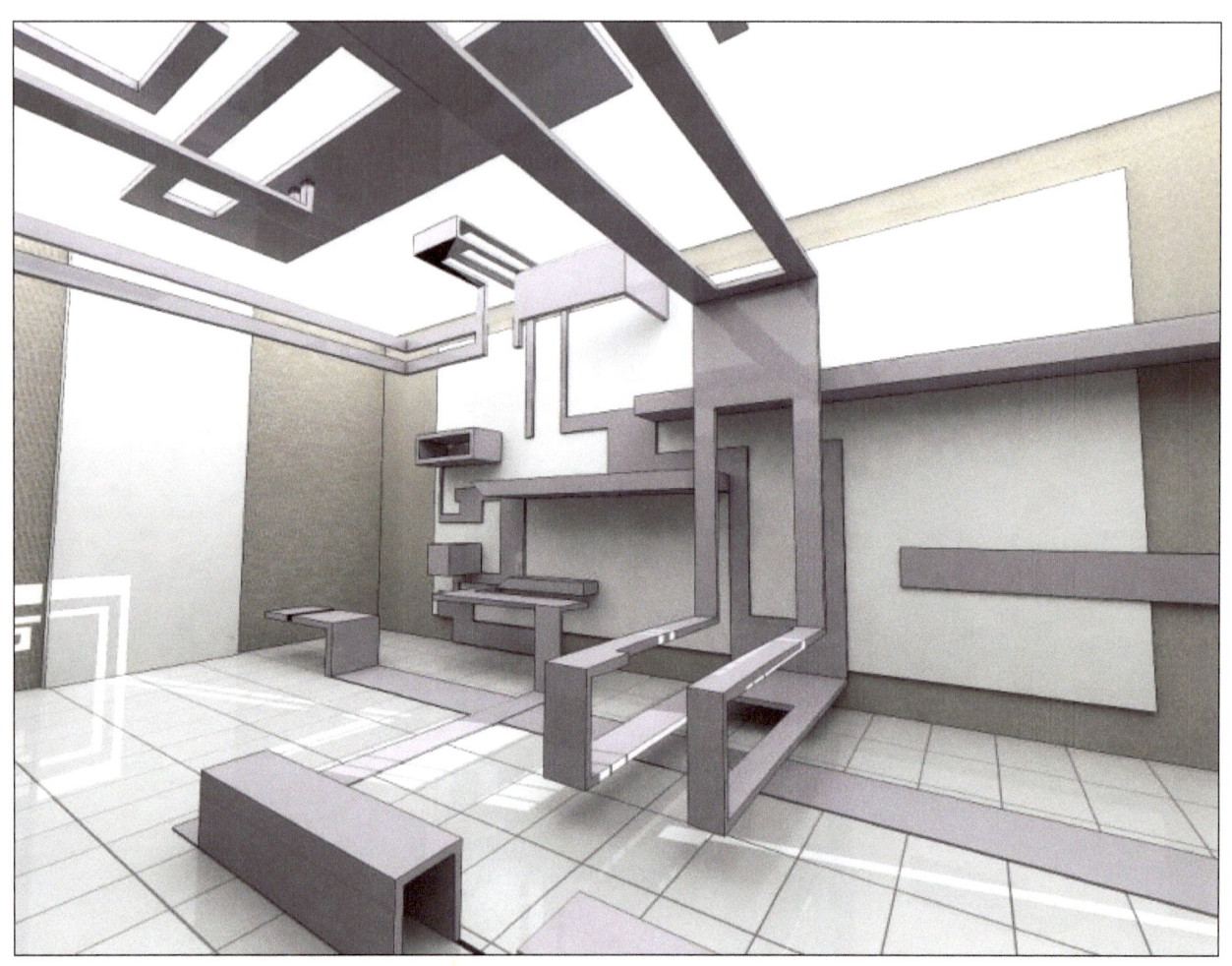

From Sketch to Architecture

At previous experiments of designing process, only evolution of an idea or a spatial structure was observed. In this part, it is tried to experience different sights toward a specified subject considering severalty of possible ideas, structures and concepts in designing process. In this experience, a shopping center has been selected as designing subject and just one of the more perfect and flexible sketches has been carefully analyzed. (Selecting of one sketch was for confining of designer and scrutinizing of designing process)

Designer's creativity evolve when he/she is capable of offering different or various structures of one concept or idea. In this experience, three narrations have been stated each of them include instructive points. A specific attitude and style was not considered in designing and efforts have been done to pay more extent attention to artist's mind facilities. Experiencing different architectural structures, non-relying of the architect to a specific pattern and style and his/her capability in offering novel ideas in different situations are regarded as features of a creative and perspicacious architecture.since it can provide answer to the problems in all conditions.

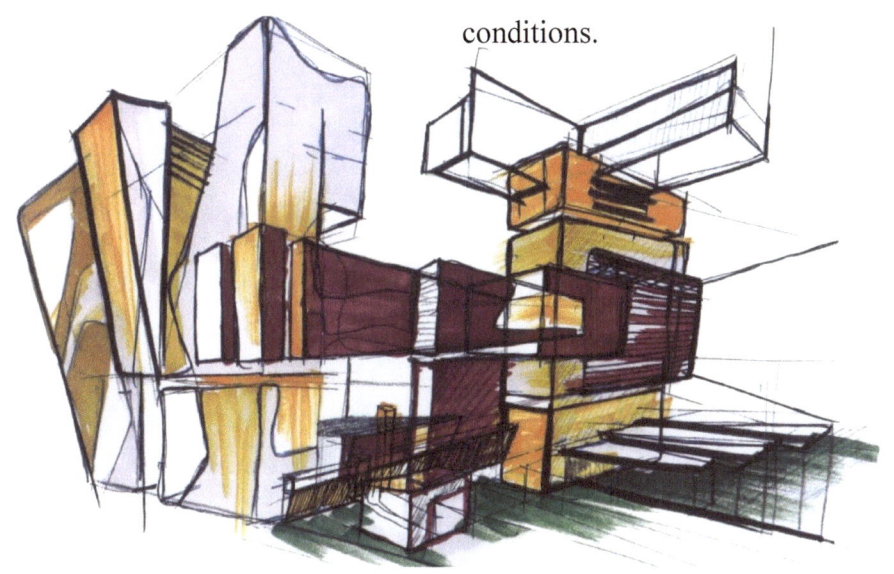

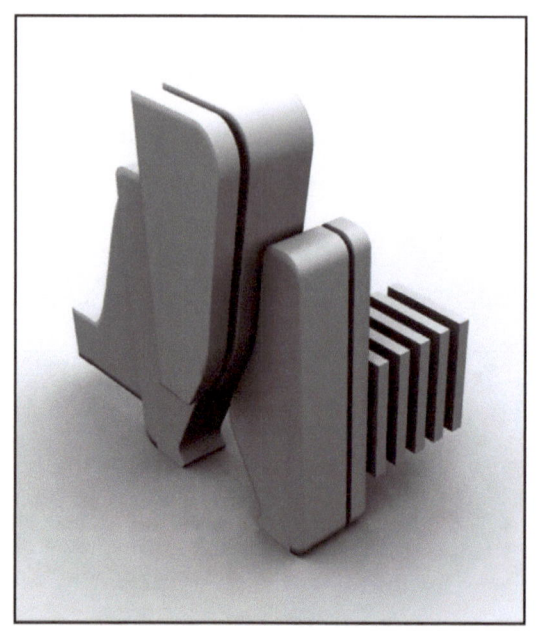

Idea Cultivation

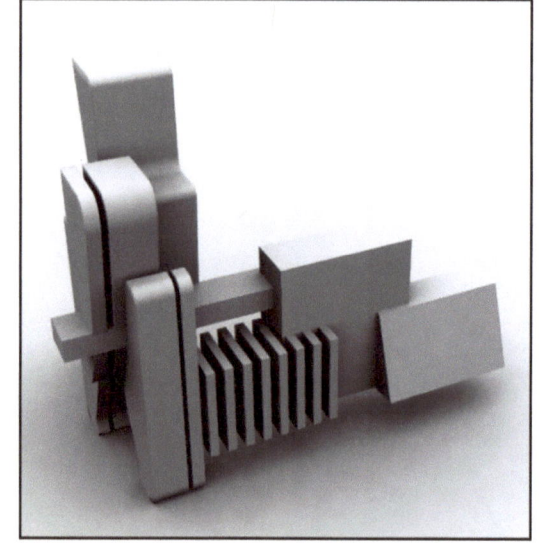

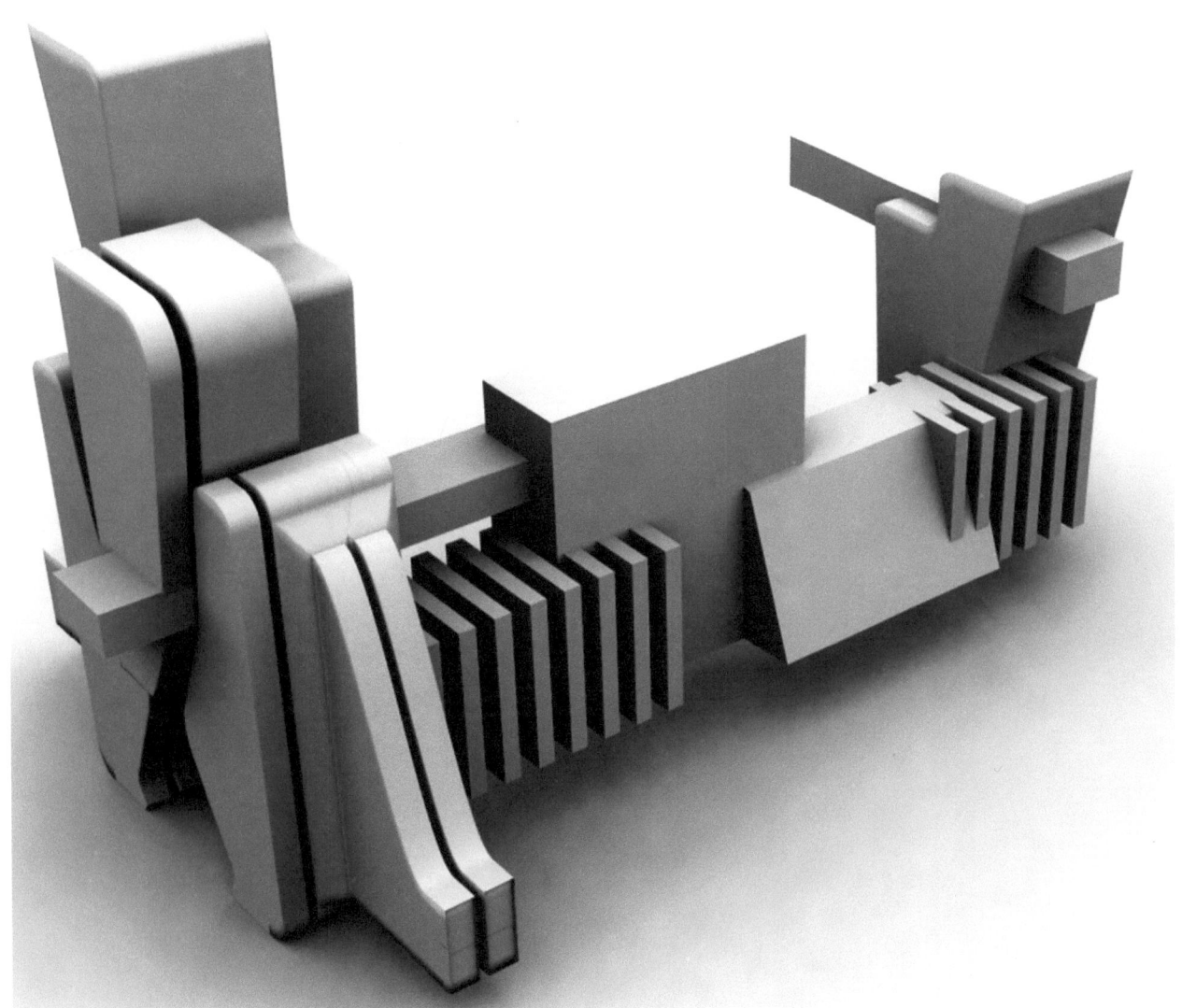

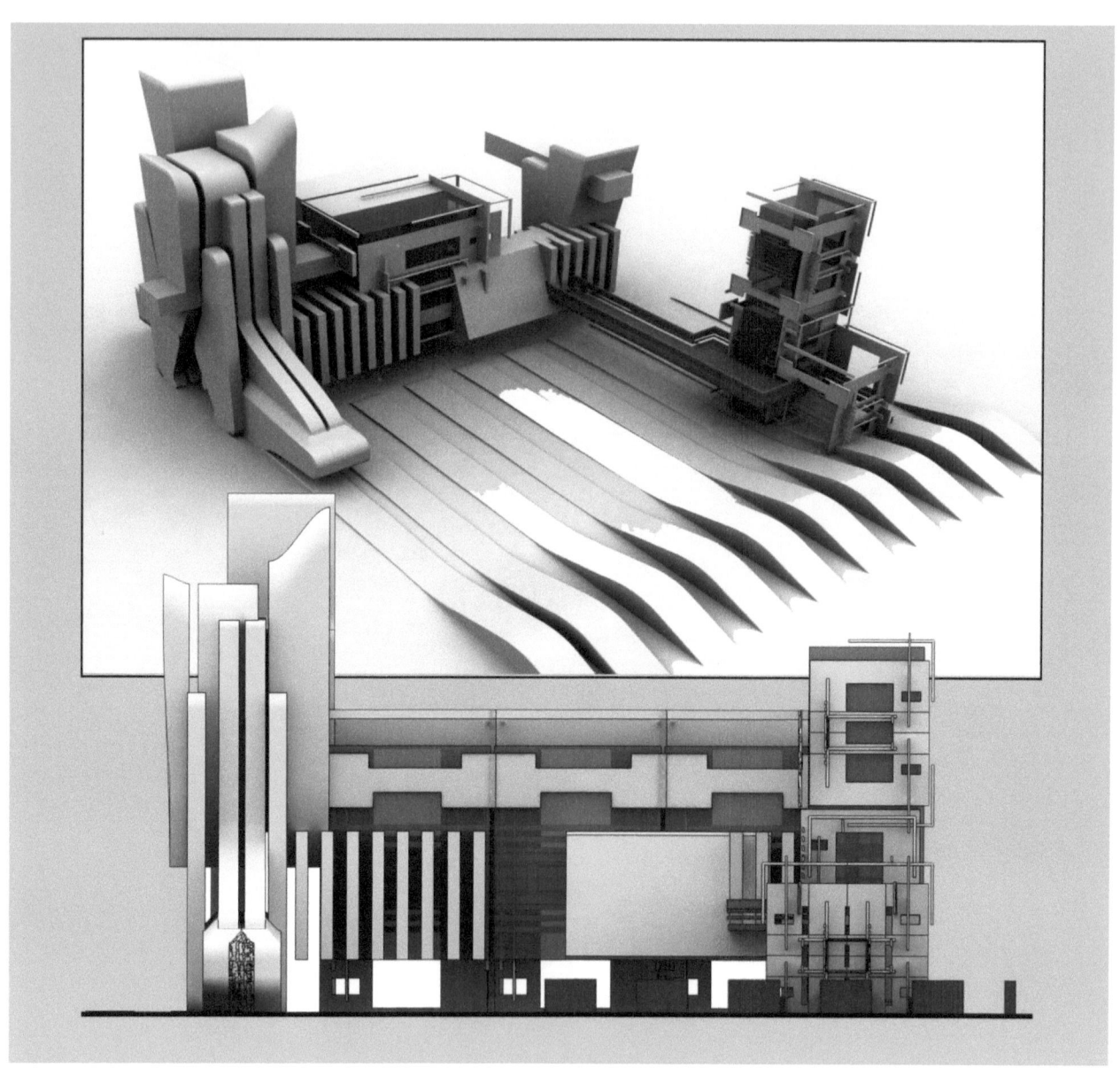

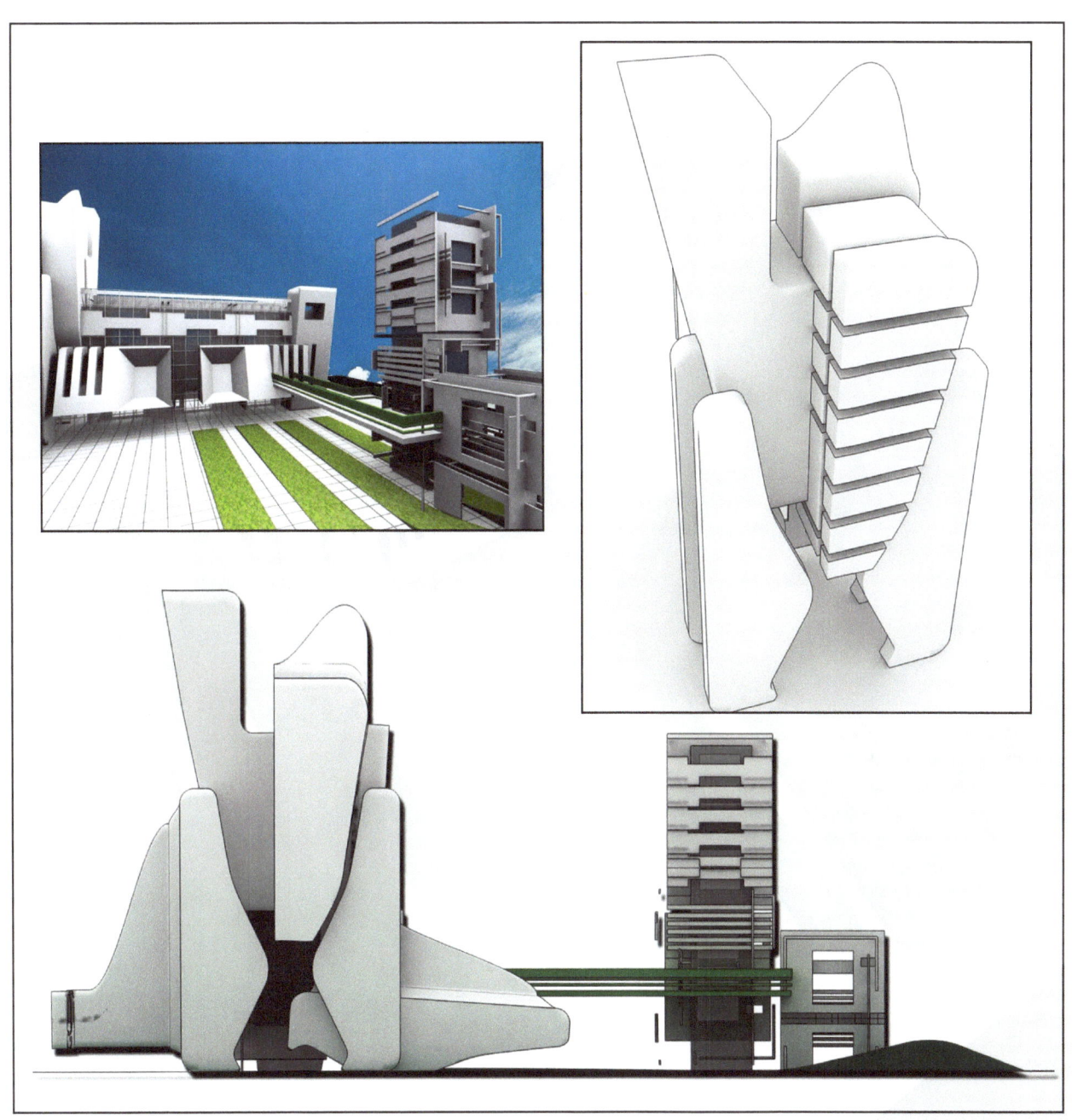

Shopping Center

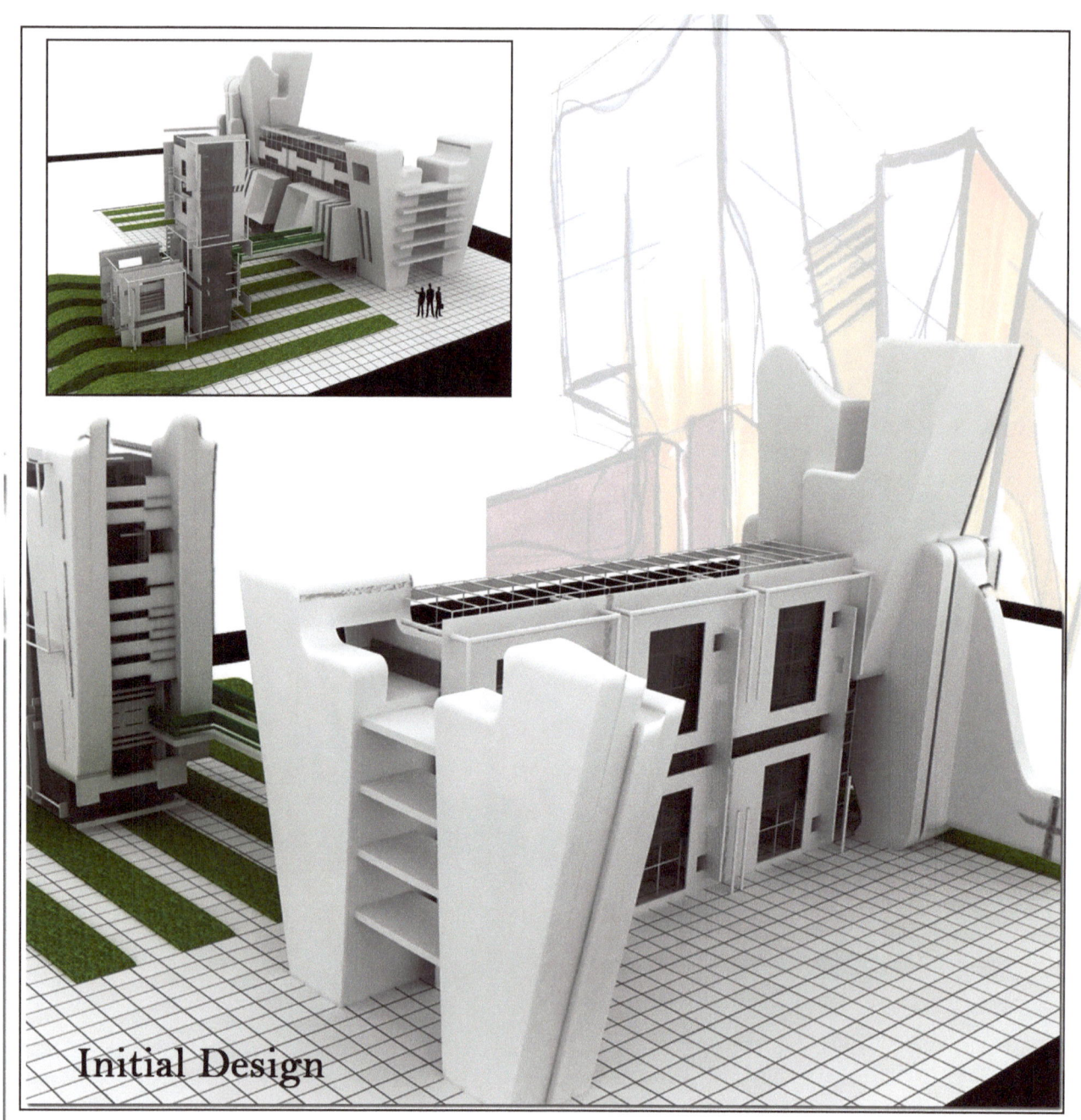
Initial Design

The Second Experience

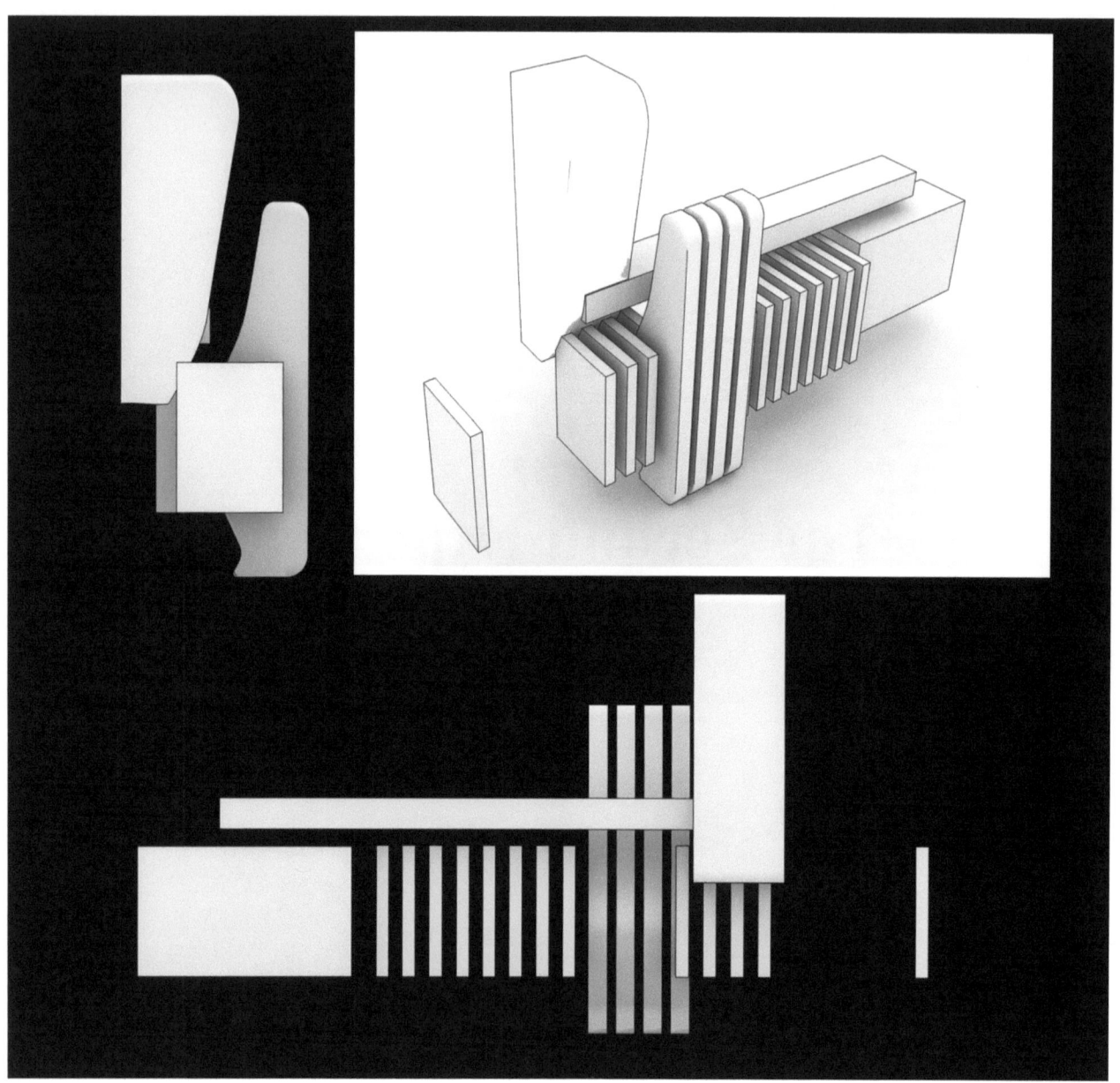

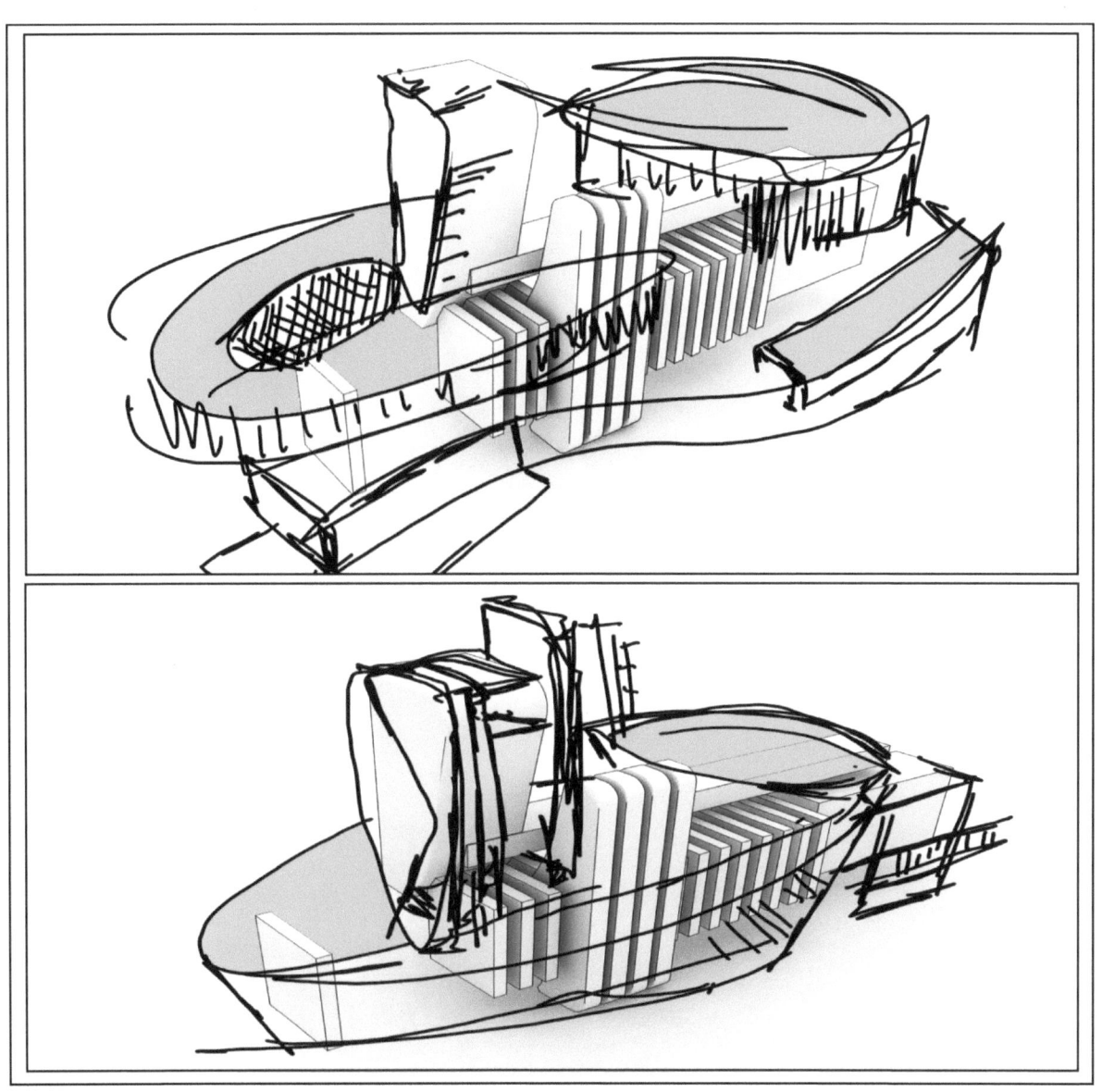

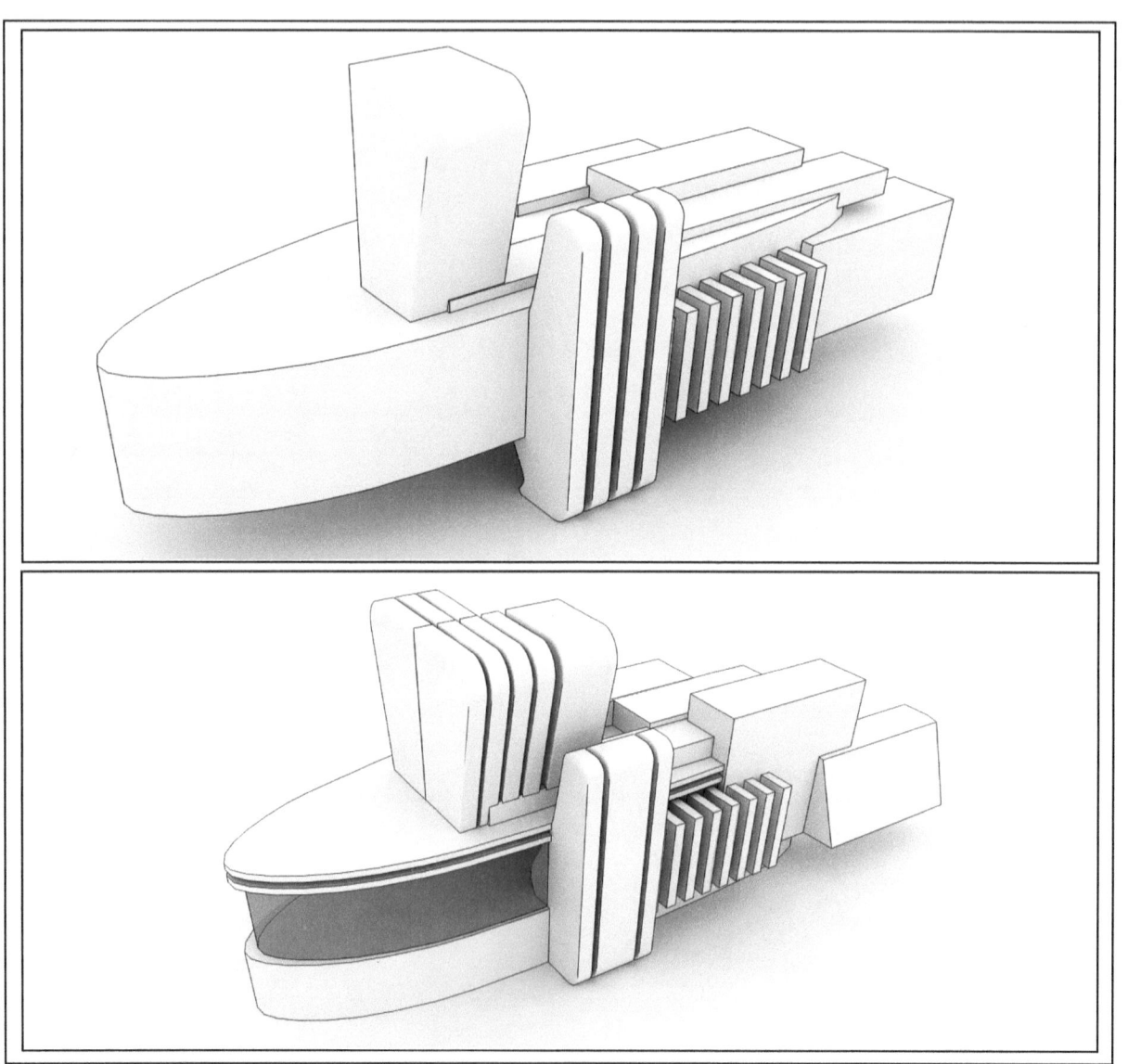

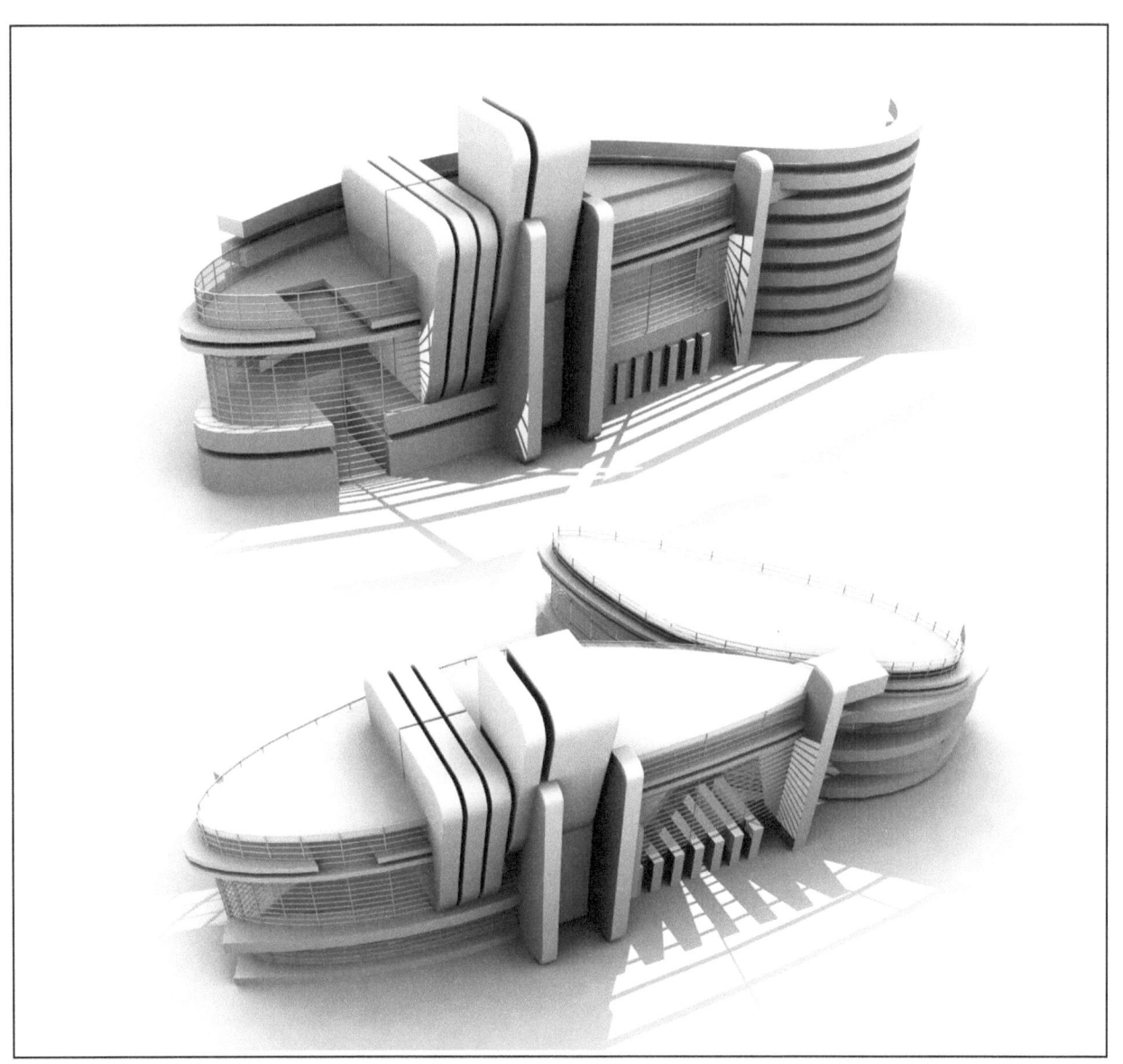

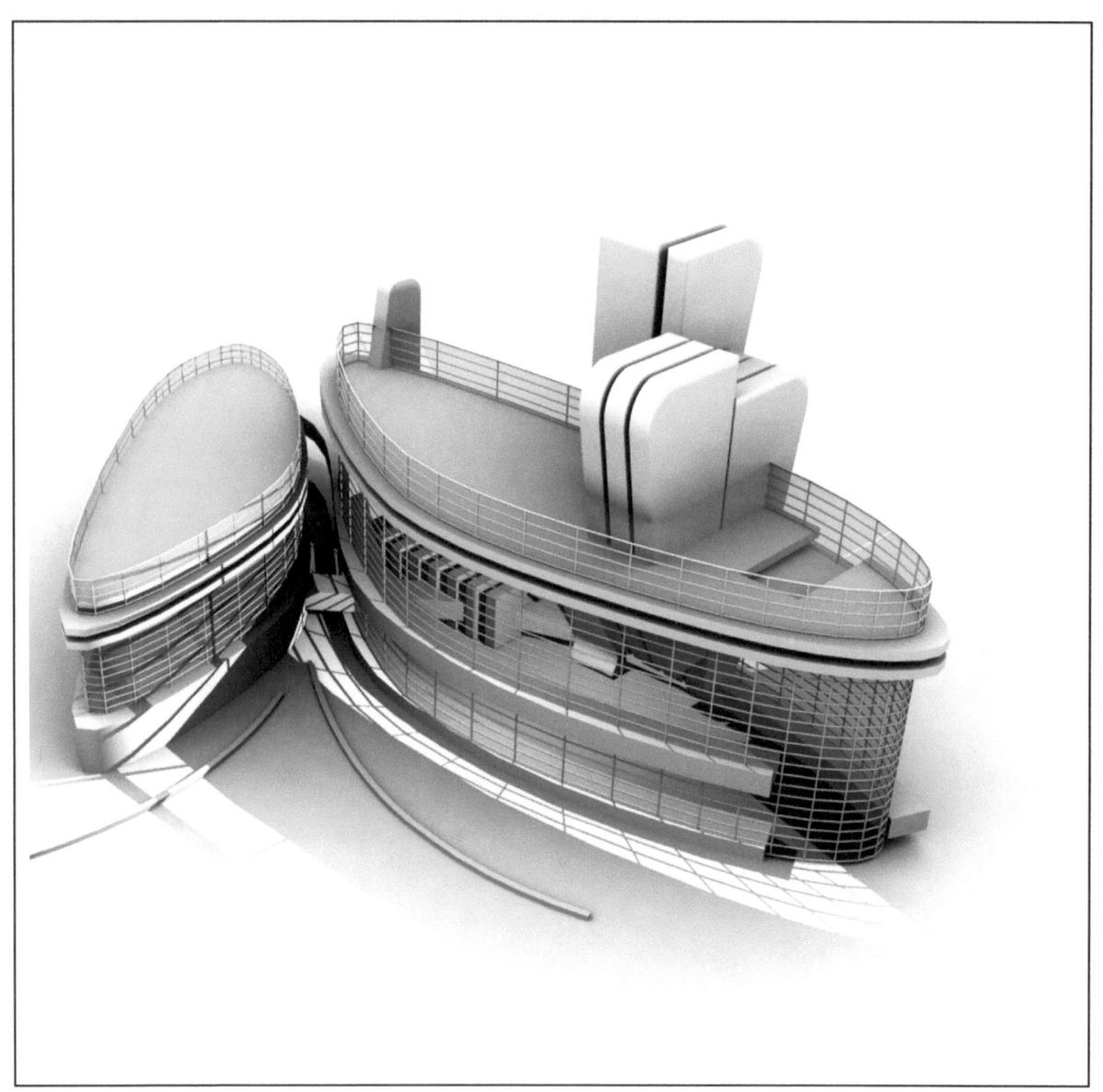

The third experience

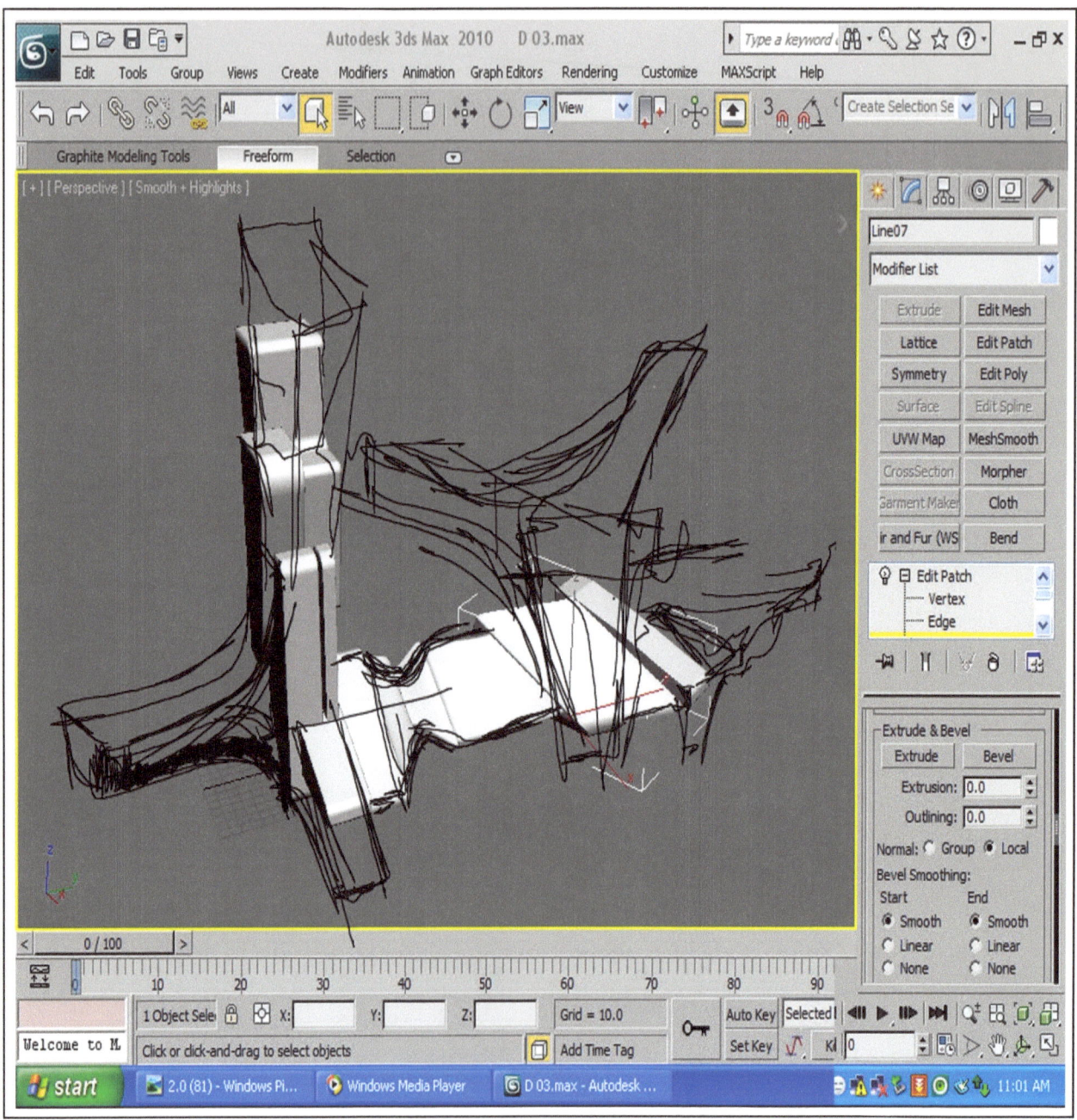

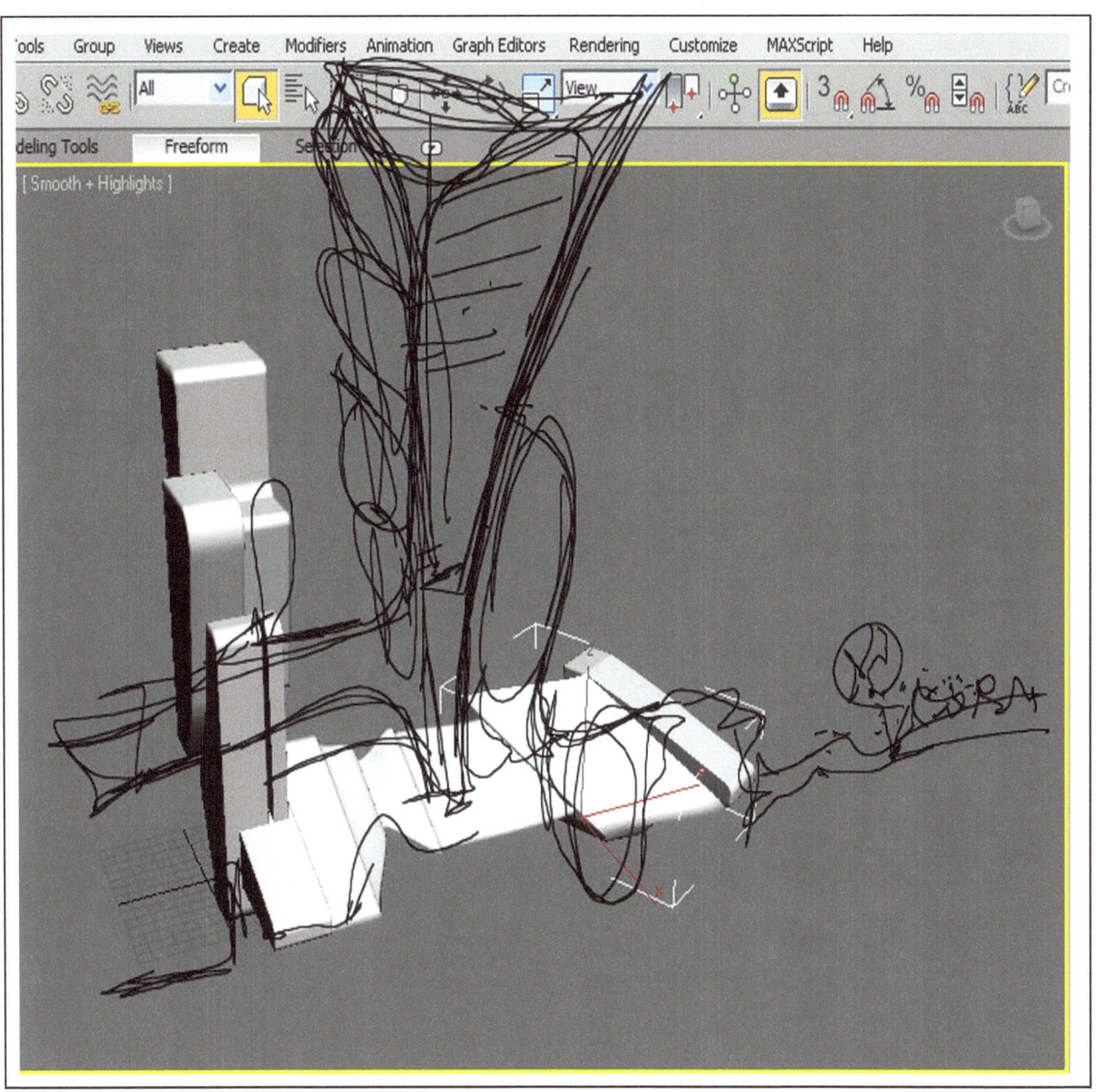

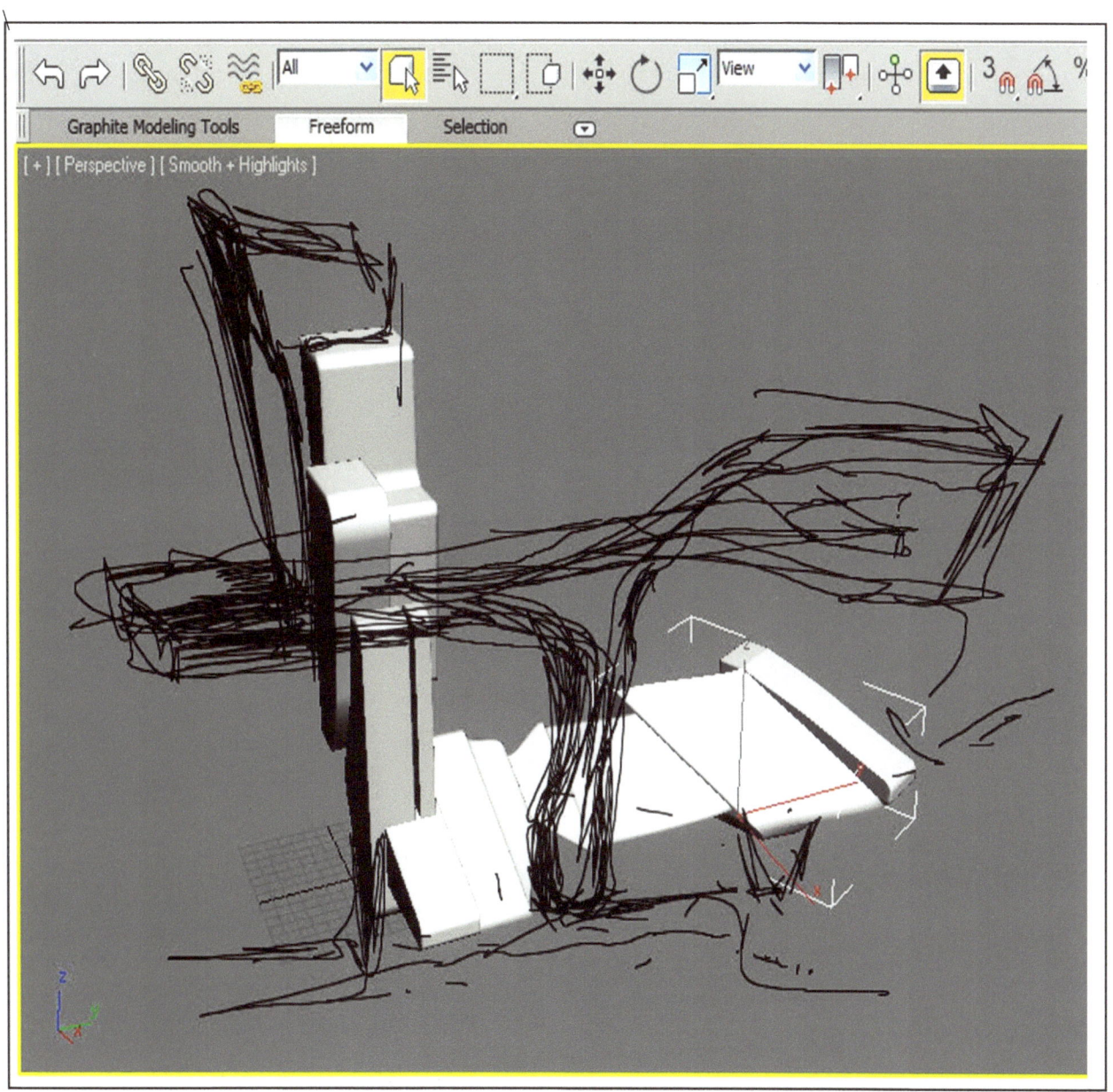

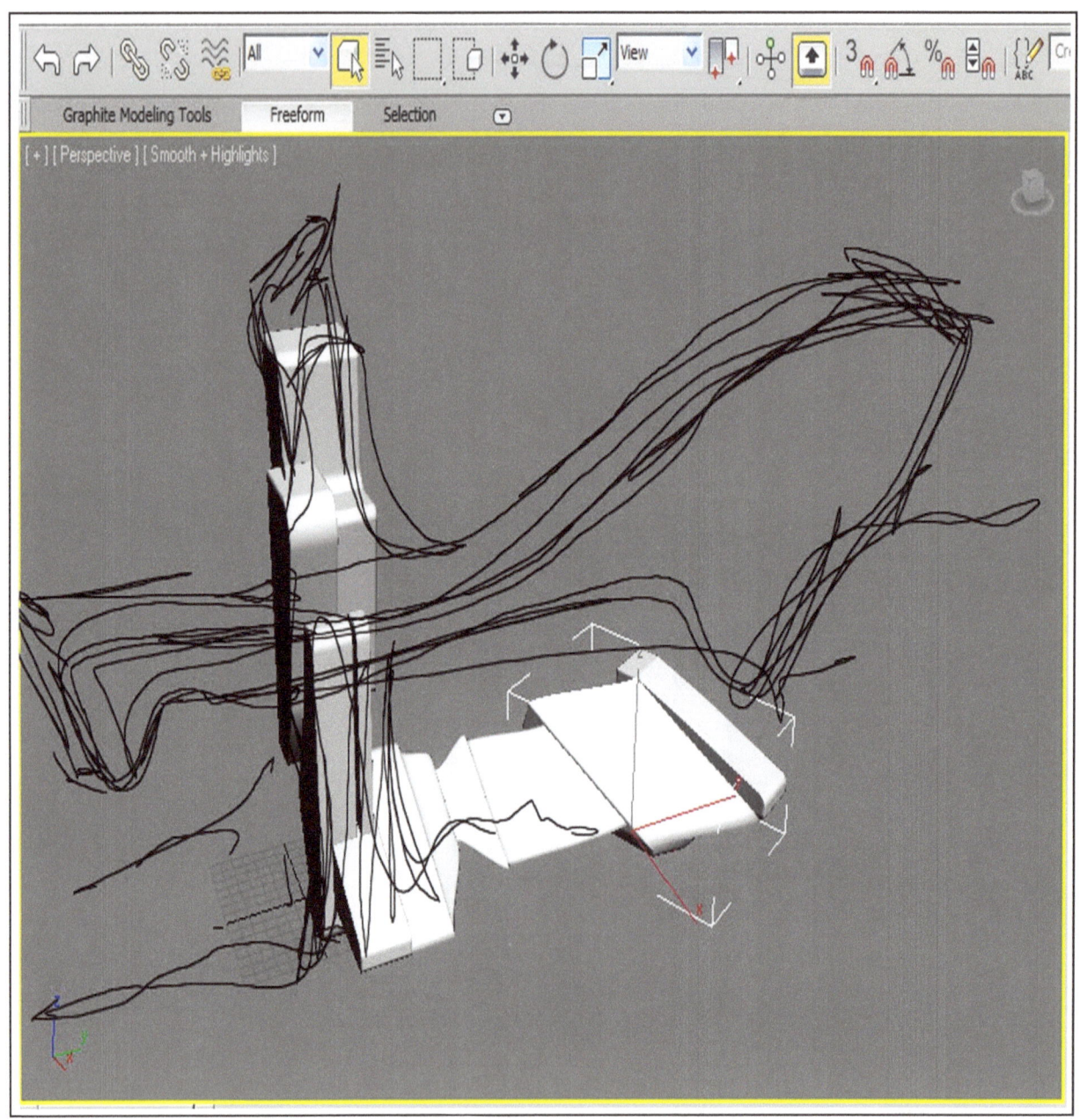

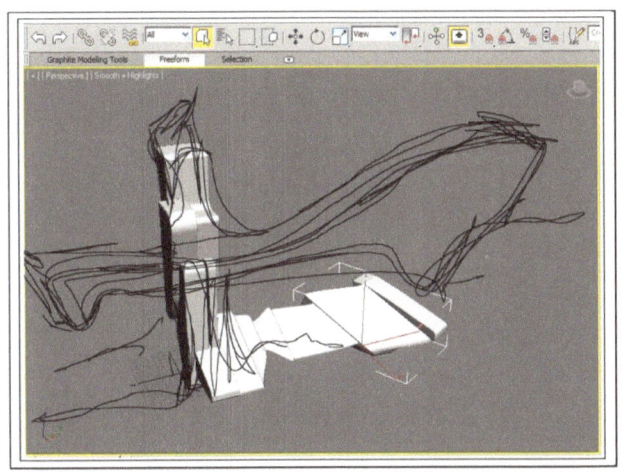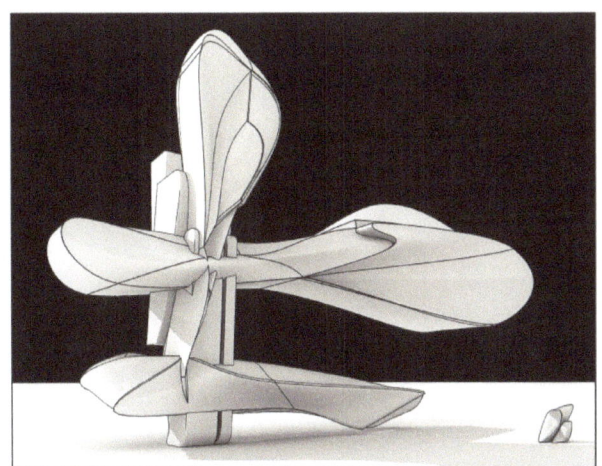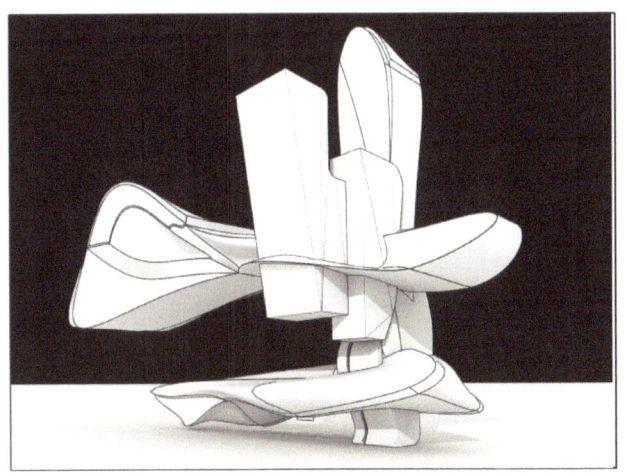

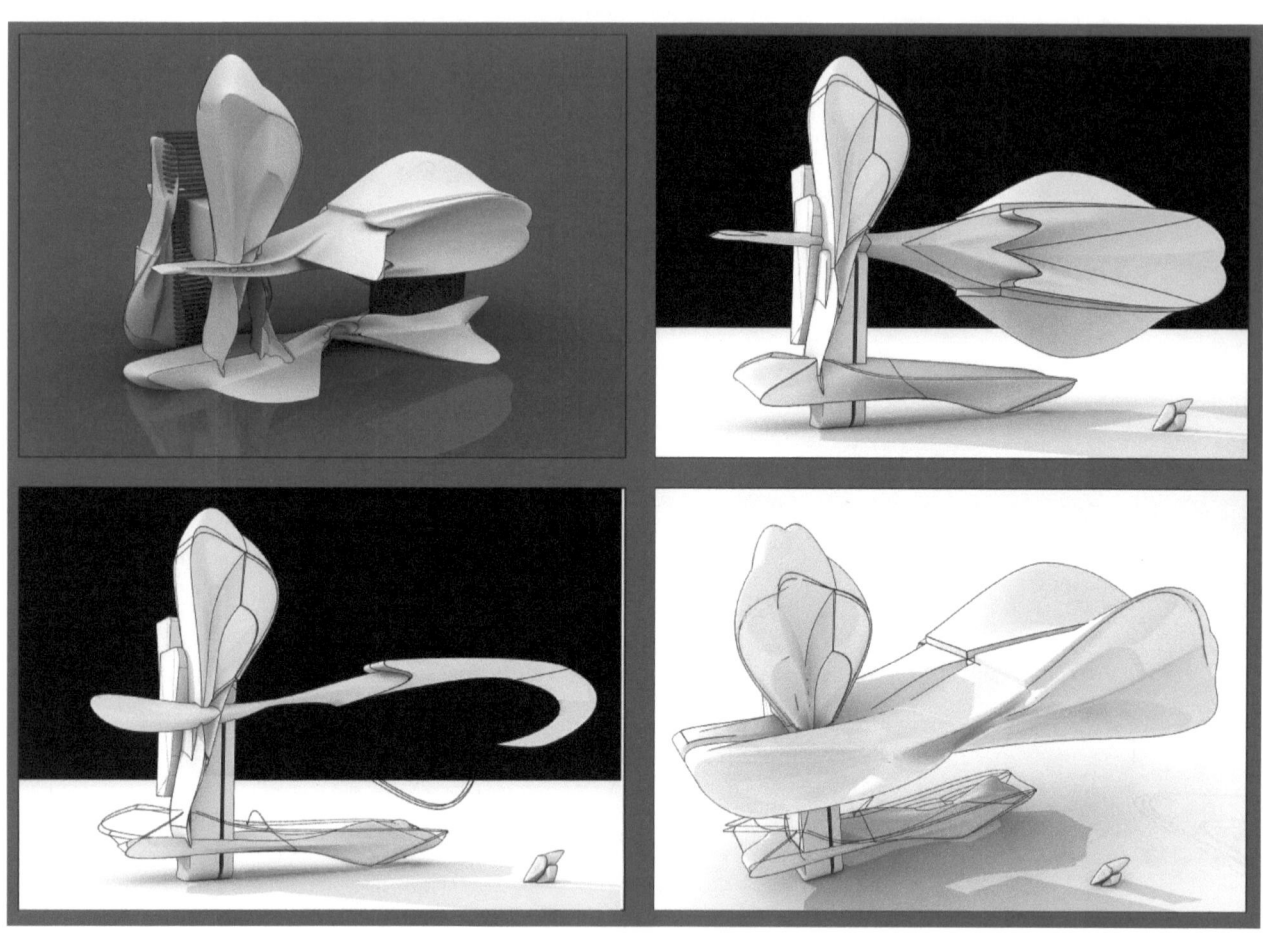

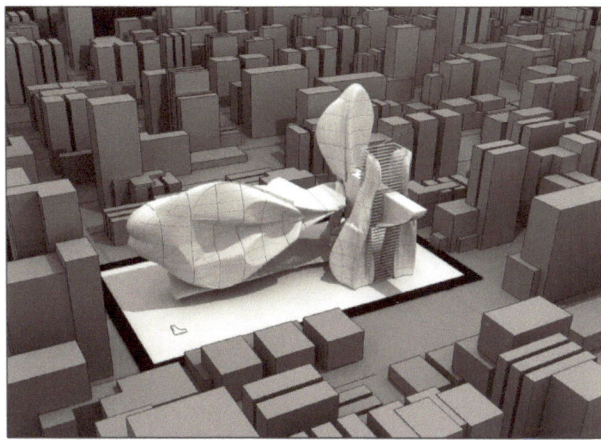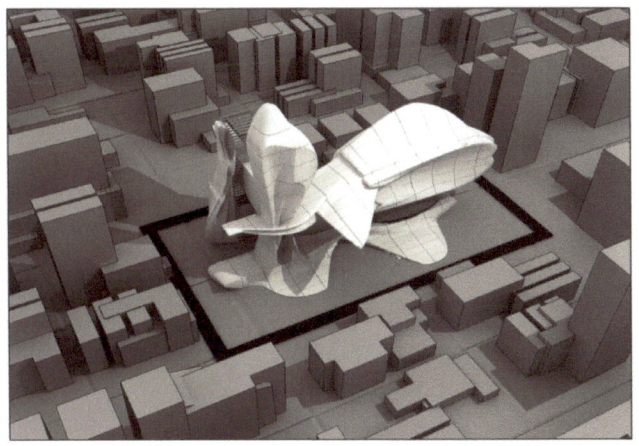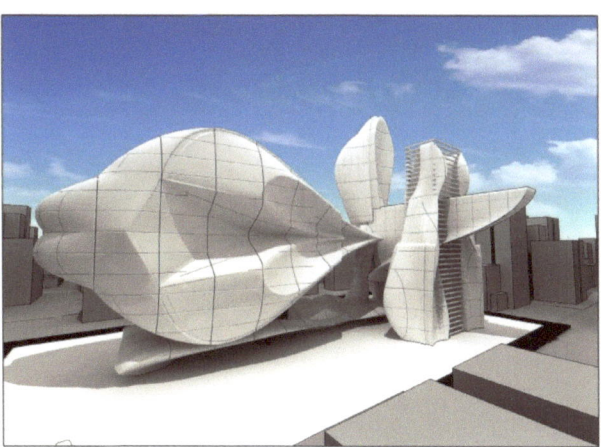

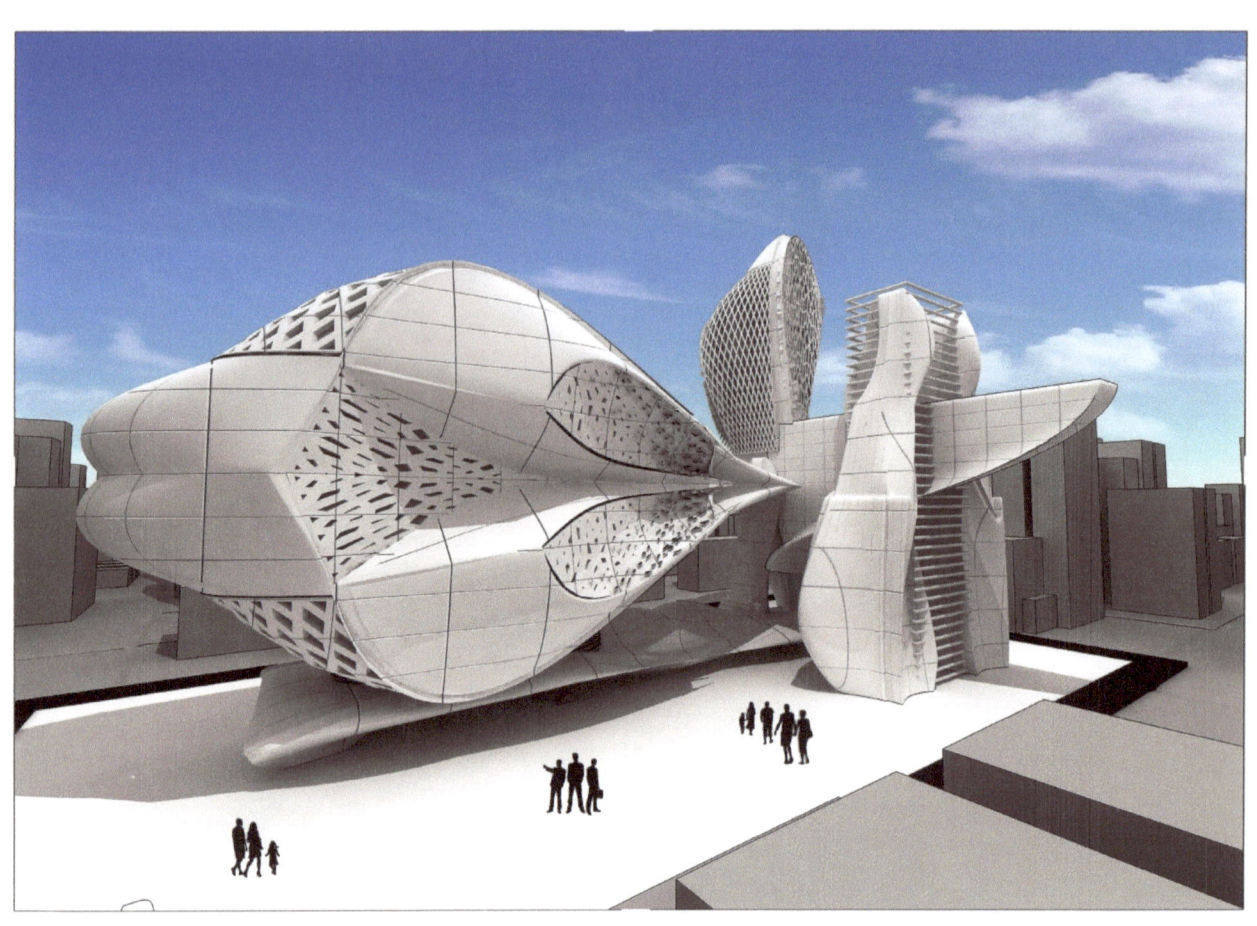

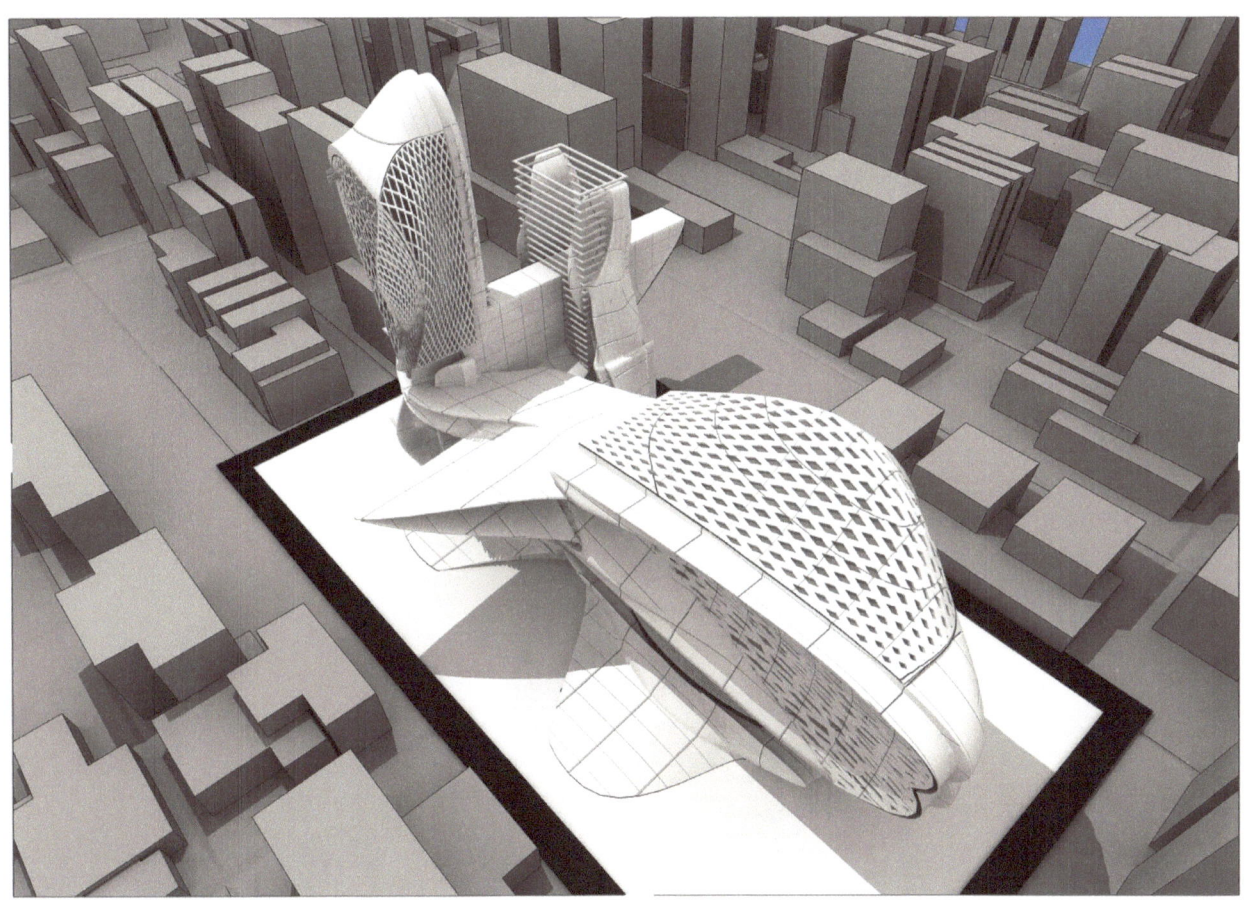

Art Center Design Process

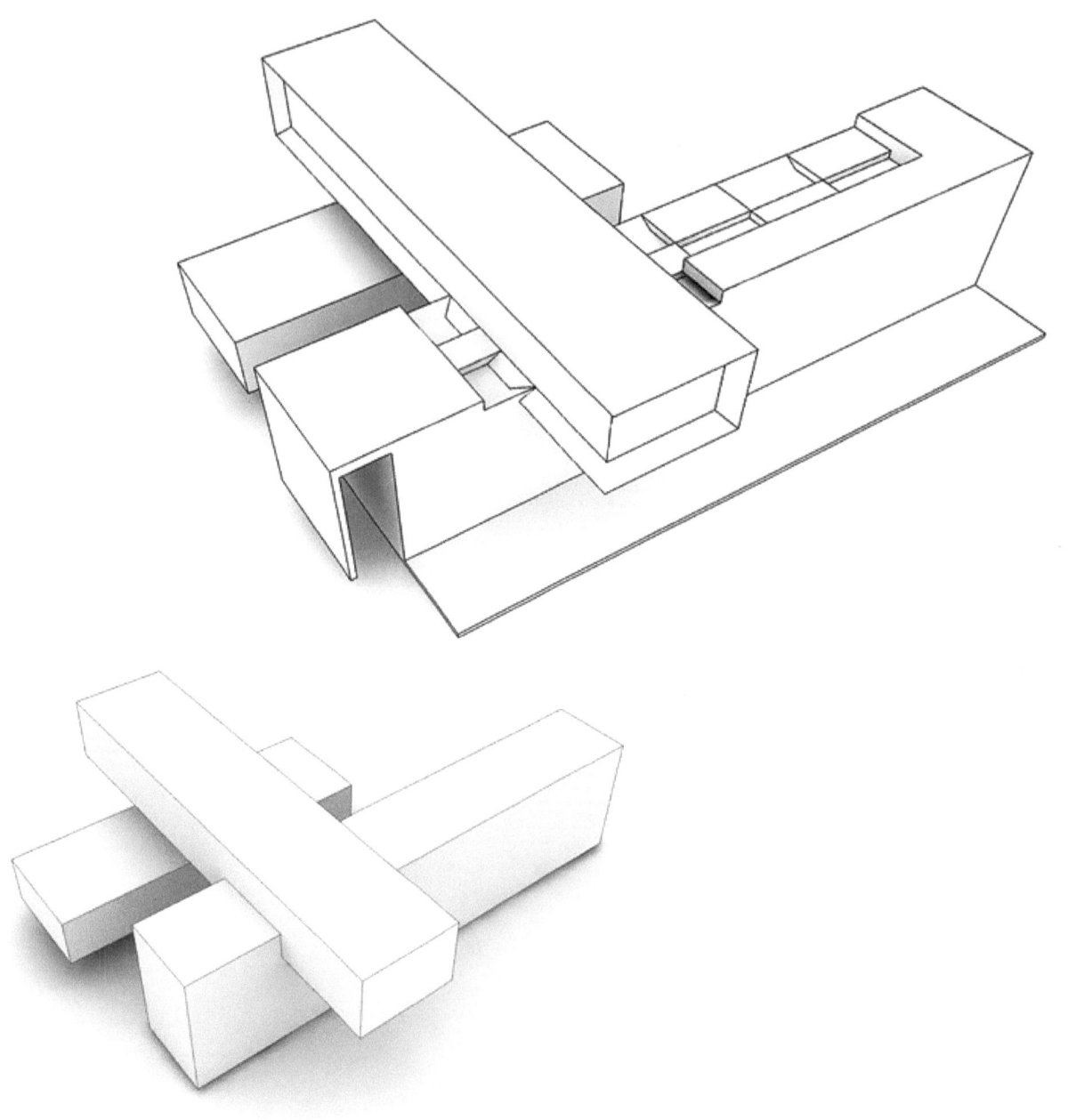

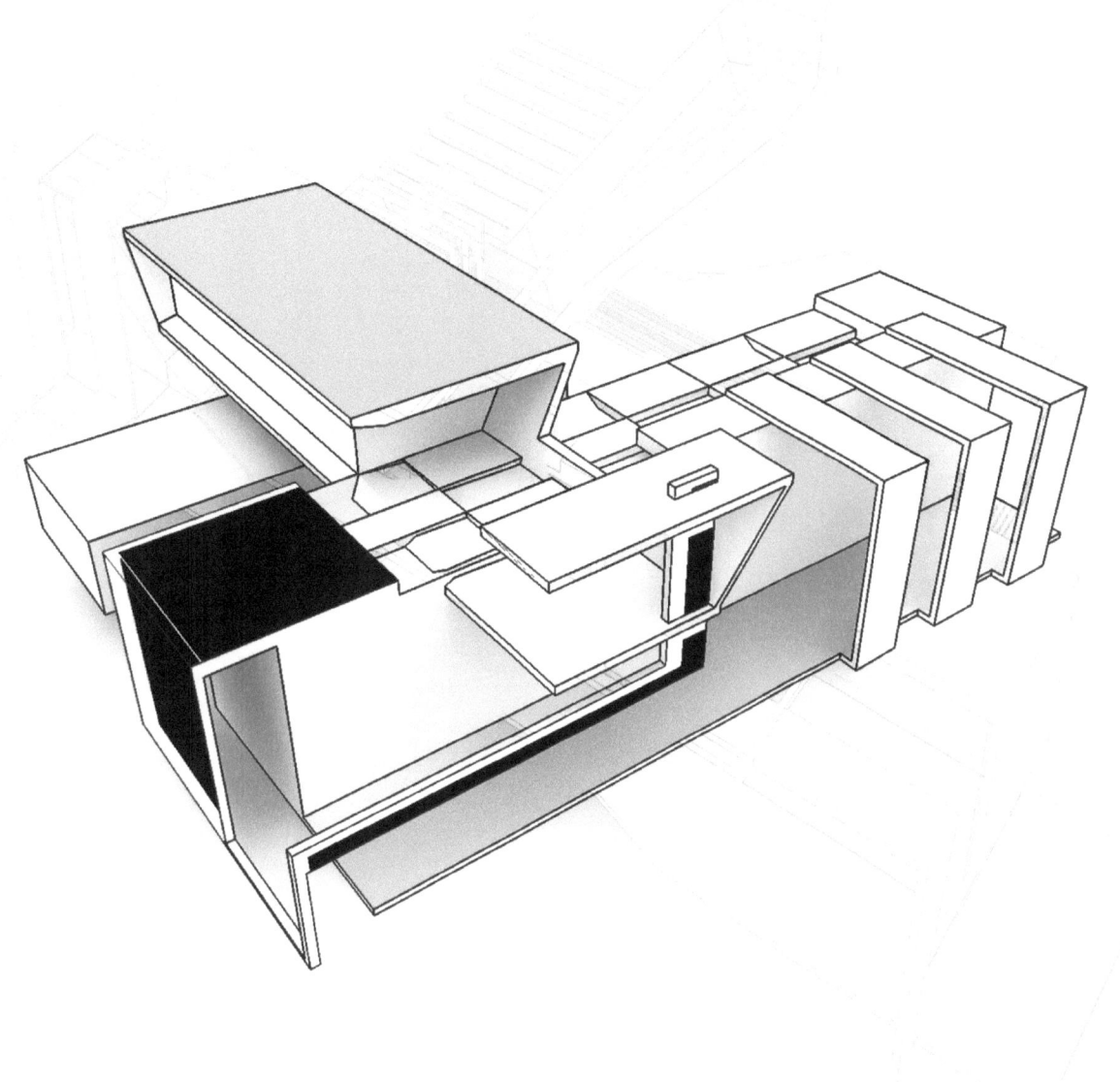

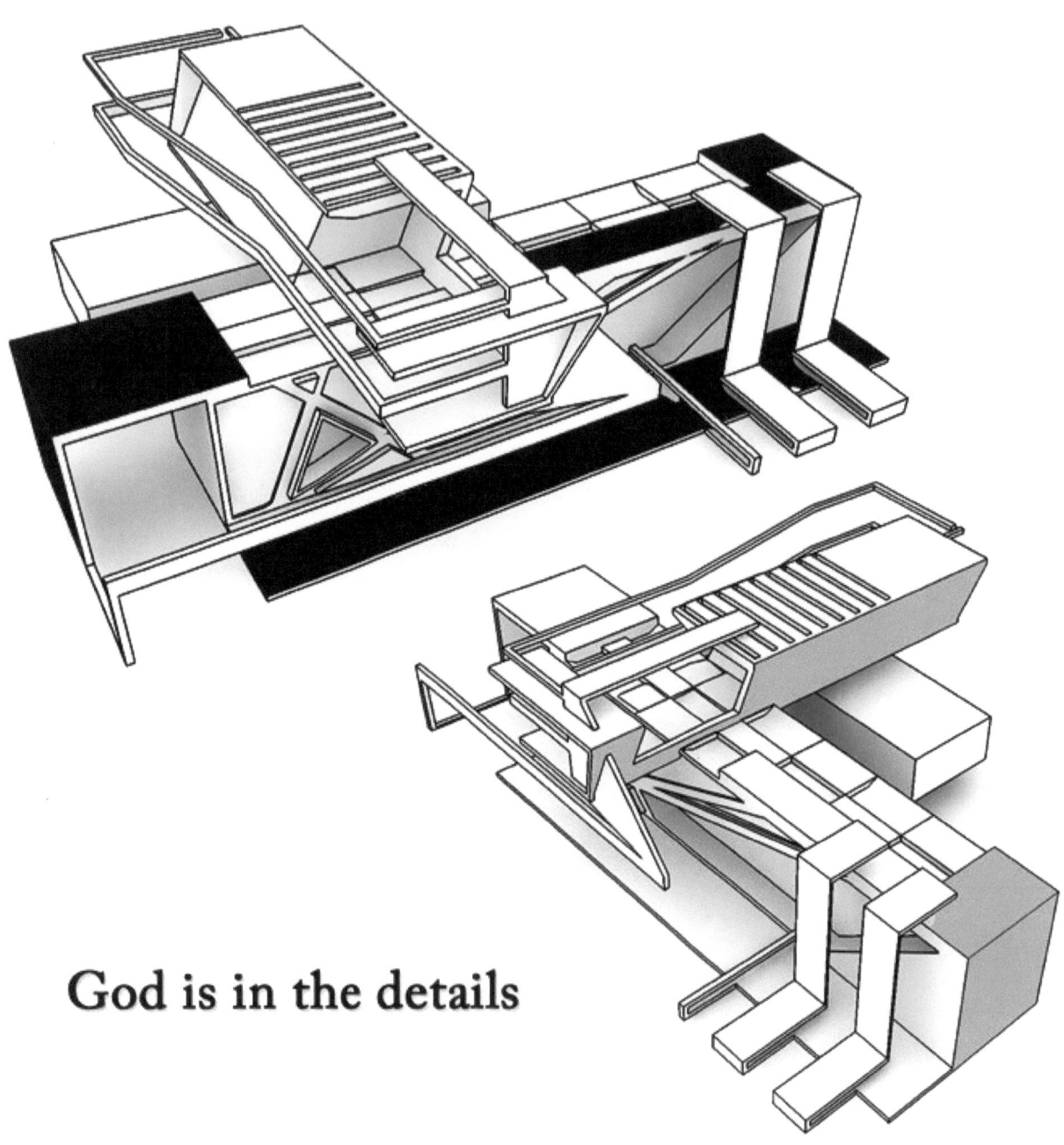

God is in the details

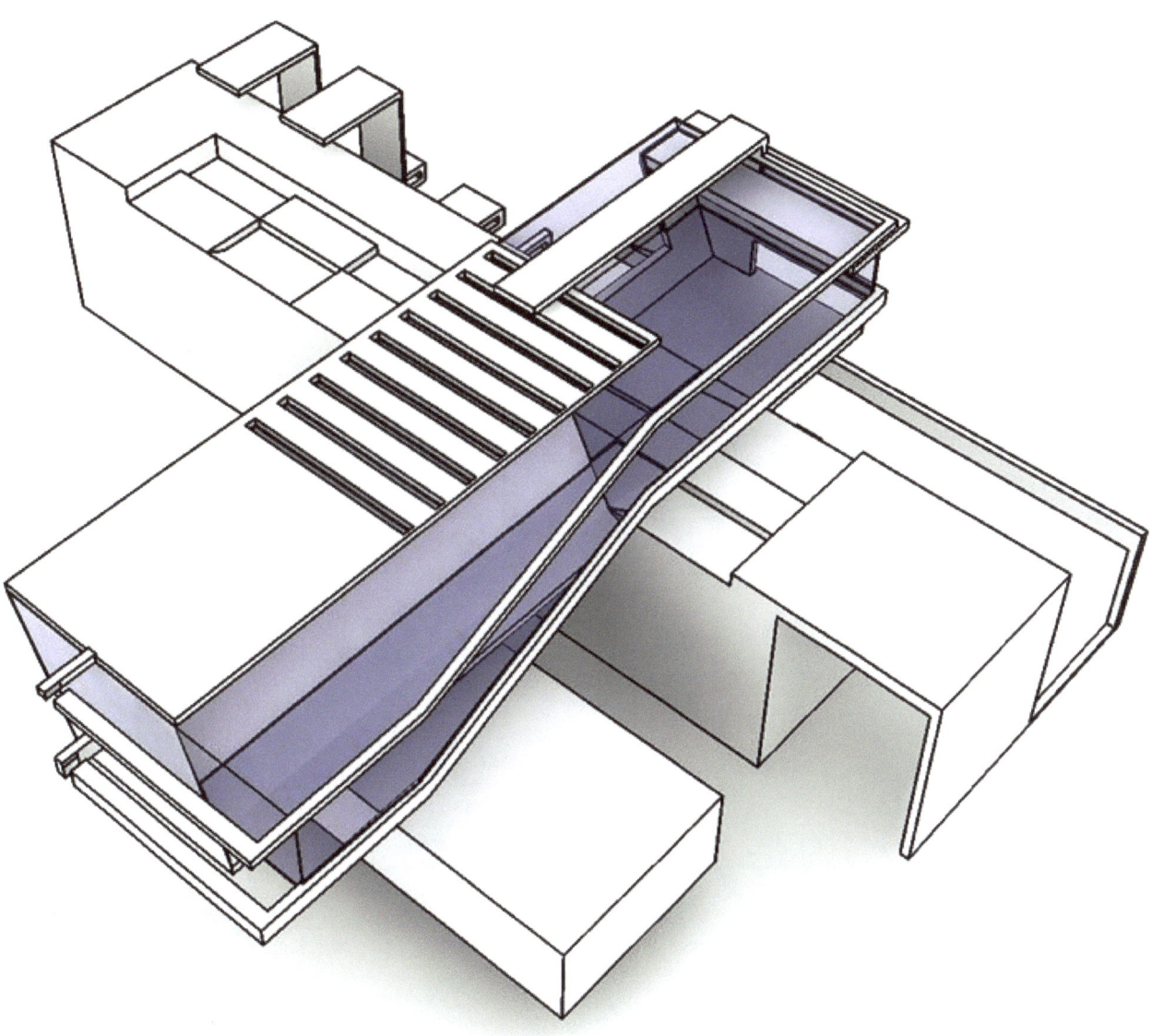

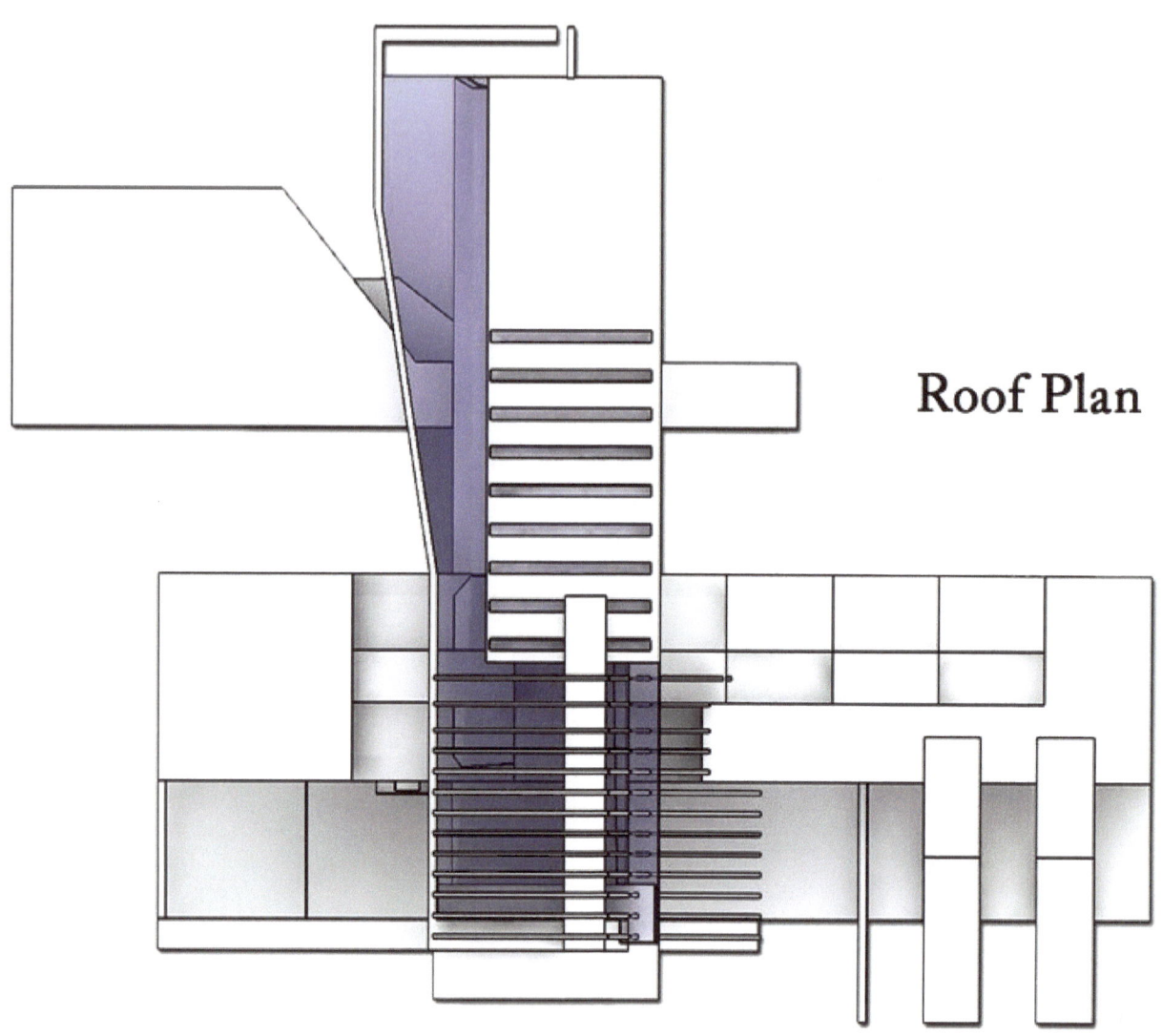

Roof Plan

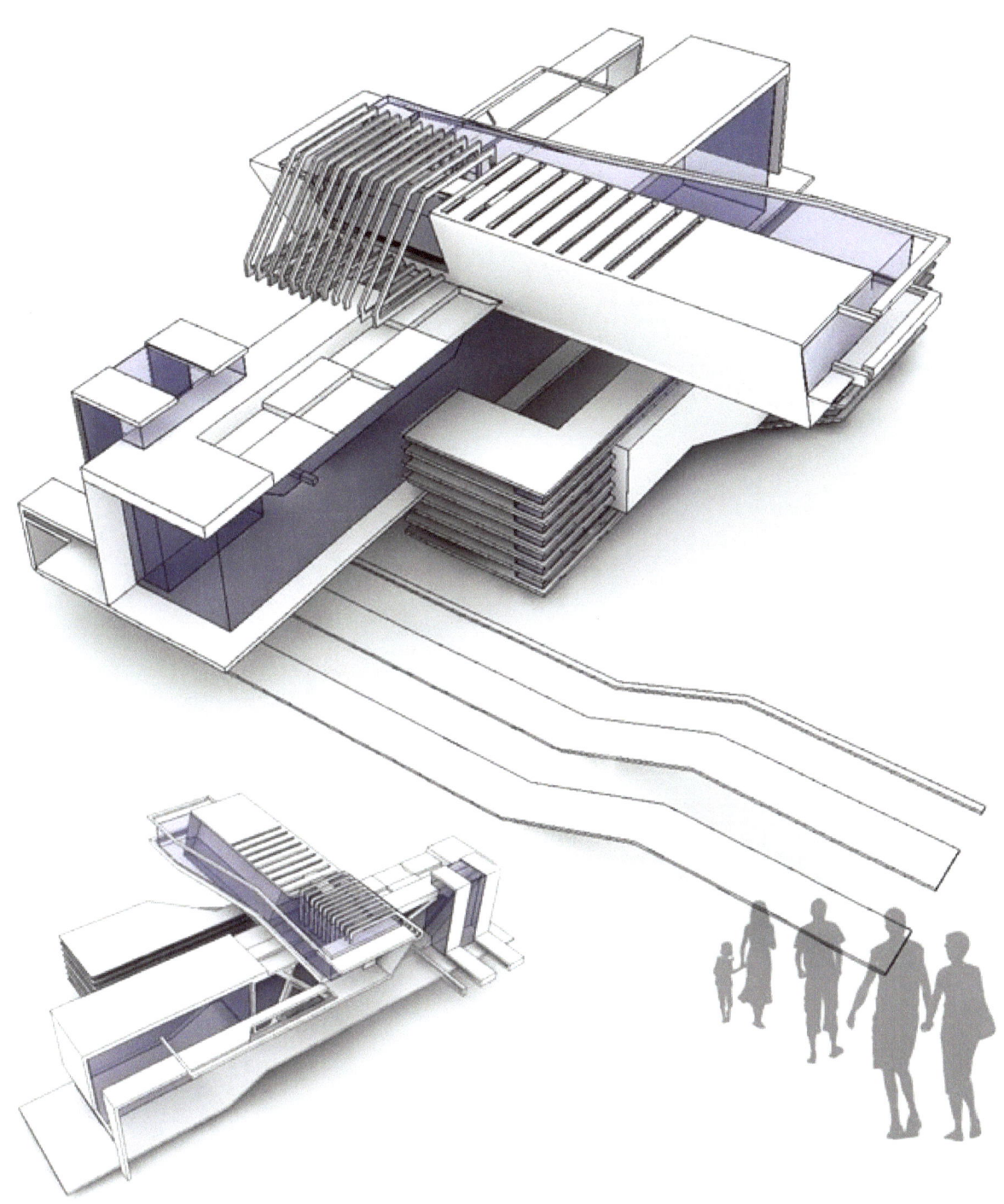

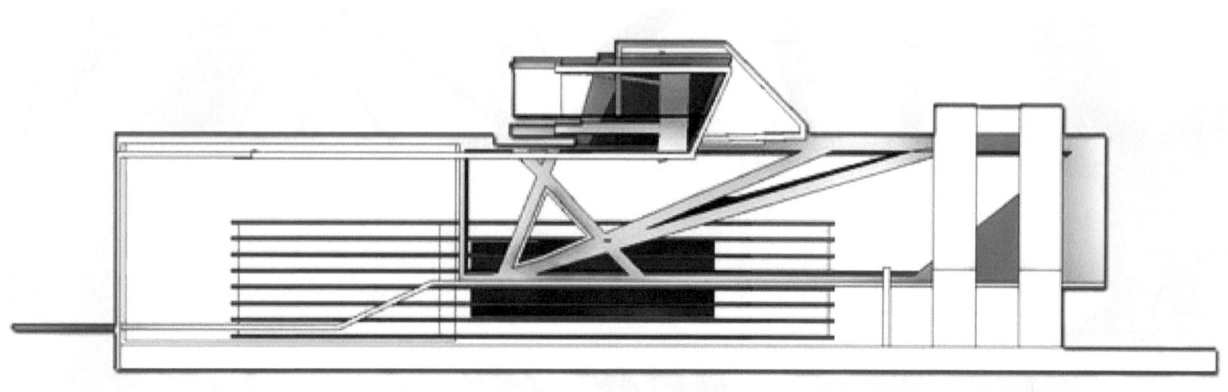
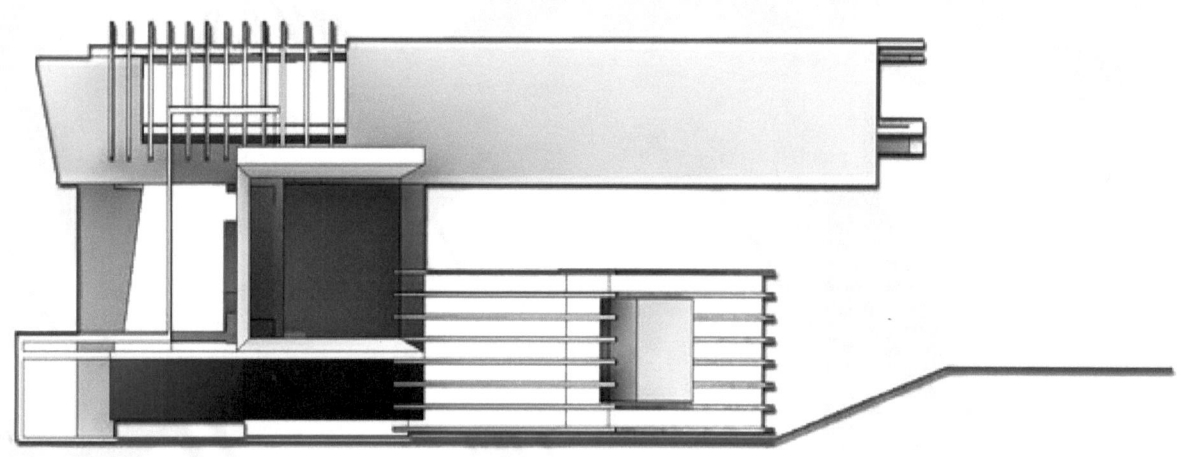

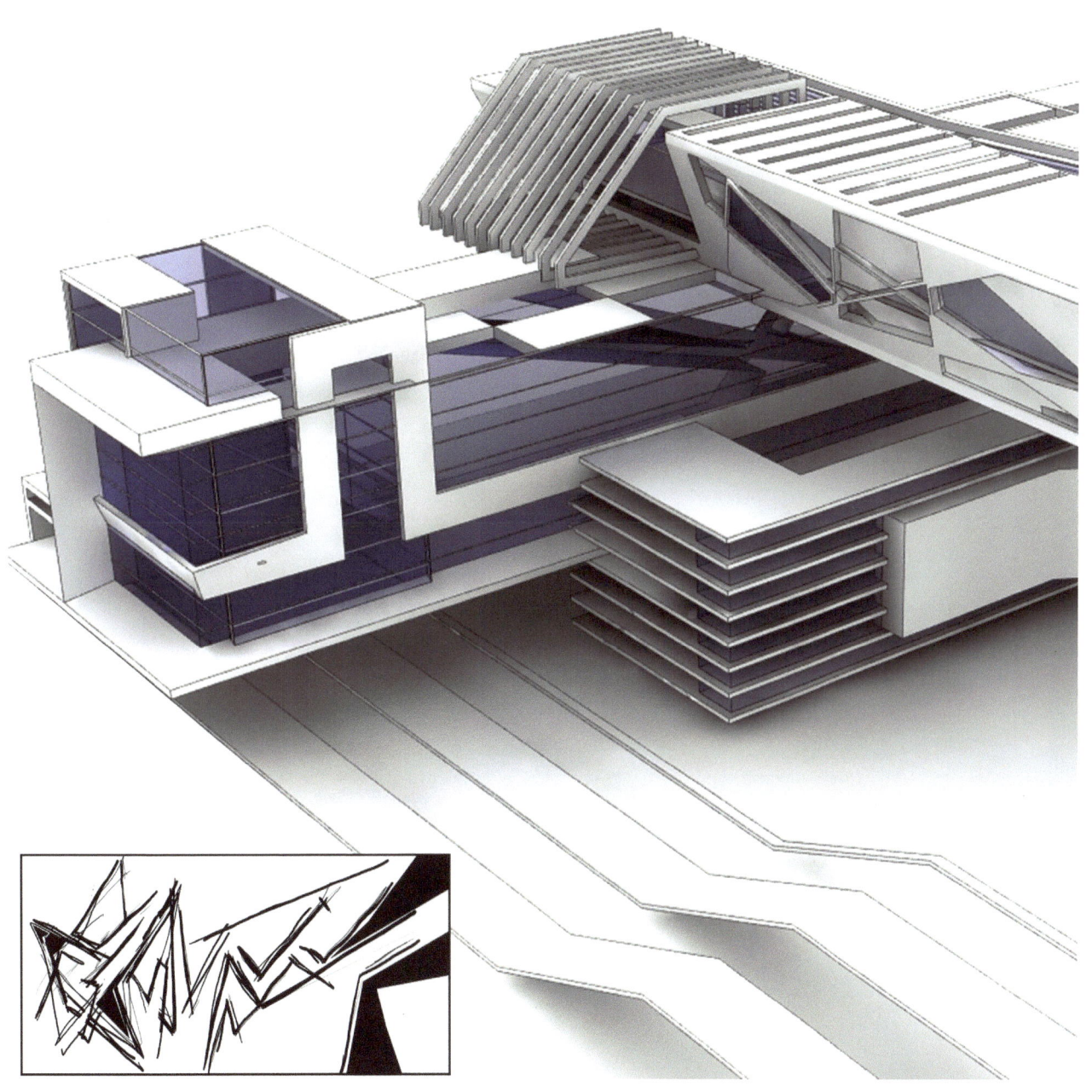

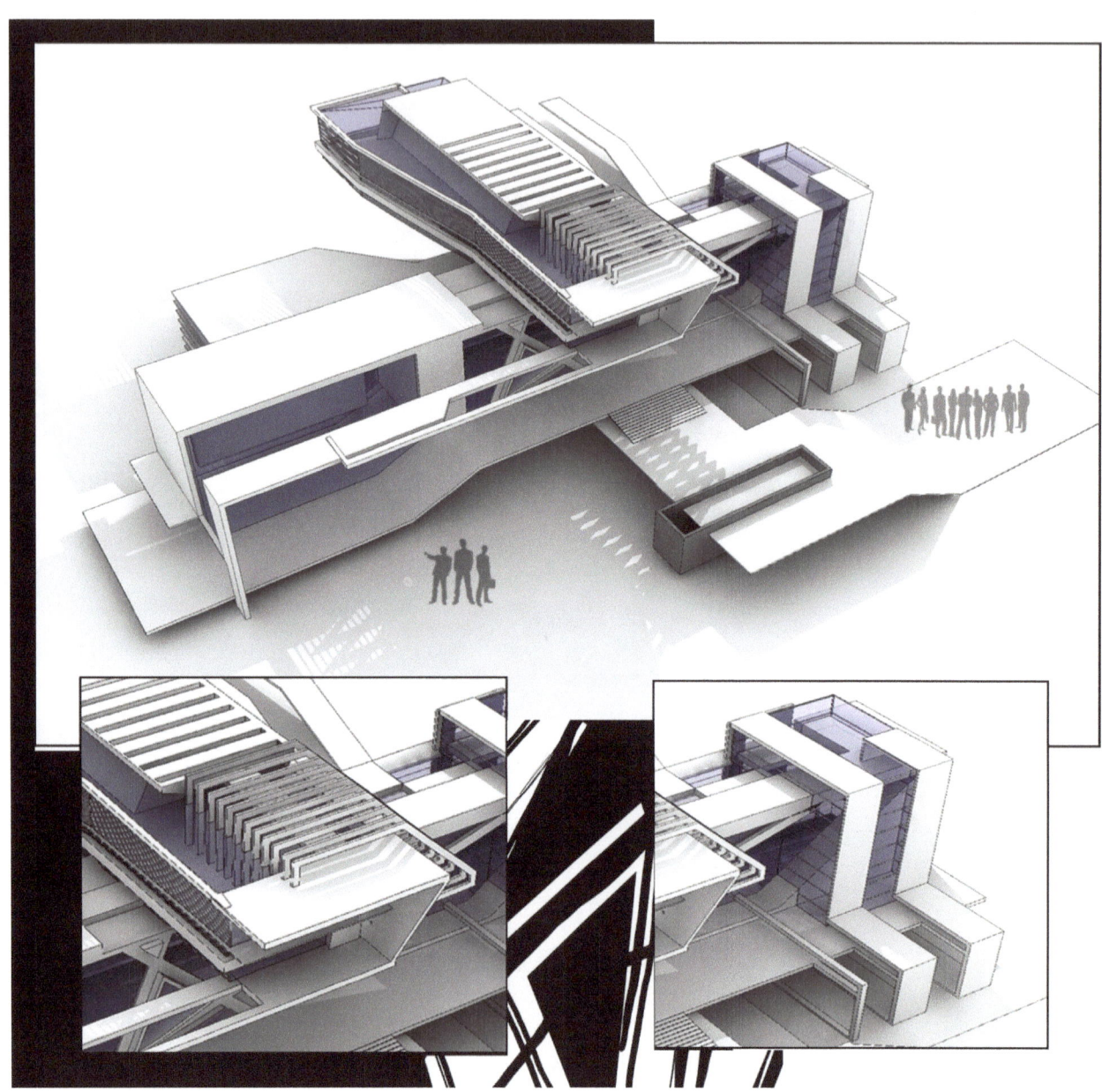

Roof Plan

References

- Bahri, H- Maknon. R, Sustainable development from Idea to practice, environment magazine, Tehran university press, number 27.
- Baker, N - Steemers, K; ventilation, translated to Farsi by: Helen Efgeie, culture and architecture magazine, number 13, p90.
- Barrnet,D, Browning, A Primer on Sustainable Building, Rocky Mountain Institute, 1995.
- Beyer, Barry K. Practical Strategies for the Teaching of Thinking; Boston: Allyn and Bacon, INC, 1987
- Bodokhti, A., Anvari, A., Creativity and innovation in peoples and organizations, Tadbir monthly, 15th year, No.152, Tehran, 2005.
- Falameki. M, Roots and Theoretical tendencies of architecture, Faza press, Tehran, 1381.
- Cameron, J, The Artist's Way, translated to Farsi by: Giti Khoshdel, Peykan(publisher), Tehran, 2010.
- Dewey, J, How we think; Mass, Heath (originally published) 1982.
- Ennis, R. H. a logical Basis for measuring critical thinking skills, educational leadership, 1985.
- Ghazi, Gh., An introduction to being human, scientific publications of Islamic Azad University, Tehran, 1990
- Ghobadian, V, Climatic research on traditional building of Iran; Tehran university press; p31.
- I.A., Poetics of architecture, Soroush press, Tehran, 2010
- Khiabanian,A, Architectural creation process, Naghsh-e-Noo art and architecture weekly-13th no, Tehran, 2005.
-Khiabanian, A, The role of creativity in architectural design process 1, Mehr Iman, Tabriz, 2010.

- Khiabanian, A, The role of creativity in architectural design process 2, Mehr Iman, Tabriz, 2011.

- Khiabanian, A, Conceptal sketches in architectural design, Supreme Century, USA, 2014.

- Khorami, M, Increasing of fuel conservation by natural ventilation, proceeding of 3rd international conferences on fuel conservation; 2004, p63.

- Khoshdel, G, Creative Visualization, Intellectuals and women's studies, Tehran, 2008.

- Lawson, B., How Designers Think, Architectural Press, Oxford, 1997.

- Madanipour, A., Urban space design, translated by Mortazaei, F., Urban planning and processing company, affiliated by Tehran municipality, 2000.

- Mahmoudi, M - Mofidi, M, Effects of climate on from of wind tower, proceeding of 3rd international conferences on fuel conservation, 2004, p247.

- Mirza, Ch, Ctritical thinking education, translated to Farsi by: Khodayar Abili, Samt, Tehran, 1995.

- Mohammadpanah, A., Recommendations of Bruce Mau, Aruna News Agency (www.aruna.ir). Tehran, 2007

- Pourali, Z., Particulars of Successful Instructors, Moafaghiat Biweekly, 146, Tehran, 2007.

- Fisher, R, Teaching children to think, Translated to Farsi by: Afsane Najarian & Masoud Safayi, Rasesh, Tehran, 2007.

- Firouzbakht, M, On Psychology, Rasa Cultural Services Institute, Tehran, 2004.

- Santrak, J., On Psychology, Firouzbakht, Mehrdad, Rasa Cultural Services Institute, Tehran, 2004

- Seyed Almasi, M, Solutions for fuel conservation; proceeding of 3rd international conferences on fuel conservation, 2004, V1, p1147.

- Shabani, H, Advanced teaching methods, Samt Tehran, 2010.

- Soltanzadeh, H., Architects' Instruction, Cultural Researches Dept., Tehran, 2000

- Watson, D - Labs, K, Climatic design, Efficient building principles and practices, translated to Farsi by: Ghobadian. Vahid, Tehran university press, 1999.

- Yasrebi, Ch, Freethinking and creativity in art education, formal base of Sore-e-Mehr publications, Tehran, 2005.

www.ingramcontent.com/pod-product-compliance
Lightning Source LLC
Chambersburg PA
CBHW041151290426
44108CB00002B/31